PAPER

HEIRLOOM

A MEMOIR

Vivian Witkind Davis

ISBN: 1496102371
ISBN 13: 9781496102379
Library of Congress Control Number: 2014905728
CreateSpace Independent Publishing Platform
North Charleston, South Carolina

For my family,

all of you.

"If I am not for myself, then who will be for me?

And if I am only for myself, then what am I?"

—Rabbi Hillel

CONTENTS

INTRODUCTION

I am mistress of a pirate's chest full of silver. Open the chest with its long brass key. The velvet-lined top drawer cherishes Gorham sterling tableware from the early twentieth century: twelve each of dinner knives, butter knives, dinner forks, salad forks, fish forks, teaspoons, round cream-soup spoons, oval soup spoons, dessert spoons, ice-cream spoons, and demitasse spoons. Run your fingers over the velvet. Pick up a knife and feel the smooth blade and gently sloped handle and then the rough, five-petaled buttercups eternally in full bloom. Engraved at the top of every knife, fork, and spoon is a bold Gothic B. The shelf below has another set of flatware in another pattern, comparatively incomplete, with a meager ten knives and a paltry two kinds of forks and spoons. A floral W emblazons each piece. In the bottom drawer, a sharp-tined serving fork is engraved, "Forget Me Not."

That should be plenty, but there is more. A drawer in the sideboard in my dining room clanks open and sags with the weight of serving spoons, serving forks, cake servers, pie servers, grape shears, and completely unidentifiable implements. At the back of the china cabinet are tiny, silver saltcellars with tiny, silver salt spoons. A magnificent casserole dish missing its glass liner occupies the bottom shelf of the front hall table. Most people in my generation have stacks of *National Geographic* in their basements; I have oddments of silver among Playbills from Broadway shows that opened long ago, closed, and were revived and closed again.

My life is twenty-first-century casual. We use stainless steel 364 days of the year. I drag the silver flatware out of its chest for Christmas dinner. The rest of the year, I worry about thieves heisting the hardwood box, though it would take a well-muscled fellow with a strong back.

Silver is a bother to polish—all those edgy buttercups. When I inherited the Gorham pattern, I had an enthusiastic cleaning lady attack it. She spent the whole day and was proud of the results, particularly the removal of the marigold-colored tarnish on the demitasse spoons, which she succeeded in excising with steel-wool pads. Unfortunately, the "tarnish" was gold plate.

Silver is the stuff of heirlooms, family relics passed down through the generations. Someday mine will be divided among my three children so they can box it up and keep it in their basements or sell it on eBay. What's left will go to their descendants, my grandchildren, probably diminished to the point where it fits in shoeboxes shoved into safe places and forgotten.

Silver gleams, but it is mute. Are you curious about what the *B* stands for on the Gorham silver? Where does the *W* fit in? What was the silver casserole used for?

Stories are heirlooms too, more informative than metal and allowing more reflection. This book is my story up to when I married in 1972. It takes chutzpah to write about oneself, so I admit to a desire to be remembered. There's a lot of that going around. Memoirs drop every day like apples from a forest of family trees. Many of them are plump to bursting with heartrending troubles. I had a rough patch myself. It was over relatively quickly. An alternate title for this book would be *Lucky from the Age of Five*. That's pretty lucky. I had a lot of help in growing up and was strong enough to use it, despite sometimes crippling shyness. Bad things can happen, yet it's possible to survive and thrive. I don't mean that there is a happily ever after: there are no happy lives, only happy days[1]—often a cornucopia of them.

A funny thing unfolds as you live through a bunch of decades. They turn into history. Whole generations think of your times as antediluvian. Thus, a third motive for this book, besides the urge to talk about my coming of age and the desire to make sure my descendants know they can often overcome adversity, is to tell what it was like being a student and young adult in the 1960s, one of the most tumultuous periods in American history.

I've kept a diary since I was nine years old, so I had written records to refer to for much of this book. They weren't always much help. I often recorded trivia and made no mention of significant events. What I wrote seems now exceedingly childish. It's not always clear which I wanted more: to grow up or to somehow avoid it. Diaries are the enemy of memoir, or at least mine are, making the past more complicated and confused than I remember it. It's not so much that I would unconsciously redesign the past in my favor. I'm sure I would, and a written record makes doing that harder. More important, however, is that the past has dead ends, strange loops, and missing connections that make it hard to construct a coherent story. I found the same dilemma with family documents and even genealogical records. They raise questions but are closefisted with the answers. As I wrote this book, I often thought it would easier just to give away the silver.

Genetic roots are simply facts. They include ugly facts, interesting facts, and facts that deserve honoring. It is a mistake to put too much stock in the seemingly perfectly formed spirals of deoxyribonucleic acid that make up your genes. Ancestry research has become a fad and for some an obsession. DNA testing is exploding simultaneously with the opening up of huge genealogical databases. In the excitement of the democratization of research, we get too much information. The facts from the databases spread backward and intertwine like kudzu. The informative value shrinks rapidly, the facts becoming indistinguishable dry leaves with nothing more than names and dates, or nothing at all. My ancestors came from Bavaria.

They came from Lithuania. They came from England and Ireland. Some did well; some not.

Each member of my family—me, a child of mine, a grandchild of mine, and whoever comes next—whether they have one X chromosome or two, can imagine being at the intersection of the two lines in the letter X, or perhaps an upright *V,* the first initial of my name, joined with an inverted *V,* also the first letter in my first grandchild's name, Vincent. The upper portion spreads backward in time through parents, grandparents, and four hundred generations or so to the early societies in Mesopotamia.[2] The lower portion is brand new and reaches into the future.

I'll tell you right now that the silver casserole often held an almond soufflé. A server brought it around a table for twelve, stopping at each guest's left and holding the heavy dish with a pair of shaky hands. Another server followed with sailor's duff sauce. I would help myself to as much of each as I thought I could get away with. If you're patient, I'll tell you more. That is the heirloom I want to pass down: stories to page through and chuckle over. No need to keep them polished.

1

A STAINED-GLASS FAMILY CREST

The anthropologist Margaret Mead said each of us contains a past and a future, which stretch back only as far as grandparents and forward as far as grandchildren—the family we know personally.[1] Anything beyond that is intangible, unobservable, and not truly a part of us. This makes it tough for me to get to know my grandfather William H. Butler. He died a quarter of a century before I was born. Writing about him is more an exercise in microhistory than memoir. I have to beat on into a past where the current carries floating junk and the pearls hug a muddy bottom.

"Every word of this is true," my birth mother, Gladys Butler Witkind, wrote me in shaky cursive some fifty years ago. "My father was due to be hanged for killing an Englishman, and they passed him house to house to get him on a boat from Ireland to America." He arrived in time to fight for the North in the Civil War, she said, and afterward made a fortune in the tobacco industry.

Relying on that letter to begin a family history invites problems, only one of which is that I have lost it. Because it was so precious, I put it in a place so safe that it disappeared. The second problem is provenance.

Gladys wrote the letter from an insane asylum. How much do you trust the words of someone who is deranged? Another issue is obvious from the dates. It would be impossible for her father to be old enough when he arrived to be a soldier by 1865 and then sire her in 1921. The guy had to be her grandfather. One of us must have gotten it wrong—Gladys in the writing or me in the remembering.

My paternal grandmother, Isabelle Theresa Witkind, or Belle, who raised me from when I was five until my teens, told me other tales about Gladys's family. Both of my Butler grandparents were "C of E" and "FF of V," she said, and from her awed tone, I guessed those were superior, if mysterious, letters. She explained that William and his wife were Church of England members, or Episcopalians, and my grandmother was from the first families of Virginia, or FF of V for short. So those credentials were classy, I figured, and meant I was several cuts above the hoi polloi. I never asked why she, a second-generation American Jew, thought my Wasp background was so terrific. It didn't seem to have done my birth mother a lot of good. William Butler Yeats, one of the greatest poets of the twentieth century, was related to me, said Belle. The Butlers were listed in New York's *Social Register.* William belonged to the New York Yacht Club. He was the commodore, even. His brother George invented the tuxedo. As a sort of society lark, George changed his clothes fifty times in one day—or two hundred maybe—and set a record. The Butlers divided their time between Park Avenue apartments and Watch Hill, Rhode Island, giving enormous parties wherever they went. That's the origin of all that silver with the letter *B.*

Some of this is true. It's taken some dredging to establish which of it is.

Wouldn't it be gratifying to be related only to good, exemplary, famous people who make your own life nobler? That's the trouble with ancestors. You can find names to drop into a conversation. Or you unearth names you want to rebury in the genealogical charts they came from. How terrific can it be to find out you are "the illegitimate son of the illegitimate nephew of Napoleon"?[2]

William Butler made a fortune and knew how to spend his gains to make himself into somebody. I can't help admiring him; however, I can't be proud of him.

❧

When Americans get rich, we want to know how because, at least up to now, large inheritances have been unlikely. It was luck, maybe—being in the right place at the right time. Or it was being extra smart.

Then there's the American tradition of stealing it. The truth in the muck of history is that William and George had the smarts to make a financial play that was dodgy then and would be illegal now. They earned a footnote in the annals of history by playing a high-stakes game of monopoly in the tobacco industry during the Gilded Age at the end of the nineteenth century. With his loot, William lived in New York with the extravagance of "the one percent" until the Depression came and he lost most of his swag.

In other words, a couple of my ancestors were robber barons. The storage box for my silver really is a pirate's chest.

If Gladys's story is true, I am also descended from a murderer. William and George's father came to the United States from Ireland when he was seventeen, by necessity, she told me in that lost letter—not the necessity of slow starvation that faced many of his countrymen in the mid-nineteenth century, but the imminent prospect of being hanged by the neck until dead. His fellows may have considered killing an Englishman an act of heroism—or at least a mistake rather than a crime—but the occupying

English were bound to see it otherwise. I suppose the native Irish passed the boy from house to house in the dark of night and finally onto a ship headed west. His son William was born in 1866.[3] That means my story goes back to the year after the end of the Civil War, a remarkably long time for someone born in 1946.

Though they were clearly Irish to the hilt, the Butlers were Anglican rather than Catholic. Anglo-Norman families, the Butlers among them, often became *Hibernis Hiberniores*, or "more Irish than the Irish."[4] There are zillions of Butler descendants, possibly including the poet William Butler Yeats, who shared with me that first Butler as a common ancestor twenty-five or so generations ago, though I doubt there's much more connection than that.[5]

The name dates back to the thirteenth century, when King John of England gave the title Chief Butler of Ireland to a supporter who accompanied him there. King John: The worst king in English history. The one who got his nobles so upset they shoved the Magna Carta down his throat. "John, John, bad King John, who shamed the throne that he sat on."[6] Along with the Butler name came the right for its owner to take a ton from any shipment of wine above a certain size that came into an Irish port. The family knew where their rake-off came from and became Episcopalians after Henry VIII broke with the Catholic Church.

With the title of Butler came a genuine family crest. I have one composed of colored glass partitioned by lead. The shield is divided into four sections. In the upper right and lower left, a trio of gold wine goblets shines against a crimson background. In the other two corners, a golden ocean rises in childlike zigzag waves against an azure sky, presumably representing the wine-dark sea the cargo traversed to reach the Butler. Above the shield is a fantastic tower of headgear. A medieval helmet is topped by a ducal crown, out of which bloom five ostrich feathers and on which rests a gimlet-eyed silver falcon with wings outspread. The falcon no doubt was meant to look fierce. To a modern eye, he looks surprised and silly. The helmet must symbolize status. With all that extra height, one like it couldn't have been used in battle; its owner might as well wear a duck on his head.

The motto emblazoned across the bottom reads, *"Comme je trouve."* That means "As I find it." The Butler brothers found *it* in a smooth-burning weed.

❧

When you've developed a taste for it, hot tobacco hits the mouth savory and sweet. The acrid scent alone is narcotic. Scientists would not discover tobacco's dangers until well into the twentieth century. The late nineteenth century boasted none of the restrictions that later burdened its sale. The rituals of tobacco give a nervous person something to do with his or her hands. At first those ceremonial activities included rolling a cigarette oneself. That process was something of an art, however. When the machine-rolled cigarette was invented in 1881, realms of production and marketing opened for entrepreneurs.

James B. Duke—from the family that named Duke University—beat his competitors to the door of the inventor of the automatic cigarette-rolling machine and cut a sweet-smelling deal.[7] Duke established American Tobacco, which controlled over 90 percent of the cigarette market and was referred to as "the Tobacco Trust." William Butler, my grandfather, probably secured his first job at a tobacco company when he was in his teens, about the time of the invention of the rolling machine. Still in his twenties, Butler became a director and vice president of American Tobacco.

It sounds like a good place to be, but Butler didn't stick around. He and his brother, George, made a move that secured their fortunes and a sentence or two in obscure annals. Duke was after 100 percent of the market, but the Tobacco Trust was still missing a few pieces; Liggett and Myers was the biggest.

Butler left American Tobacco to serve as president of a brand-new company, Union Tobacco, formed by a financier who appears to have specialized in various ways of duping the public. Insider trading and watered-down stock were among his operating methods.[8] Union Tobacco told the world that it intended to become a big player in chewing tobacco. However, it did not produce a single chaw in its existence of less than a year. What the company manufactured was an exquisite feat of arbitrage.

I've done a bit of arbitrage myself. Ohio State football tickets are sold at a fixed price, but some games are worth more than others. I can take a pair of tickets for which I paid seventy dollars—say, for an important Big Ten game—and, if I find I can't use them myself, sell them for much more online. I have made a risk-free profit taking advantage of price differences in two separate markets. I suppose it's cheating, but it's not illegal.

Union Tobacco accomplished arbitrage on a rather larger scale than reselling tickets to the Ohio State–Michigan game. First it acquired the Blackwell Company and its famous Bull Durham brand. Then it went after Liggett and Myers.

The Butlers had help from another man who was also starting his career. Bernard Baruch was still in his twenties. He went to Saint Louis, Liggett's headquarters, sometime after December 1898. George Butler was already on the scene. Butler began regularly to call on Colonel Moses Wetmore, president of Liggett, in his lodgings at the Planters Hotel. Meanwhile, Baruch cultivated Liggett's heirs. Saint Louis was more southern than northern in those days, and, according to Baruch's autobiography, the strategy was suitably indirect—to wear the colonel down with "amiability."[9]

In other words, Butler's job was to schmooze with the colonel, playing cards and telling stories.[10] I imagine them all sitting by a fire, playing whist or poker under gas lamps, drinking good American corn whiskey,[11] and smoking Chesterfields as they talked. Perhaps George told how his father was wanted in Ireland for killing an Englishman.

Perhaps he had tales of the battles his father fought in the Civil War, and he and Wetmore could compare notes. Wetmore, a Democrat and eventually the campaign manager for William Jennings Bryan, might have talked about free silver. Butler would have sympathized with the plight of poor Midwestern farmers weighed down by the gold standard, whether or not he agreed that silver should become currency.

Butler and his colleagues came away with an option to purchase more than half the stock of Liggett and Myers for $6.6 million.[12] American Tobacco then paid a highly inflated sum to buy the Liggett option from them. Union Tobacco got $20 million out of the deal and was immediately dissolved.[13] Baruch was on his way to becoming an extraordinarily successful financier and adviser to US presidents.

William and George were on their way to living it up. No evidence points to their engaging in any significant philanthropy. No university or hospital. No college gym. No fountain in an emergency waiting room. Not even a brick in a pocket park.

Sometime during this period, William married his much younger wife, probably within a few years of his financial sleight of hand. Gladys Berry was born in 1885 in Maryland. The Berry family in America goes back to the early seventeenth century, or about as early as it gets on this continent for Caucasians. The family had social standing and probably some money as well. They were indeed C of E and FF of V. The Berrys before the Civil

War must have held people as property—they were slave owners. Berry men fought for the South in the Civil War. So I have ancestors on both the Confederate and Union sides. William and Gladys had one child, also named Gladys, nicknamed Bunny, who was born in 1921, when William was in his fifties. That Gladys was my birth mother.

In the interim, William and George faced the little unpleasantness of the Sherman Antitrust Act, passed in 1890, the same year as the founding of American Tobacco. The act at first appeared to be mere window dressing, a toothless answer to citizens' concerns about far-reaching trusts. It didn't stop the new industrialists from inventing the modern corporation. When you have a monopoly and the means to keep other companies from starting up, you get to jack up prices and restrict supply. Plus you don't have to invest a lot in innovation. Monopolies are a bad deal for consumers.

It was the populist president Teddy Roosevelt who figured out how to use the Sherman Act to counterattack the mammoth agglomerations put together for the benefit of the people of the robber-baron class. William Butler's latest company was among those accused. He testified at the hearings that challenged American Tobacco's hold on the cigarette business. The Supreme Court broke up the Tobacco Trust in 1911, the same year it dismantled the Rockefellers' Standard Oil. I don't think Butler slowed down at that point; as far as I can tell, the family continued to live well.

Butler may have had one final fling. "He sold guns to the Germans in World War I," my birth mother wrote me from her psychiatric hospital room. I don't think she was proud of that story. It was one more chapter in her father's exuberantly piratic life. If the story is true, wasn't the munitions trade a betrayal of Butler's country? But the United States didn't enter the Great War until 1917, three years after it started. You also have to remember the family's loyalty to Ireland. Above all, Butler hated the English. He wouldn't mind helping gun them down.

William and Gladys Butler became members of "the 2,000," New York City's elite, or Chateaux Society.[14] It was not the original exclusive inner circle, but the circle as redefined by the aggressive nouveaux riches of the day. People like the Butlers. Four hundred had been the magic number of New York society's ingroup.[15] Then someone smart launched the *Social Register*, multiplying the number of acceptable people fivefold. The directory listed folks with new lucre along with those whose money had been around long enough that people forgot whether it was made legally, illegally, or in some anything-goes frontier where freebooters duked it out. A complete set of *Social Register*s from the early part of the last century was among the peculiar artifacts that arrived on my doorstep after my birth mother's death. They sat in the basement for a decade or so before someone needed the bookcase they were stored in and tossed them.

To own a yacht, then or now, is like hoisting a signal flag that means "superrich." As the saying goes, if you have to ask how much a yacht costs, you can't afford one. William Butler bought a yacht and became a member of the New York Yacht Club, which ran the America's Cup Race, the foremost international yachting competition. He was never commodore, however, despite what Belle, my grandmother, told me. The William Butlers divided their time between New York City and their summer house in Watch Hill, Rhode Island, near Newport, the capital of the Gilded Age. Gladys Berry Butler showed Chihuahuas at dog shows. They journeyed by ocean liner to England, France, and Italy.

George did not invent the tuxedo, as my grandmother had told me, but he and his brother wore them to fetes large and small. The story of his setting a record for changes of clothes in one day is possible. I have heard the exploit is recorded in *Ripley's Believe It or Not*. I am not sure whether to believe it. Or not.

William lived through the Roaring Twenties to see his fortune destroyed in the Great Depression that began in 1929. Perhaps, given time, he would have remade his money. I wouldn't put it past him.

◈

My grandfather was a swindling, munitions-dealing self-aggrandizer trading in carcinogens, the son of a murderer, himself descended from unscrupulous, rapacious middlemen raking in state-sanctioned graft from soul-destroying alcohol in the service of the combined stupidest and greediest monarch ever to sit on a throne. And he married into a slave-holding family, yet.

A fitting translation of *"Comme je trouve"* could be "Take whatever you can grab."

None of this history affects my descendants, whether biologically related or adopted. A person doesn't share many more genes with a great-great-grandfather than with a random stranger in Times Square.[16] The story of William Butler is entertainment, a paper heirloom.

The guy was more interesting than your plain old cattle thief, though. And I can't help indulging myself in looking at the story another way. William was a shining example of American get-up-and-go, wasn't he? It's what the country is about, right? We call it entrepreneurship, don't we? I like to think of those years when the fortunes of William and Gladys crested. I have a newspaper cutting with the headline "New York Dogs Take Laurels at Newport" and a photo of "Miss Gladys C. Butler with her Chihuahua Marata";[17] a gift card, perhaps once accompanied by flowers, that says, "Wishing my dear Bunny a pleasant trip to America and back to Monte Carlo, Uncle George"; and a newspaper clipping with a list of the steam yachts, sloop yachts, and cutter yachts that came to anchor at City Island in Long Island Sound, or left for Larchmont, or simply bellied by and were noted, including "Passing east May 29, 1895, was a steam yacht owned by William H. Butler." Her name: *Forget-Me-Not*.[18]

2

A Teddy Bear
Named Henry

"What are you doing out here?" the neighbor asked me as he struggled with his kid's bicycle in the rapidly dimming light. I didn't answer. The question was a rhetorical aside in the middle of frustrating work, perhaps reattaching a pedal that had come loose. The neighbors were used to the unsupervised four-year-old I was at that time.

The dad finished by flashlight. Headlights floated through the street. The lamps had come on in the courtyard of the brick post–World War II development in Hempstead, Long Island. When the dad and the other children left, I entered my high-rise, walked up the three flights of stairs, and quietly opened the back door.

My mother leapt at me like a lioness. She was weeping scarily.

"Vivi, I was frantic. Don't ever do that again." She held me crushingly close as she choked out the words, tears pouring down her cheeks.

I knew I had done the right thing. In that moment, as Gladys held me tight, I realized I was on my own. I would have to watch out for myself. I'd been smart to stay out long enough that she wasn't babbling and screaming in terror, which would put me in the way of blows. When Gladys did that, she addressed somebody else, somebody I could not see, and I couldn't understand what she was talking about. Hiding under an end table with the cat might have been enough to keep me out of whatever was going on, but the cat didn't like it and would escape from my arms. The cat could find a really safe place to hide. I was better off outside. It was a neighbor parent who took the training wheels off my bike and another who applied stinging mercurochrome to my knee when I scraped it trying a hard turn at a corner of the courtyard.

Several years later I had a word for that strange time when I was dependent on a caretaker who vacillated between the predictability of helping me serve tea to my teddy bears to raging tears and angry, pleading arguments with an invisible presence. The word was "uts-nay." It helped to use pig Latin. By the time I could use that emotionally distancing label, Gladys was distant physically—institutionalized. Several more years afterward I had the beginning of an explanation for the underlying trigger for her craziness. The trigger was crazy too, but even a little knowledge can lighten a dark load.

William Butler was middle-aged when his only child was born. Gladys Vivian Butler arrived in 1921 to a world of the New York *Social Register,* a Park Avenue address, and private schools. She hung on to that provenance throughout her sad life, like post–Civil War Southerners did, wishing for the return of antebellum privilege. It was a validation of self-worth through her years of psychosis.

They named her Gladys after her mother. I imagine the first few years of her life as princess perfect, living on Park Avenue in an elegant apartment with sparkling silver, vacationing at the estate in Watch Hill, and making the crossings to England and France. That ended when my grandmother died in Paris in October 1927.[1] William had stayed in New York. The coffin went back to the United States by sea with the six-year-old girl and her nanny.

It was a horrible voyage, Gladys said. It must have been, with her mother suddenly gone and the body somewhere below in the bowels of a steamship for an endless five-day Atlantic crossing. The hours stretch out for a child on a ship at the best of times, even now with video games and swimming pools. She must have consoled herself by playing with her teddy bears. She must have read what was available, perhaps wrapped in a blanket on a deck chair in the chilly Atlantic spray. Finally, the boat steamed into harbor on the west side of Manhattan, and she could see her father far below on the dock.

When Gladys's father died in the early 1930s,[2] his fortune largely lost, Gladys was still in her teens and truly alone. Her uncle George seems to have moved to Monte Carlo and was out of the picture. George's daughter, Gloria, eventually ran a tennis club in Monte Carlo, and I don't believe Gloria and Gladys were in communication after their fathers died. All Gladys had was a guardian, whom she called "Uncle Billy." Enough leftover money sent her to boarding school at Miss Hewitt's Classes and then Dana Hall in Wellesley, Massachusetts. Girls in her set weren't expected to go to college; "finishing" school was sufficient. Gladys rounded out her education with a year in Italy.

I wonder when Gladys started to show signs of illness. Did she have more than the usual mood swings as a teenager? Did she have days when she didn't get out of bed to go to classes because she was too sad to move? She had plenty to be sad about, alone in a world that denied her great expectations. I wonder if anything terrified her then, or if any particular people made her overwhelmingly guilty, foreshadowing what was to come.

In 1950, the time of my first memories, Gladys was on her own, in despair and besieged in a way I could not comprehend. Yet, I believe she tried her best to be a parent.

"You're a real live baby girl," she would repeat to me with delighted wonder that, I suppose, echoed her introduction to the new infant at my birth on February 15, 1946.

She showered me with whimsically named teddy bears. Herbert and Anatole were tiny Steiff bears, one white and one bronze. Henry, a medium-size yellow fellow with a pointed noise and working joints, was my favorite. He still lives in my closet on an overhead shelf with my pocketbooks. He looks a bit ragged, particularly the bald patch where I once gave him a haircut. Teddy Gold and Teddy Diapy were brothers. "Diapy" stood for "diaper," though he must have been out of diapers because he was enlisted to help me learn to use the toilet.

"See, Teddy Diapy can sit on the potty," Gladys would say, holding the small tan bear over the pot.

A Scottish nanny had taught Gladys how to behave, and she passed it on. "Wash behind your ears, or potatoes will grow," she told me. "You're nae sugar, nae salt, and you won't melt," meant you shouldn't fuss about going out in the rain. A saying I took to heart was, "Children should be seen and not heard." It suited my personality and my situation. Disturbingly, my mother had eyes in the back of her head, though when I snuck a look at her curls, I couldn't see the eyes.

I know Gladys read to me and the bears and recited poems to us in French and Italian. She must have gone through all the regular fairy tales. Perhaps I thought she was enchanted or being harassed by an invisible witch.

A couple of the older children in the neighborhood went to school. I wanted desperately to go to school or for my father to take me away.

❧

"There's Daddy," said Gladys. We were at the window of our constricted Hempstead apartment. I looked down across the courtyard and saw my father, tall and as handsome as a daddy should be, leaning against his parked car. I was high above him, and he was as tiny as my little finger. If only I were Rapunzel and could let down my hair and escape with him. Instead, he took us both out for a spin, then left. He was always a man uncomfortable with young children. He visited regularly, so I knew he cared about me, but I doubt that I was ever alone with him in those couple of years or that he asked me how I was doing.

When Gladys met Richard Jules Witkind in 1945 at the age of twenty-four, she must have been in an "up" period. She would have been pretty, with curly hair and a ready laugh. She would have been witty, often bitingly sarcastic, and have had a decidedly upper-crust accent, the kind you hear in movies from the 1930s that star Katherine Hepburn or Clark Gable. Dick would have been delighted at Gladys's patrician background. He considered his Jewishness a shortcoming, like a clubfoot that needed to be disguised by walking extra carefully.

Gladys would have easily fallen for Dick, especially when he was wearing his naval officer's uniform. His calm demeanor spoke of competence, decisiveness, and even valor. He would have seemed reassuring to someone who was already a little edgy. Dick could be deeply serious but had a sense of humor that often turned puckish. A solid six feet tall, he had thick eyebrows, dark hair, and deep-set eyes. He was lean and fit. Gladys would have figured out quickly that he was well educated. He spent his high school years at Horace Mann in New York City, a private school named for the famous educator. His bachelor's degree was from the University of Virginia, a gentlemen's school at the time.

The uncertainty of wartime makes acting fast seem important. Gladys and Dick fell for each other hard and married in 1945. I was born the next year when he was at sea. When I was about two years old, Dick divorced Gladys in Idaho, one of the few states where it was easy to do so. From the time I could think about such things, I knew it was good for him to get out of the marriage.

I don't know what happened to get me out, only the incident on which my childhood self fixated. Gladys socked me hard in public, and it took on the clarity and power of a personal myth.

She and I were in a department store near the elevators. Whatever four-year-old behavior I was into, lollygagging or whining or begging, was sufficient for her to lose control. She hit me hard. I screamed. I pulled away, but she had me by the left arm and hit me again. Maybe she meant to slap me on my bottom, but nothing cushioned where her hand came down with untempered anger. The episode ended abruptly when an elevator door opened. Gladys "beating me up" became my most essential memory, a part of myself locked up safely like a small, precious shard of glass. In it lay my sharpest fears, an aching sorrow, and a conviction that I was an extremely special person, like one of those beautiful, lonely little girls in the grim stories.

The department store incident could have been what got the attention of other adults. Or perhaps Dick had already figured out intolerable sickness darkened the apartment in Hempstead. Perhaps it was Dick's mother or one of the neighbors. It could have been Gladys herself who said she could not go on.

Whoever the precipitator was, Gladys was taken somewhere. I was immensely pleased that she got what she deserved: suitable punishment for treating me badly. And I was wounded to the soft center of my tiny self by being separated from my adored mother, the one who taught me not to eat the icing first on a piece of cake because then I would not have it to look forward to.

I moved in with Dick's mother, Belle, who had a huge apartment at 888 Park Avenue in the city. Henry and the other teddy bears came along. The bad time was over, though it would have repercussions in my own bouts of despair and fear.

᠅

Researching the story of Gladys's parents, I found an entry in the 1930 US census for a household in a Park Avenue apartment that included William Butler, age sixty-four, head of household; Gladys Berry Butler, age nine, daughter; and Elizabeth Jackson, age forty-two, nurse, birthplace, Scotland.

It was the Scottish nanny, the one who'd said, "You're nae sugar, nae salt, and you'll nae melt" if you go out in the rain. The nanny was a real person. For the first time in my life it occurred to me that this Gladys Berry Butler listed by a US Bureau of the Census worker over eighty years ago was a real child, living with her father and a caretaker.

I was sixty-five years old, and it was the first time I thought of Gladys as something other than a mental patient. I wondered what she would have been like without her illness.

I had already come to terms with the period of blows by then. That happened in my early forties, when I'd turned miserably sad and went to a psychiatrist. She wanted to give me medication, but I refused—that would make me a mental patient, which I wanted to avoid. I did, however, dredge up my most essential memory.

"She beat me up," I told the shrink. I expected horror and commiseration. Instead, the therapist said it wasn't too surprising, considering how ill Gladys was. She calmly asked if police had come, if I'd gone to the hospital, or if I had scars. In the quiet of the psychiatrist's office, sitting on a comfortable sofa in low light, the mantra of "Gladys beat me up" lost its cosmological grandeur and became connected to a world where people could ask reasonable questions about what happened.

"You just took away my most essential memory," I told the shrink with amazement. My immediate relief, like from a migraine headache after an injection of Imitrex takes hold, is the best single piece of evidence I have ever had of the value of the talking cure.

Many people have difficult times. Memoirs are loaded with them. Without Gladys's illness, I would be less aware today of how lucky I am. But at the age of four, I had no words, no context, no one to talk to, and no way out.

3

MY ROCK IN
CENTRAL PARK

I had a rock in New York City. I can't throw in the rock as part of my legacy to my descendants along with the silver spoons. Excavating the thing and getting it out of Central Park would cause all kinds of trouble. I can, however, tell you where it is and leave you the stories that make the rock mine.

With my grandmother or babysitter as escort, I would head for my rock, through the Seventy-Sixth Street entrance to Central Park from Fifth Avenue, via a winding path. From a distance, my weathered granite outcropping was an enormous gray mound shaped roughly like the letter *C*. Up close it was a wedding of white, black, bits of red, and sparks of light, warm from the summer sun. Inside the enfolding curve, the ground was bare, thanks to the sneakers of kids like me who comforted their dolls with tiny plastic bottles or defended their forts with cap guns as raging Indians tried to breach the wall. Inside, slightly to the right of the middle of the *C*, a jagged crack snaked from bottom to top. Within the crack, a stone sliver gave a foothold. The sliver was shaped like Manhattan Island, with the surrounding ribbons of dirt the Hudson and East Rivers, cloistered from the outside world.

I would reach up and grab the wall with my fingertips and arc my right foot as high as it could go. That allowed my knee the angle and my small thigh the leverage needed to push my toes against the slightly loose sliver and rise to a victor's stance.

I stood on top of my rock, overlooking the vast veldt of Central Park surrounded by the pillars of an empire. I was five years old and at the center of the universe.

My claustrophobic confinement as a preschooler alone with Gladys was over. By the summer of 1951, I was living with my paternal grandmother, a solid, stable woman. The local telephone exchange serving Belle's Park Avenue apartment was Butterfield 8, the name of a movie that emphasized an Upper East Side location.

Belle had been in my life from the beginning. Unlike William Butler, this grandparent was someone I knew, even if I didn't appreciate what she did for me until later. Gladys stayed with her while Dick was overseas in the navy and I was born at Lennox Hill Hospital. Belle, like Dick, kept track of me when Gladys and I lived in Hempstead, Long Island. In her fifties, her three children long raised, she took me in.

Belle was one of five children—four girls and a boy. Her father, Julius Shapiro, arrived in the 1890s from the town of Kaunas, or Kovno, which was in Lithuania when it was a country and in the Russian region of Kiev when Lithuania was subsumed by the Russian empire.[1] Julius's father was "the chief rabbi of Kaunas and a respected intellectual leader of Lithuania."[2] Jews in Lithuania dated back to the tenth century.[3] You won't find them there now. They had ups and downs during the czarist period, but Hitler's final solution finally did them in. Over two and a half million Jews left Russia, Lithuania, and their neighboring areas between 1881 and

1914.[4] They were the smart ones. When Germany invaded in World War II, the ethnic Lithuanians were enthusiastic and successful in helping the effort to exterminate the Jews.

Shapiro was changed to *Speyer.* The newly surnamed Isabelle Speyer and her family did their best to blend in and indeed flourished as Americans. All the sisters had postsecondary education. Two were nurses. Belle attended Columbia Teachers' College and worked as a secretary. The son, Archie, became the family sorrow, marrying a woman the sisters considered uneducated and anti-Semitic. The sisters found solid Jewish citizens to wed. After a bad first marriage, which I never heard Belle talk about, and the birth of one child, Blanche, Isabelle married Charles Witkind and had two sons, Richard (Dick) and Lloyd.

Dick's father died suddenly when he was nine, a huge blow that he never talked about. It happened in 1929—a good year to pop off, in a sense, and avoid the misery of the Depression, but not so good for your wife and three young children.

Belle dated her life by Charlie's death. "When Charlie was alive...," she would say. When Charlie was alive, the family had an enormous house complete with gazebo and topiary gardens in Deal, New Jersey, to which they repaired in the summer. She had to sell the summer house after he died, presumably along with other accoutrements of a wealthy life. In that, the Witkinds were similar to the Butlers. Rental properties, particularly around Columbia University, were the source of family income and remained steady enough.

"We're comfortable," Belle would say to me, or, "We're well enough off." She meant we had enough to live on, though things weren't the same in the post-Charlie era.

In investigating online records through Ancestry.com, I was shocked to be guided to a reference in the 1940s to an Isabelle Finck. I talked to Dick's first cousin Chuck Cooper. He confirmed that Belle had married after Charlie's death, this time to a lawyer named Finck who had children. They lived together as a household. That had to be only shortly before I was born. I was stunned. I knew I was missing information on the first husband—and on the sainted Charlie, in fact—but no one, certainly not Belle, ever said anything about a third. It was one of those strange branches in the tangled vines of genealogy.

᳀

Belle had help caring for me in the gentle form of Inez Jenkins, a tall, zaftig African American woman who had no children of her own. Many years later I asked Inez how she felt about my arrival.

"Your grandma looked at me, and I looked at her," she said. "And we kind of shrugged our shoulders and said, 'OK, the two of us together can do it.'"

Inez had no New York accent herself, nor a southern one, which might have been expected at the time. She didn't get the title of nanny but was called the maid and always wore a uniform. Inez took me to the park, held me on her ample lap, and played silly games with me.

"The weatherman says it's going to rain a bit today," Inez would say when she arrived in the morning.

"Who is the weatherman?" I asked her one day.

"He's a nice old fella. He gives me a wave every day on my way to work."

"Where does he live?"

"On Eighty-Sixth Street."

It was good to know the weatherman was close and keeping an eye on things.

Belle cooked three meals a day, starting with eggs and bacon for breakfast, and worried that I did not eat enough and was growing only by quarter inches.

I felt safe. Even better, one of my greatest wishes was about to come true. I was going to school.

❦Belle took me to visit the Town School, where an interviewer asked what I thought were stupid questions, like what the difference between a hippo and a rhino was. She showed me a Babar book.

Belle boasted afterward, "And she said, 'This one is Pom, and this is Alexander, and this is Flora.'"

Pom and Alexander were boy elephants drawn exactly the same, so I knew I'd been guessing. I did name Arthur, who was larger and wore a beret. It was one of those worrisome times when someone said how bright I was, which was important to them and made me special. Living up to it was already a concern.

I wouldn't turn six until the following February and was small and immature for first grade. But the school was suited to me. The Town School in 1951 was "progressive," meaning the teachers put academic achievement into the context of nurturing a whole child. The classes were tiny. My fourth-grade graduating class had seven students. The school was a model for others, including the Lower School at the Columbus School for

Girls. We called our enthusiastic teachers by their last names and ending with a *y*, like pets or friends: Houcky, Wrighty, Youngy, and Mavey. It was a perfect combination of a new world, support from kind adults who were all like surrogate mothers, and regimented predictability that I desired as much as anything.

I took to reading like a bird to song and wrote down the name of each book I read in painstaking print. After Christmas, the kids in the class who were deemed ready received arithmetic workbooks. I loved the touch of graphite on paper as I completed page after page of addition and subtraction with the physical satisfaction of a stonecutter building a wall. By the end of first grade, I had forty-eight books on my list and knew my father and teacher were proud of me.

My father was the handsomest man in New York. I know that because the *New York Daily News* once called his brother, Lloyd, a hanger-on in the city's café society, the second-handsomest man in New York, and Dick was the better looking of the two. He had bushy eyebrows, a velvety bass voice, and a demeanor that was reserved and serious yet could switch suddenly so that it was still low-key but twinkling with humor. Hearing him speak you would be sure he could sing beautifully; in fact, he could not carry a tune at all. Lloyd's voice was even deeper and more resonant, so deep you could imagine him saying "CNN" at the bottom of the bass range. This was probably the result of the couple of packs of cigarettes he smoked into the dawn in all those cafés and in the late morning over his coffee, checking to see whether he had made the society section of the papers. I've never seen the *Daily News* story naming Lloyd the second-handsomest man in New York. Maybe it didn't exist, but I like to believe it.

Along with the possibly mythical newspaper article, I have the word of a somewhat independent observer, a cousin in New York who married into the family during World War II. Bea Cooper, Chuck Cooper's wife, told me how she remembered seeing Dick and Lloyd for the first time. Together they had entered a synagogue for a bar mitzvah, Dick in his navy uniform and Lloyd an air force lieutenant.

"I thought to myself that I had never seen two more handsome men in my whole life," she said.

Dick was not a roué and bounder like Lloyd, but he did have a series of girlfriends. I knew about them but usually did not meet them. I wonder whether he told them I existed. Dick dated librarians and UN translators. His brother held the attention of models and aspiring actresses.

World War II was tough on my uncle. Lloyd was a bombardier on a B-29, and one day the crew went on a mission that did not require a bombardier, leaving him on the ground in Australia. The others did not come back. My uncle didn't have photos on his bureau of any of the models, but he did keep an eight-by-ten black-and-white picture of the young, smiling crew posed beside their aircraft.

I never saw Dick's apartment, but I knew he had a busy life beyond my ken. He was a "customers' man," meaning a stockbroker, at Bache & Company on Wall Street, one of those brokerage firms that has long since merged with other companies. I think of his string of girlfriends, not all of whom I met, as being tall and beautiful, with names like Gloria and an elegance I knew even then I would never attain. One, a Chinese woman, worked for the Library of Congress, and Dick would take the train down to Washington for the weekend to visit her. I imagined her charm and worldliness and how she would have read a lot more books than I.

I assumed it was normal for fathers to be away a lot, and in the 1950s there was some truth to that: mothers were supposed to stick to homemaking. The lengths of my father's absences were unusual, however.

Although they were not supposed to be especially involved in child rearing, the fathers of my classmates went to work and came home to dinner. I was delighted that Dick visited regularly on Tuesday evenings. Belle made sure the cupboard had a box of Mallomars, a deliciously bulbous cookie with a graham-cracker bottom, marshmallow filling, and dark-chocolate coating. Eating directly from the box, he would consume all nine Mallomars with a glass of milk.

Every Saturday that he was in town, Dick took me on an excursion. Our outings usually commenced at Hamburg Heaven on Madison Avenue for a lunch of juicy hamburgers with red relish. We walked down Madison, probably to Doubleday's bookstore, which I think was at Fifty-Seventh and Fifth, my father shortening his stride so I could keep up. I chattered all the way, thrilled to be with him, to hold his large hand and try to impress him with all I was doing and learning.

Dick posed questions as we walked, such as how to identify signs of spring. In the city in March, the harbingers of gentle weather were not always as obvious as buds on the caged trees along the sidewalks. Were the roasted chestnut hawkers gone, replaced with an early Good Humor truck? Were the doors of some of the boutiques open to the bracing air? Were the men wearing felt fedoras or, sensing winter's demise, boldly sporting straw Panamas?

Dick would buy me a book, ordinarily for one dollar, at Doubleday's— probably one in a series, such as biographies called *The Story of...*about people like Andrew Jackson or Thomas Alva Edison (almost all white males except for the occasional George Washington Carver or Florence Nightingale) or a Black Stallion or other horse book. A new Pogo book was the greatest find. I read the comic books about the possum who lived in the Okefenokee Swamp over and over at bedtime, eating Mallomars (four one night and five the next) and drinking a glass of milk, feeling close to my father.

Once I selected a bigger book, *Exploring Nature with Your Child*.

"That's too expensive," Dick said. It cost four dollars, a whole lot. He bought it for me anyway.

He never followed up on the book the way I'd hoped. Even so, as I think about it, Dick did explore nature with his child—not a lot, but enough to count. In the summer he took me to Jones Beach on Long Island, driving the convertible sports car he owned jointly with Lloyd. We hiked from the parking lot to a spot that was not too crowded or too far from the water. He threw down a faded, blue US Navy bedspread for our place on the sand, weighting the corners against the wind with objects from the beach bag. The waves were frequently an overwhelming sight, but I'd learned to swim when I was six during a summer in Florida with Belle. Dick taught me how to dive through waves that were too large for me to swim over, yet large enough to knock me down if I faced them straight on. When the water was brutal and white-capped, he beached me.

He taught me to dig for sand crabs. The harmless crustaceans follow breakers, scuttling just below the surface of the sand as the water recedes, making small moving lumps. Captured, they were no bigger than Dick's thumb, but they filled my whole palm. The crab would be still for a moment as I grabbed it, but when I held it in the water, it would wiggle for freedom, tickling my hand with its antennae and feet. We built small pools for the crabs and collected them, although there was no way to keep up with more than three or four because they were constantly attempting to escape into the sides of the pools. Sand crabs can swim backward, which made it harder.

When hungry, we walked barefoot to the concession stand for fat hot dogs, which Dick said were best with lots of relish and mustard, but no ketchup. The sand was painfully hot, but the journey was worth it. We finished with ice cream, oddly sold as rectangular blocks of chocolate or vanilla jammed into round cones. The first years we went to the beach, the ice cream melted more rapidly than I could manage and would drip stickily onto my hand. I learned to eat at exactly the right speed to avoid drips but savor each slow lick.

Every year at Christmastime, as we stood on the second floor of FAO Schwartz watching the big-gauge Lionels labor in elaborate loops, Dick would ask, looking down at me with amused hope, "Are you sure you don't want a train set for Christmas?"

"Whoo-oo," their horns called brightly, and the metal wheels clacked on metal rails. The display was surrounded by rapt fathers and their kids, mostly boys. I tried to pay attention and enjoy the way the electric trains crossed intersections within seconds of each other without crashing. They rose over bridges. They disappeared into tunnels and magically reappeared. The engines, coal cars, and freight cars exhibited signs like Southern Pacific and Burlington Northern. The passenger trains had tiny windows for the tiny occupants to look through and admire the miniature train stations, model villages, and rolling scenery. I liked lots of boy games, but I drew the line at train sets.

Dick would look down at me sideways, expectantly.

"No," I would reply, feeling it was an assertion of my separate self. To Dick's credit, he did not use me as an excuse to purchase one. How we could have fit it into the apartment I do not know.

As we rode home in the Town School station wagon driven by Mr. Mounter, known, of course, as Mounty, a girl named Harriet inspected the gold locket with my initials—VMW, for Vivian Mary Witkind—that Gladys had given me. It was the kind that opened to reveal photos, though it had none.

"You can tell real gold by how hard it is," she said. "Give it to me."

I gave the locket to Harriet, and she bit it.

"See," she said. "It's not real gold."

The tooth marks were real, and are to this day.

"Where is your mother, anyway?" asked another child another time in a classroom.

"In a rest home." I wasn't sure what a rest home was, but that's what I was told.

"Why?"

"For cruelty to children," I said, as Youngy looked at me with narrowed eyes and a shallow frown.

In art class, I painted watercolor sunsets over and over.

"Could you try something else besides sunsets?" asked Wrighty, who handled the art, as I gave her my latest.

I could not. I took a new sheet of thick, yellowish paper and gave it a thin strip of brown, arid land at the bottom and then a thinner strip of fast-disappearing sun. I moved the thick brush upward and painted a thick horizontal band of bloody pink, then darker pink and red and deep blue, and finally a broad stripe of despairing black.

Belle began to take me to a psychiatrist once a week, perhaps at the school's urging. At least I was told she was a psychiatrist, though her sobriquet was "Mrs." Mrs. Enterman practiced out of a brownstone about ten blocks uptown.

Mrs. Enterman seemed perpetually bored. She quietly played solitaire at the beginning of our sessions while I made up dramas with various small dolls. After a while she would invite me over to her desk and, still playing solitaire, try to draw me out. She rarely looked up from the game. I suppose she was being patient as well as playing Patience.

She recommended that Dick and Belle buy me a punching bag. It had a wooden base to stand on, so a child's weight kept it stable. A flexible pole inserted into the end of the board held the bag, and I socked the daylights out of it.

Mrs. Enterman sent me a present herself. It was an unfinished dollhouse with instructions and equipment for painting it and putting in wallpaper and carpet and, indeed, making it into a comfortable, safe place for the lucky dolls, who had a real home and family. I worked for weeks cutting, pasting, painting, and furnishing.

I knew what a real home was, and not only from reading *The Bobbsey Twins* and other children's books where happy families are all alike. Belle was close to her sisters, and their children had kids my age in the suburbs: Mahopac, Scarsdale, and Mount Kisco.

The trips to Mount Kisco were the best. Eddie and Grace Marwell lived in a rambling, weathered prewar house. They had few neighbors, and the back of the house bordered a wide field. The house jumped with four stepping-stone kids. Stuart, the oldest, always had ideas for new games. I participated with the joy of someone acting out her dream life. They even had trees to climb, though I found I was scared of heights and could not go up very high. The only thing missing was horses. I wished that someday I had a home like my cousins', with a husband, lots of children, trees, fields, and a stable.

❦

"Who is your second-best friend?" asked Mrs. Enterman, moving a red ace up and flipping the card underneath. She knew my first-best friend was Carol.

"Carol."

"Aha! A slip of the tongue," she said with great excitement for a change. It was probably her best Freudian detection of the day. "Who is really your first-best friend, then?"

What I meant was that Carol was my first-best, second-best, and truest friend. Carol lived with her father, and her grandmother—his mother—helped out with sitting and cooking, while I lived with my grandmother and saw my father once or twice a week. Carol's mother was a psychiatric patient in the care of the state of New York and came home briefly every once in a while, drugged to the point of zombiism. I couldn't have pinpointed the difference between a mental hospital and a rest home, but I knew Carol and I were in the same predicament.

Carol and I watched *The Snakepit*, with Olivia de Havilland playing a patient in the insane asylum. At one point in the movie, she is put into a bathtub to calm her down, one of the strange treatments of the time. While forcing her into the tub, one nurse says to the other, "She's uts-nay."

"It's not nice to call a person uts-nay in a place like this," said de Havilland.

Carol and I laughed ourselves silly. If we'd been able to replay the film, we would have gone back to that scene over and over, but that technology did not exist. Instead, we regaled each other with "uts-nays" as conversation stoppers or starters or random outbursts.

The word did not come up in our imaginary worlds, however. Narnia came ready to inhabit via the C. S. Lewis stories. A new book in the series was published each year. It was a superb place for queens, kings, horses (some of them talking horses), and adventures. It wasn't my only fantasy world, however. I reported in the first of many journals that I had three made-up worlds plus twenty-five imaginary dogs with pedigrees.

I also ran a ranch using plastic riders and horses, many sold as representations of historical figures. Rows of books from my two bookcases, tented to stand on their sides, became stables and paddocks. Thus it was that Annie Oakley became the boss of stable hands who looked remarkably like Robert E. Lee (on Traveler) and George Washington (on his white horse).

At the end of *The Snakepit*, de Havilland's character is allowed to leave the insane asylum, and the song "Going Home" fills the asylum's eating hall. The last thing *I* wanted was to have my birth mother come home.

Blessedly, Gladys did not visit in these early grade-school years, but Belle hauled me up by train to Stamford, Connecticut, to see her a few times, which was a few times too many. Stamford Hall indeed seemed restful. It had a pleasant garden, and the residents must have been delighted to see a child in their midst. One time, Gladys and I were sent to her room to be alone together. I did not go gladly.

"Those are fleurs-de-lis," Gladys said as I gazed neutrally at the pattern on the wallpaper. "They're a symbol of royalty. The Bourbon kings."

I took in the information but kept quiet. Children should be seen and not heard. I had mentally added "no sudden moves" to the list of aphorisms. In her restful room, my mother was calm, and I wasn't going to get in the way of that. As far as I was concerned, we were separated by a clear wall as tough as Mrs. Enterman's heavy wooden desk.

❧

By the time I was in fourth grade and about eight years old, Belle and I moved from the expansive apartment on Park to a somewhat smaller one at 142 East Seventy-First Street. It was the only apartment building on the block bounded by Third and Lexington Avenues. If you kept the single apartment building out of the viewfinder, it was an iconic New York City street of cozy two- and three-story brownstones with outside staircases and decorative courtyards. The producers of *Breakfast at Tiffany's*, the midcentury movie, figured that out and used our street as Holly Golightly's home. They closed the block off to shoot, which meant that for two days I could not run free with my gang.

I'd zip down the back stairs of the apartment and meet my friends on the sidewalk for handball, stoopball, hide-and-seek, or cowboys and Indians. The brownstone houses had stairs, sunken front yards, low walls of various heights, and openings that easily translated to hills and arroyos. I owned a cowgirl outfit and six-shooters with fringed and sequined holsters.

We played two varieties of handball, American and Chinese, each with three or more players. The outer wall of the apartment building made the backboard for the game, and the clearly marked squares in the cement formed the boundaries for the hits. In American handball, the server slapped the ball directly against the wall with no bounce and into the court to his or her right. In Chinese handball, the ball had to bounce once before it hit the wall. We used Spalding "high-bounce" hollow rubber balls, red and a little smaller than tennis balls. Just as golf courses had roughs, we also had a big rough—Lexington Avenue. It was unnerving to see a ball that looped awry get crushed by a fast-moving bus coughing up diesel fumes as it headed uptown. When that happened we went around the corner to the toy store and bought another ball for about a dime, the amount of my weekly allowance.

Bruce was our leader, the one who came up with what to do next and what the rules should be. Bruce and I agreed that we would marry when we grew up. It didn't work out. Bruce went away to boarding school eventually, and I lost track of him.

"You're not like the other girls," he said, my first clue, well before I read *Little Women* and wanted to be like Jo, that the opposite sex did not always want a frou-frou form of femininity. Bruce was a couple of years older than me and had no sisters, only a younger brother named Keith, who by the age of four was busy selling his artwork—watercolor sloshes on kindergarten paper—from their brownstone stoop. When Keith was low on art, he diversified his product line and sold Kool-Aid in paper Dixie cups. The passersby thought he was adorable and were often, as I viewed it, suckered in. I wouldn't be surprised if he grew up to be a captain of industry.

In the name of prepubescent research, Bruce suggested we show each other how we went to the bathroom. That gave me good visual information, but he was disappointed.

"There's nothing to see," he complained, so we went into a closet for a more equal exchange of views.

୬

The fourth grade at the Town School was a milestone because that was the highest grade it had. Everyone adored Mavey, one of those splendid teachers often found in fourth grade.[5] I suppose Mavey would have been a corporate lawyer or hedge-fund operator if those paths had been open to women in the 1950s. Because Mavey was from Norway, the last year at the Town School was also an indoctrination into the achievements of the Vikings. The word *Sweden* never came up. We learned poems with lines like "Our sea-steed through the foam goes prancing / While shields and spears and helms are glancing." The accompanying assignment was to draw a picture of a Viking ship thrashing its way through the waves. We learned, "Washed and well fed should a man ride to the Thing, though he be not so well dressed." Mavey explained that the Thing was the precursor of democracy, a forum where everybody had a say and decisions were made for the good of the community. For many years I was convinced that Norway was the one and only fount of the idea of constitutional government.

The highlight of every fourth-grader's year was when Mrs. Mavey undid her waist-length braid and let her silver hair hang down her back while we listened to Wagner's "Ride of the Valkyries."

With only seven of us in the fourth-grade class, Mavey gave me my head, allowing me to get the class to put on a play I wrote and letting me form a "nature club" under the auspices of the Museum of Natural History. The other kids went along with it, though I bet they saw me as a teacher's pet.

By the end of that year, I was reading at the twelfth-grade level. In other words, I got every question right on the reading test and thought I was really, really smart. That made up for the kids who called me a shrimp because I was so short.

An objective observer, Mavey, perhaps, would have found words to say I was short in grace and empathy and tall in fear of change. For one thing, I sucked my tongue. I didn't actively suck it; I slipped it between my front teeth like an infant ready for a nipple. I didn't even bother to wait until people weren't looking. I sucked when I drank, whether or not I had a straw. On the positive side, the teachers must have liked my exuberance for school. We didn't have homework, but I would cram a backpack full of books and comic books anyway, pretending I had more work to do, like older children did. From my vantage point in the present, it's hard to believe a child so babyish and so determined to stay that way would ever become a functioning adult. I was lucky to have the Town School as an incubator.

Mavey allowed me to carry Henry, the teddy bear, at the fourth-grade graduation ceremony.

❧

Throughout the Town School years, Central Park beckoned. In the winter I sledded near the Seventy-Ninth Street entrance from Fifth Avenue. On the hottest days, I would play in the circle of shooting spray from a fountain in the playground. Inez would sit on a bench and watch. Or Belle would, accompanied by a sister, a friend, or Aunt Belle.

"Why do I call her 'aunt'?" I asked.

"She was your grandfather Butler's mistress," she answered.

That was sufficient. I did not ask how Belle van Loan came to be with William Butler or whether it was before or after his wife died. I must have heard about mistresses, though I had no idea of the sexual aspect. Though ancient, Aunt Belle had an aquiline nose and a dramatic *poitrine* that fit my idea of a mistress. Belle and Aunt Belle seemed like the grandmother and courtesan aunt in *Gigi*. Remembering Aunt Belle now, I wonder how she fits in the family tree. What do genealogists do with mistresses?

Roller-skating was a major sport in the park. My small, unskilled hands had trouble turning the key that tightened the metal bands over my shoes so I could travel along the concrete walkway on eight metal wheels. A grown-up would have to complete the job to ensure that the bands squeezed deep into the shoe leather. Cracks in the road were big risks, and my knees were often skinned.

Inez or Belle took me to the Central Park Zoo, where my favorite animal was Rose, a hippopotamus. I loved the joke of naming an ungainly, ugly animal for a delicate flower. At the seal pond, I watched in rapture even when the seals only lay in boneless poses sunning themselves. I'd keep my patient adult in hand as I hoped for one to arc his whiskery head and bark. Best was when one, then two, then three decided it was time for a swim and slid awkwardly into their moat to become creatures of fluid grace.

And of course, my rock was ideal for entering Narnia or becoming a perfect house in the country (with horses). Which would I gravitate toward: a safe imaginary world or a risky real one?

In the early spring of 2000, my husband, Jack, and I took our youngest child, Charlotte, and Julie, a friend of hers, to New York to see the sights, traveling east from our comfortable home in the suburbs (without horses). The girls were twelve, and I was determined to stuff them with theater and art. We had fifth-row orchestra seats to see Bernadette Peters in a revival of *Annie Get Your Gun*. It was rainy, so we spent two days at the Metropolitan Museum of Art, exploring most of its dark corridors. On the afternoon of the second day, I asked Julie, who was standing against a cold, dark museum wall, deep into a collection of Neolithic objects, what she wanted to do next.

"I want to see the sun," she said and slowly slid down the wall in dramatically restrained agony.

"I'll take you to my rock," I said.

My personal igneous intrusion on permanent exhibit was a fifteen-minute walk from the museum. There it was, a natural dolmen of mysterious meaning, a wedding cake of red and gold orthoclase feldspar, plagioclase feldspar, black basalt, white quartz, and sparkling mica (I'd taken geology in college). As I stood with the girls, the realization poured into me like lava down a cliff—my rock was only four feet tall. The ground within the half circle, once flat, was concave from fifty years of pounding by small, active feet. And the sliver of rock that gave me purchase to climb from the inside out was gone, worried free, as if Manhattan were no longer the center of the universe.

4

AN ORIGINAL-CAST RECORDING OF *ONCE UPON A MATTRESS*

Right about the time that puberty socked me in the gut in the middle of seventh grade, my well-defended life was shattered. Gladys reappeared, then fled to another continent in a bewildering blaze of craziness. Dick jilted me for a stepmother. Stepmothers were by definition wicked—I was sure of that.

Change was coming whether I wanted it or not. I'd lost the ability to get into Narnia. I was in deep trouble.

I had started fifth grade in the fall of 1955 at Miss Hewitt's Classes, an all-girls independent school. Gladys had boarded at Hewitt's, which was one reason for the choice. The Town School also suggested to Dick and Belle that I would do better in a small school, and Hewitt's had about twenty students per class. I picked up a couple more years in a cocoon, spoiled by Belle and Inez, escorted by Dick on Saturdays, and safe from Gladys, who was in the Connecticut "rest home."

Unlike the Town School, Hewitt's called for fitting in rather than standing out. Authoritarianism agreed with me. The more rules and hierarchy, the safer I felt. I liked the bells that announced classes. I liked seeing myself as a middle schooler with an infinite ladder of girls ahead of me all the way to twelfth grade, which was forever.

Miss Hewitt hailed from England, and the school was more Anglican than the archbishop of Canterbury. I adored curtsying to the homeroom teacher every morning before we said the Lord's Prayer in unison. I didn't mind that the teacher sometimes stalked down the rows to make sure every girl said every line of the prayer. The Episcopal version had four more lines than the Catholic one at the time. In what passed for protest against regimentation in those days, sometimes one of the few Catholics would bravely seal her lips rather than voice, "For thine is the kingdom" and the rest. Counting me as half Episcopalian and half Jewish, there were one and a half Jewish girls in my class, more than in many at Hewitt's. That was unusual for a private school in New York City.

In fifth and sixth grades, our uniforms were navy-blue tunics worn over white blouses and navy bloomers—baggy shorts gathered above the knee. For recess or gym class, we shed the tunics. In seventh grade, we graduated to navy wool blazers with light, plaid cotton skirts in the fall and spring and dark wool ones in the winter. If a girl won a sports award, she could have a white "HC" sewn on a pocket.

Skirmishes over the uniforms occurred, of course. Independent schools are always fighting dress-code violations, and the assault in the late 1950s was from crinolines—stiff petticoats under the pleated skirts. Girls piled up three or four of them and looked like pears. I wore one, but not more, and did not mind when crinolines were forbidden, a rule that probably stayed in the dress code long after anyone knew what the word meant.

Our white blouses had Peter Pan collars. I assumed at the time that they were named for the new musical with Mary Martin. In fact, Peter Pan collars were more or less in vogue for little girls from early in the twentieth century. The bloomers dated from the nineteenth century. They allowed modesty without being shorts, which were for boys. Barrie's fantasy did have an influence: three of the girls in my class of twenty or so were named Wendy. Teachers used the first initial of their last names to distinguish them. Peter Pan can hang out in Neverland; Wendys have to grow up.

Wendy J. was my new best friend, an ebullient girl, though no scholar. On school mornings I walked from my grandmother's apartment on East Seventy-First Street to Wendy's apartment building on Seventy-Second Street between Madison and Fifth, and we went on together to Hewitt's on Seventy-Sixth between Madison and Park.

My former best friend Carol was at the Nightingale-Bamford School uptown. We saw each other, but our interests had diverged. Carol had a ferocious crush on Boris Karloff, the horror movie actor, and was only slightly less madly in love with the other stars of the genre. My dreamboat was Jackie Cooper, the star of a TV comedy called *Hennesy*, about a handsome navy doctor in a white uniform. *Hennesy* had a laugh track. Nothing remotely scary happened, ever. And in an episode I anticipated with romantic fervor, his nurse got to marry him.

Carol scheduled her weeks using *TV Guide*'s paper listings of scary movies to be shown on the recycled movie channel, one of the seven channels we had in New York at the time. I don't suppose the old Frankenstein and Dracula movies would frighten a middle-school child today. They scared the bloomers off me. Worse, Carol liked to go out to see the new horror films in the movie theater. I tried it a couple of times, cowering in my seat with my cardigan pulled over my eyes, while Godzilla made a mess of Tokyo or the Blob from outer space silently surrounded and sucked up human beings and expanded its gooey girth to the size of Philadelphia.

⚓

By the time I started seventh grade, Gladys was out of stir, but I was in no danger of having to live with her. I suppose Dick and Belle could see that would be too much for Gladys, as well as for me. Gladys seemed happy to be a visitor to the apartment on Seventy-First Street. She was living somewhere in Connecticut and working in sales at Bloomingdale's. In retrospect, that she had a period in her adult life when she was able and willing to hold a job is amazing.

"Mom is great," I wrote in my red-leather diary with the brass lock. Each page was a day of the month, with twenty lines divided into five sections, each labeled 19__. A page was meant to cover five years' worth of that day. In the cramped space allowed, notations were bound to be cryptic, though they did not have to be banal, as today's tweeters know. Mine were almost always trite—how well I slept, what friends came over, and what I purchased at the five-and-dime store. The brief entry on Gladys is exceptionally informative. If I was happy, though, I was wary as well. We took part in no mother-daughter talks. I don't recall any hugs or kisses. We kept our distance.

One Saturday afternoon Gladys summoned me to Belle's living room, saying I must listen to *Der Meistersinger* on the weekly radio broadcast of the Metropolitan Opera. I settled into a chair and tried to attend to it, but Wagner was cacophonous. Perhaps Haydn would have sounded like cacophony as well, since my exposure to music consisted of hymns and musical comedy. The afternoon taught me nothing except that long ago a German wrote noisy music, though I proudly recorded my listening accomplishment. Gladys didn't sit with me to listen to the radio, but that afternoon was the closest I ever felt to my birth mother, who grew up in

43

a social set where everyone went to the opera whether or not they were in tune with the music.

At our apartment Gladys found gemütlichkeit, the warmth and social belonging she craved, not from Belle or me but from my cousin Bob Wacht, the youngest son of one of Belle's sisters. He was living with us. Bob's day job was a real-estate broker, and presumably apartment rentals were slow. By night he was in café society, wearing a tux and escorting women like Hope Hampton, a former silent-movie star and socialite, to the opera. Bob checked the morning newspapers regularly to see if he had made the society page.

When Bob eventually moved out, it was to live with a man named Butler Miles (I always had to remember it was not "Miles Butler"). Bob decided the spelling of his last name should be "Watt," hardly unusual. Rather more oddly, he said he would like to be called Caithness. The word *gay* at the time meant lighthearted. *Coming out* was what debutantes did. What was I supposed to make of my cousin? I took my cue from Dick, who enjoyed Bob and loved the idea of calling him Caithness. I understood from Dick that Bob's living arrangements were part of the spice of our sophisticated city. I already knew that to be a New Yorker was to be superior to the rest of the world.

Gladys and Bob would commune in the living room through endless cigarettes, both their noses in the air as they inhaled. In appearance, they were dissimilar: Gladys, a blousy blonde of five feet four or so with hair the color of dry sand and whose curls refused to go one way or another; Bob, a tall, flagpole-lean man-boy with hair the color of wet sand. Their plummy voices were synchronized, however. Both affected the snobby, slightly British accents one hears in black-and-white movies of the 1930s and '40s. Think of Cary Grant and you have Bob; a chunky Katherine Hepburn, Gladys. I loved the way they handled their Chesterfields, holding them artfully between thumb and index finger and flicking bits of ash effortlessly into ashtrays at their sides while they gossiped. They laughed frequently, laughs filled with cynicism and delight. I mistrusted both of them. The books I read were hard on snobs, and that's what they seemed to me. I lacked the empathy to see a façade, but I recognized falseness.

Caithness-to-be and Gladys agreed on many things, one of which was that Belle, who cleaned out the ashtrays, was exceedingly stupid.

"Grannie is so dumb," Gladys told me as an aside, with a ruthless, rueful smile. The smile probably held kindness as well as amusement, but I took it as a just indictment and justification for my treating Belle like a servant.

Much later I realized that although Belle was no scintillating raconteur like Caithness, she took care of all three of us. Her cooking was as bland as her personality, but she served us nutritious, if not always appetizing, meals. Sometimes the chicken parts were a bit raw at the bone. The vegetables were boiled into gray submission. Desserts tended to be chocolate pudding, tapioca pudding, or Jell-O, all from boxes. The mashed potatoes were yummy—what can you do to mashed potatoes? Sometimes we went out to eat at Schrafft's, where the chicken salad was good. The revolution in American cooking wouldn't arrive until the next decade; few families then were adventurous.

ϾϾ

A bunkmate at summer camp had started menstruating the previous summer. Anxiously, she confided to me that she'd gone through all her clean underpants and was going to have to tell the counselor. I swept the cabin floor while they had their talk and wished I knew what was said.

Breasts budded like promises on my skinny chest. I tried putting two tennis balls into a dress front to see what fulfilled ones would be like. The effect in the mirror was something like a woman, although the hard, round balls were uncomfortable and prone to slip. It was difficult to anticipate what else was coming.

"You can tell when someone is having their period," Wendy J. informed me.

"How?"

"Remember when I bounced onto Wendy B.'s lap? I could tell she was wearing a pad. And I could smell it."

So periods had pads. And a smell.

In tribal societies, rituals, ceremonies, and initiations accompany the onset of adolescence. They must be reassuring. I had Belle, who subscribed to the euphemisms and elisions of the Victorian age. Her condescension to bodily functions was a linen handkerchief she kept tucked in the long sleeves of her black dresses.

"We're going shopping this week," she told me one day, and I found myself with my grandmother in the sanitary-supplies section of a department store, where a knowing salesperson brought out garter belts, disposable napkins, and a pair of plastic underpants. I didn't ask questions. On the bus ride home, Belle sat with her hands folded in her lap. Her eyes did not meet mine, and I did not want them to. I was going to get through this myself.

When we got back to the apartment I tried on a garter belt. It was no wider than my thumbnail and immediately etched a sharp red line on my stomach. The belt had clips fore and aft to hold a sanitary napkin. It was going to be difficult to get the clips right. The plastic pants were immediately itchy and way too tight in the waist and legs. Perhaps that was necessary, I thought, because they would be filled with blood, like a balloon, and had to be tight as a tourniquet to keep that bright red goo from pouring down the inside of my leg into my white socks at the most unfortunate possible moment, say while I was in chemistry class holding a full glass beaker with nowhere to put it down and the teacher was engaged with a Bunsen burner and unavailable to ask permission to go to the bathroom.

This was going to be bad.

It wasn't. Not immediately.

"I'm so excited," Inez said and gave me a hug.

"About what?"

Her smile turned quixotic. "Go look in your underpants."

I'd missed my coming of age in the form of a nickel-size spot of pink. Menstruation wasn't going to be a problem after all. I didn't know that sometimes it starts with a light harbinger before ovulation and the real deal. It's too bad I didn't put more faith in Inez and talk to her about what was happening to me. But I thought of her as a servant, not a confidante.

Could Gladys give some advice, something that shared the experience and made it more routine?

"I hear you've gotten the curse, dear," she said. "Don't worry. It happens in the best of families."

I recognized the comment as her skewed vision of an aristocratic past. Even superior women were stained by a bodily function suited to the hoi polloi. This was no help at all.

Worse, suddenly Gladys was gone. She left for Florida sometime during the winter of 1958, soon after my periods started. A letter arrived addressed to me, Vivian Mary Witkind, in her small, thin handwriting. The contents of the letter were too bizarre to deflect and brush off, which was my standard strategy. Gladys apologized for "beating you up at Bloomingdale's." I knew that when she hit me that awful time, it was in a department store, but not which one, and I was surprised it was the company she'd been working for in Connecticut.

But that wasn't the shocker. She was leaving the country. She'd tried moving to Florida, but that was not far enough, and she would go on to Ireland. She explained, and I'm sure I had to read this explanation twice, that she was in terrible pain from the "death rays from Myron Taylor's television tower in Long Island aimed at my head."

This was one I couldn't keep to myself. I took the letter to Belle.

"That's Mommy's delusion," she said. "She thinks someone is trying to kill her."

Watching scary movies with Carol was nothing: Dr. Frankenstein's monster stalking desperately through the night with frightened townspeople waving fiery torches, Dracula leaning over a virginal white neck with his razor-sharp canines, Godzilla tromping through Tokyo while screaming hordes attempt to flee and the electric grid explodes in flames. Gladys's letter was horror.

If I'd allowed myself feelings, they would have been mixed. Fear, of course. What was it that made "death rays" real to her? Was it contagious? Did growing up mean becoming like her? And I would have felt pain on her behalf. The visceral connection was down there, even if I had abolished it, and somewhere I must have known she was in agony. Feelings had to be submerged. I could not allow myself questions such as whether it was worse being around Gladys or separated by an ocean. I locked up. My diary has no entry for the letter or the departure. I had to take care of myself, or it was uts-nay for me.

In Dublin, Gladys started out at Buswell's Hotel, writing me letters that sounded as though she was drinking like an Irish construction worker. It wasn't long before she landed in Saint Patrick's Hospital, a renowned mental institution founded by Jonathan Swift.[1] She remained there until her death in 1982.

After Dick died in 2003, I found in his effects a paid bill for a grave in a Dublin churchyard and a map showing the exact spot. Jack and I went to Ireland and found Gladys's resting place. All the other spots were marked with tombstones in a long, neat row. Gladys's spot looked like a tooth was missing. We asked a taxi driver to take us someplace to buy a stone and ordered one for $2,000. I had them engrave "She had moments of glad grace" on the tombstone. It's from a William Butler Yeats poem.

My grades plummeted. My seventh-grade homeroom teacher took me aside to ask if anything was wrong.

"No," I told her.

My periods started in earnest. The nonovulating dress rehearsal was over. Cramps took root in my abdomen like a pit full of snakes. Doubled up in agony in bed as I prepared to die, I called on Belle to pity me and telephone the pediatrician. Surely Dr. O'Reagan needed to make a house call before I exsanguinated.

I looked up at her from my rack of pain. Belle pursed her lips and shook her head gently. So that was it. If I made it through the next couple of days, I was doomed to the medieval torture chamber once a month for the rest of my mortal life.

My birth mother was as rational as a bowl of pecans, my grandmother was a mouseburger, and I was going to bleed to death under some full moon before I reached eighth grade. I'd never live in a rugged country house like my cousins the Marwells did in Mount Kisco. I'd never become a playwright with my name in lights on Broadway. I'd never find my prince in a white uniform.

I needed a new strategy. Sucking my tongue (which I was down to doing secretly and only at night) and hiding in my room eating Mallomars and reading Pogo books over and over wasn't going to do it. I couldn't articulate it, but I needed help. I needed mothering.

It was a few months earlier, sometime in 1957, that my diary sprouted entries about going out with Dick and "friends of Dad's." Looking back, I know the "friends" had to be Char—Charlotte Lazarus Gorman—and her three children.

Dick had dated numerous women. The most recent had been a member of the French delegation to the United Nations. She won my acceptance, if not admiration, by giving me lovely dolls dressed in the traditional costumes of French provinces. She was posted to Algeria in the spring of 1958, I believe, and Dick never contacted her again. My cousin Cornelia Marwell, who worked in the admissions office at Columbia and volunteered at the League of Women Voters with Char, introduced Dick and Char.

Dick wasn't inclined toward a long-term relationship. He probably would have been happy to go around with Char as he had with his other women friends, maintaining his bachelor and man-about-town status.

There is no diary entry for the Saturday I accompanied Dick, Char, and a couple of her kids to *Once Upon a Mattress*, an off-Broadway production starring an unknown actress named Carol Burnett, the boisterous comedienne who went on to TV success. The story is about the princess and the pea—a girl so delicate she spends a sleepless night because of the unbearable irritation of a tiny pea under her soft mattress. Burnett's character, a princess of improbable royal credentials, arrives at the castle dripping wet. The drawbridge is up, so she swims the moat.

In the crucial scene in act two, the robust, intrepid heroine has to climb a ladder to reach the topmost of not one, but twenty mattresses. She doesn't know it, but her supporters have added a few things besides the pea, such as ox yokes, plows, battleaxes, and full suits of armor. Burnett sang in her booming alto voice about how she could use magical intervention if she was ever to win the hand of Prince Dauntless: "I don't have a fairy godmother. I don't even have a godmother. Fairy godmother, godmother, *God* mother, where can you be?"

After the show, Char stood a foot away from me, talking straight at me. Her eyes were funny. She pointed first one at me, then the other. She was only a little taller than me, so a bit over five feet.

"Wasn't that a wonderful score?" asked Char. "I think the best song was 'Sensitivity.' You hear five-four time so rarely. It's really hard to write. Wasn't Carol Burnett amazing?"

She was asking for my thoughts. She was talking to me as if my opinion could be interesting.

Like in act one of *Hello Dolly*, when Dolly Gallagher Levy rolls in from stage left, perched on a Model T and wearing an outrageously glamorous dress and a pink hat as broad-brimmed as an umbrella, Char entered my life.

No way was Char going to take Dick as a perpetual date, not with Bobby, Donnie, and Babsie to care for. It was marriage or nothing. They scheduled the wedding for the evening of the start of Yom Kippur, the holiest holiday on the Jewish calendar. Char was from a Jewish family, though she, like Dick, was not observant. Char's father, Robert Lazarus Sr., called Pop-pop by the grandchildren, nixed the date. He was not particularly observant himself, but did not think it would go over well, especially in his hometown of Columbus, Ohio.

Char wrote songs for big occasions, and her wedding song to Dick went to the tune of "I'm Getting Married in the Morning:"

> *Almost got married on Yom Kippur,*
> *Dingdong, the bells were gonna chime.*
> *Pop-pop got nervous,*
> *Called off the service,*
> *But we all had a real good time.*

Except me. I didn't have a real good time. "Dad is going to marry Char," was my bleak diary entry a few weeks before. "Darn." The word *darn* in dark-blue fountain-pen ink looks like the unvented dome of a volcano. I bought the long-playing record of *Once Upon a Mattress* and memorized every cut. But I shoved the real-world disastrous turn of events out of consciousness as much as possible. I don't remember a thing about the wedding at the Sherry Netherland Hotel on September 22, 1958. Char told me later I was a morose, silent being.

I had no idea yet what I had gained—a functioning mother lustily engaged with all the world had to offer: family, friends, food, the constant battle for truth and fairness, sports teams, novels, gossip, and laughter. Char was, above everything else, a fan, and once she included you in her sphere, she was your fan. She was determined to woo me into her loving domain.

Char was "Char" to everybody, including her children. The youngest, Babette, or Babsie, who was seven in 1958, recalls Char explaining that "Char" was better because when a kid called for "Mommy" at the playground, she couldn't see well enough to know whether it was her kid or some other mommy's. Char's eyes were indeed crooked; she had a bad nystagmus, a wiggle to her eyes, and was only somewhat more sighted than a garden mole. Ordinarily she looked at you more or less with both eyes, though if you paid attention, you could figure out which one was doing the work. If she fixed you with a single eye, that usually meant you were in trouble. Donnie, eleven that year and the one closest to my age, was the one most at risk of this dubious attention.

"It's the evil eye," Donnie would say as Char gave him a look that told him, at a minimum, to "calm up." "Calm up" was one of the family phrases. Wordplay was a family habit.

The explanation about the playground was nonetheless worrisome: Char was saying she could not keep even one eye on her child. I doubt that she took children to the playground much, however. That was for the household help to do.

Bobby also had an explanation for Char's moniker: Char thought the only mother and father deserving of a title were her own. He cautioned me several years after the wedding, when I was in a period of rapturous admiration for Char and mimicking her in in every way, that idealizing your parents forever and never separating from them was neurotic, unhealthy, and limiting, That was when Bobby was thinking about becoming a doctor and perhaps a psychiatrist like the Gorman kids' father, Warren.

Bobby had arrived in wartime, 1943. The army posted Warren to various hospitals around the country, and rather than serve by standing and waiting, Char handed her firstborn over to her mother, Hattie Lazarus, known as Hoo-hoo, and father, Pop-pop, and followed Warren. *Pop-pop* makes sense as a name for a grandfather. *Hoo-hoo* takes explaining. Their house at 2075 Fair Avenue in Columbus had a second-floor corridor about as long as an airport runway. The grandparents' room was at one end and Bobby's at the other. His grandmother would call "Yoo-hoo" from down the hall. Bobby heard it as "Hoo-hoo" and called back.

"At the end of the war, these people who said they were my parents showed up and took me away," said Bobby. He was four.

The explanation I like best, and therefore believe, was the one Char gave me. She was who she was, and labels like "Mom" and "Dad" were old-fashioned, limiting identifiers. As Char, she was there for me exactly as she was for her other kids.

It was perfectly natural that Char wanted me to move to the apartment on East Ninety-Sixth Street. It would require cutting the dining room by a third to make a small bedroom, but she knew it was the right thing for me to live with them.

I resisted Char's perfectly natural idea with all the wiles a twelve-year-old could muster. I would not be delivered into the bright light of constant company. My bedroom in the Seventy-First Street apartment was a private safety zone, complete with my parakeets, my bookcases filled with horse and dog books, and the chair that folded out into a bed when friends stayed overnight. Belle and Inez were at my beck and call. I knew the weak point in Char's plan—Dick. To say I sulked would be inadequate. I turned to stone at the whisper of a suggestion that a move might be in order. I made my father miserable enough that he gave in. The deal was that I would go to their apartment every Tuesday for dinner and join them on weekends. They would not forcibly remove me from my girl cave.

On the face of it, Dick—and Belle, who agreed to continue to provide me safe harbor—made a poor decision. If they simply gave in to my demands, they were indeed wrong. On the other hand, they were familiar with my queasy personality.

Perhaps I could have gotten along with one new sibling up close: calm, thoughtful Babsie, perhaps, who was much younger but in many ways more mature than I was. "She's been here before," said Constance, the cook, who subscribed to Jamaican theories of reincarnation.

Or funny, energetic Donnie. The two of us played knock hockey, a game on a board on the floor until we had all the angles down and could score at will.

Bobby also would have been fine to live with. He was older, self-assured, and easy to admire. I liked to lean over the top of the upright piano in the front hall and watch his fingers as he practiced jazz.

But it wasn't only the Gormans I'd be moving in with. The twelfth floor of 17 East Ninety-Sixth Street functioned like a high-rent commune. The Gormans occupied the unlocked 12D. In the unlocked 12C lived the Freunds: Charm and Seelig and their children, Debbie and Johnnie. A fifty-foot telephone cord ran between 12A and 12B so adults convening in the Freund apartment could answer it as the kids flowed back and forth across the hall. Dick and Seelig, a general surgeon with a Park Avenue practice, hit it off quickly. They both loved cameras and cars. Charm and Char had a friendship with considerable give-and-take. Char complained that Charm was neurotic, but they happily and energetically engaged in mutual projects and child-care issues, Char providing free psychiatric help as called for. From living with a psychiatrist, Char had concluded that she was one. Charm was one of her patients, as indeed were I and the numerous others who came for advice.

Charm was thin and exquisitely coiffed, the kind of woman you see on the first floor of Saks Fifth Avenue expertly evaluating the Hermes scarves. She constantly fiddled with the long, gold chain she wore around her neck. When she reupholstered the living-room furniture, she saved enough material to make herself a dress so she would match the chairs. Charm was not meant to be an at-home mother. In an era kinder to women, she would have been director of the New York Port Authority or something equally complex and her anxiety directed toward making trains run on time rather than making sure that Seelig's ties went with his suits and that his medical journals were neatly stacked rather than accumulating at the foot of their bed.

By the time I joined the family, Bobby was trusted to babysit. Debbie Freund, now president of the Claremont Graduate University, recalls that things could get wild, what with five kids, often plus an older boy who lived downstairs. They played darts, for example—real darts with two-inch points. The dartboard hung over the bookcase in Donnie and Babsie's room. To this day you can find children's books in our houses whose spines are pierced with the wounds of long-ago misses. According to Debbie, one night the older children, led by Bobby the babysitter, decided to make a "kid sandwich." The younger children were enticed to lie on the box spring of a bed while the older kids put a mattress on top of them. It must have been a giggling, wriggling, and screaming sandwich.

So maybe it wasn't an abandonment of child-rearing principles to exempt me from the general mayhem. Instead, I could fancy myself a visitor.

Dick was also something of a visitor at the Ninety-Sixth Street apartment—or tried to be. He did not take an active role as stepfather.

Like many men of the World War II generation, he was aloof and silent, maybe a little more than most. He kept his distance from children insofar as possible. Since he was entering a matriarchy, it worked out fine that he had no interest in actively rearing his stepchildren.

Anyway, the place was a bit wild. Here was Babsie, for example, careening around the apartment, a stark-naked five-year-old in the midst of a game, while Char and Dick were at the lunch table.

"Stop that," said Char. "Can't you see he's eating?"

Babsie stopped short, not so much for the command as to try to figure out what eating had to do with it. She still wonders.

❦

Rather than losing my father, I saw more of him than I ever had. My new siblings called my dad "Dick," so I did too.

Everyone was busy during the week. Char worked as second vice president of the New York League of Women Voters, a volunteer job that was close to full time. Dick continued to be a customers' man at Bache. The Gorman kids went to school at New Lincoln, an independent school known for its innovative curriculum and diversity of students. Few black children attended any of New York's private schools in those years. It was important to Char that her children study in an integrated one, which just about left only New Lincoln.

Weekends were opportunities for family excursions.

Char missed her hometown of Columbus, where college football was a big deal. She had to make do with the Ivy League. On bright fall Saturday mornings, I sat in the back seat between Bobby and Donnie, with Dick at the wheel. (Babsie was deemed too young for the high privilege of attending a football game.) We headed downtown to pick up heroes, the sandwiches called "subs" in other parts of the country, at the place Char had determined sold the best in the city. Driving was one of Dick's jobs, one he did happily.

Well provisioned, we headed uptown to Columbia University to tailgate in a parking lot. I had to use both hands to hold a sandwich packed with salami, pastrami, tomatoes, provolone, and pungent peppers. Char always had extra napkins as I dripped tomatoes down my arms. We'd wash down the heroes with seven-ounce glass bottles of Coca-Cola, sweating beads of icy water in the hot September sun. Baker Field had wooden bleachers, and the crowd stomped their feet to make a roar for the Lions, our team. Dick bought me the away teams' pins, round buttons with their logos dangling gold charms in the shape of footballs and ribbons in the correct colors. Columbia did not win often, but we had great fun singing "Who Owns New York?" "Roar, Lion, Roar," and the alma mater.

Constance had the weekends off, so Char was inventive about Sunday night meals. Not that she cooked herself. Char laughed about her one foray into the kitchen. "Don't you come in here. You'll burn yourself," said Constance. Char did not try that again.

Often on Sundays we ate Chinese food, opening up cardboard buckets of fried rice and moo goo gai pan at the dining room table while the adults drank beer and the kids had Coke. Beer was what went with Chinese food, Char said, not wine, their usual libation. Some Sundays Dick drove us out to Long Island to pick up steamers—clams. At home on Ninety-Sixth Street, we dumped them in an enormous iron pot to boil just until they opened.

The first time, the idea of eating clams was off-putting. I looked down at my plate of wide-open clam mouths. The clams did not look happy. Neither was I. I stalled by sipping my soda, trying to drink rather than suck. I watched Char as she skillfully wrested a clam from its shell with her fingers and slipped the ridged black skin off the tail in one movement, then, holding the naked crustacean by the newly shiny tail, shook it in a bowl of water to remove any remaining sand, dipped it in drawn butter, and popped it into her mouth.

"Delicious," Char said and reached for another.

I liked butter, and I liked eating with my fingers. Dick was looking at me to see if I would take up the challenge. Despite the risk of sand and slime, I took hold of a clam, pulled away the tiny grips it had on its shell, clumsily peeled off the tail skin, washed it, and, holding the newly shiny tail, dipped the clam in the melted butter and popped it in my mouth. Delicious.

Char's parents had a fifty-foot swimming pool at the bottom of the hill below their house in Bexley, a suburb of Columbus. Char and her siblings were popping out children yearly, and Char believed that the best way to keep them from drowning was to teach them to swim as soon as possible, by age five or so. Her method was direct. She would throw a child into the deep end of the pool and see if he or she came up. The children almost always did—they were ready to swim and didn't quite know it. One, Robbie Rosensteil (later Robbie Sirak), failed the test. Char threw him in, and he went directly to the bottom, lying on his stomach over the drain. Char had just come from the beauty parlor, so her hair was newly poufed. She thought for a moment before diving in to rescue her nephew. I can read the event as an early warning sign about Robbie. In his late teens, he began to fall apart, and he spent most of his life in a mental institution, dying in 2013.

Char had the same approach to information as to swimming. There were things children needed to know. She could tell it was up to her to give the lowdown on sex. I'm pretty sure it was the summer after they got married, during my second trip to Columbus (I'll tell more about my first trip, in the summer of 1958 before Char and Dick were married, in the next chapter), when Char took the opportunity to educate me. In a single, long session in August 1959, she gave me a thorough, enthusiastic dousing.

Char was an expert on menstrual cramps. She swore that hers as a teenager had been similar to the early stages of childbirth. There were medications to help. Codeine was good, and she would make sure I had some.

When I met a boy I really liked and wanted to have sex with him—my decision, not his alone, and not likely for a number of years—I must use birth control. The pill had yet to be invented, and Char went through the available options one by one. Condoms were effective, but you mustn't count on a guy to use them, she told me. Spermicidal jellies were no good used alone. Intrauterine devices were available and trustworthy but had to be inserted by a gynecologist. The best alternative was a diaphragm combined with spermicidal jelly.

"I've never gotten pregnant on a diaphragm," she said. She had no faith in statistical analysis. Her own experience was always enough to draw a conclusion. When the time came, I should go to a Planned Parenthood clinic and be fitted—no need to consult her or another grown-up.

Char threw in extra advice. Sometimes you should have sex in the morning. Men often have erections when they wake up, she said, and it was a kindness to oblige them, even if you didn't feel like it that early. Never say the name of the man you're with during intercourse. In the excitement, you might call out "Marvin" when you were sleeping with Irving.

So it was that I rewrote my wish list, which I maintained in a secret code and kept taped to the back of my bureau. A diaphragm went to number one.

Sex education was one thing. My birth mother was at least as mysterious a subject. Char had talked to Belle and Dick about Gladys and winkled out essential information. Maybe they were relieved that someone else could take on the task of talking about the bats and the nuts, as well as the birds and the bees.

"Myron Taylor is a real person," Char said, speaking of the guy whom Gladys identified as aiming death rays at her head from a television tower. He was the president of US Steel at one point, and Gladys's parents would have known him from New York society. Char believed that at the fateful moment when Gladys raised her hand against me by the elevators at Bloomingdale's, the real Mrs. Myron Taylor emerged from one and saw us. This was still nonsense and begged for further explanation. How did Char hear about Mrs. Taylor? Did Belle tell her something? What else happened? I've never found out.

I was not rid, on the spot, of loathing and avoiding the very thought of Gladys. Nor did I suddenly see her as a human being. What I felt was gratitude and adoration for Char, my new, vastly improved mother.

"You're not likely to turn out like Gladys," Char said. "You seem like a sturdy kid to me."

I doubt she fully believed that. I'm sure I wasn't convinced myself. The truth was that I wasn't all that sturdy but did have strengths to build on. A fearful kid, she may have been thinking, whose eyes could get wide and scared. Awfully short—probably wouldn't reach five feet. A locked-down, walled-off kid who needed drawing out, which Char was sure she could do. Also a sycophant, which Char did not mind. On the plus side, the kid was a reader, even if some of that was for escape. Char was a reader. We had that in common. The kid was a hard worker, Char would have observed, and extremely determined to succeed when she went at something. Those were good qualities that Char sometimes wished she had more of herself.

Char's words were fresh air. They gave me hope. I felt like a kid who'd been lying on the bottom of the pool and realized she might be able to swim.

5

DOROTHY GOINS'S RECIPE FOR ALMOND SOUFFLÉ

"You're going to like Columbus," my soon-to-be brother Donnie told me as we tossed a football in the narrow hallway of Char's apartment, soon to be home to my father as well.

It was the summer of 1958. I wore Donnie's catcher's mask and chest protector because I was afraid of the pointed ball. I could have used the mental equivalents of these guards to deflect the drastic changes coming at me hard and fast.

"There's Ohio State," he added.

What did he mean by Ohio "state"? A park of some kind? When he explained, I was not impressed, knowing that the only colleges that counted were in the East. The only *anything* that counted was in New York. New Yorkers are the ultimate provincials. My walks to the new orthodontist in the East Fifties to check the progress of my braces and the effectiveness of the brutal device I wore at night to curb my tongue sucking were as far south on the island of Manhattan as I had gone regularly. Char and

Dick's apartment, all the way north on East Ninety-Sixth Street, was a mile farther north than I was used to, aside from summer camp in New Hampshire. I'd never been west and didn't know there were distinctions like Midwest. I'd hardly gone to the west side of Manhattan. Caithness, my fay grown cousin, liked to say that one only made the trip to the west side to see a show or board a transatlantic liner. I was too young to have seen *Oklahoma*, but I had the record. Farmers and cowboys were out there somewhere. And waving wheat.

Columbus, Ohio? Would I be going on the *Pinta* or the *Niña*?

Yippee-kai-yay? No way.

Char, Dick, and we kids arrived in Columbus on an evening plane on August 27, 1958, after camp and before the wedding. The dark air was hot and humid and smelled of wet grass. I noticed the quiet; there were no traffic and no horns.

"This is Bexley," Char explained as the car headed down Maryland Avenue. "It's an enclave of Columbus."

"A what?"

"It's a suburb surrounded by the city of Columbus."

We arrived at 2075 Fair Avenue. In the limited lamplight, I didn't get a sense of Char's parents' house, except that it was white-painted brick and at least as big as one of those transatlantic liners. The bedroom that Babsie and I would be using was as large as Belle's bedroom and mine combined plus the dining room.

In the morning I swung out of bed, and as my bare feet touched the carpet, I found myself in a new world. The pile was as deep as grass and soft as a blanket. At home Belle and I had thin Oriental rugs and bare wooden floors cold to the toes. The carpet at Hattie and Robert Lazarus's house was cut to run an even foot from the wall, revealing dark, wood flooring. I recognized the style as elegant and unusual. Light flooded through a bay window. I hadn't realized until then that my apartment at home was dark. I was staying in what I learned was Char and my new aunt Babs's childhood bedroom. The beds, chaise longue, and partner's desk in the alcove were made of a light-blond hardwood. I didn't notice it then, but if you opened the partner's desk to reveal the red-leather working surface, you could discern penmanship embedded, as if children had pressed down hard with a dull pencil on paper that was long gone. It said, "Char, Babs, Jean and Bobbie. Don't we write nicely?" Char was the oldest of four. Babette, or Babs (or "Big Babs," as she was sometimes called to distinguish her from my sister), lived in Tucson, Arizona, at the time, and Jean lived in Cleveland. Their brother, Bob—Robert Lazarus Jr.—was nearby in Bexley.

I pulled on some shorts quietly so as not to wake Babsie in the other twin bed. I went down the curved staircase, my hand sliding along the smooth, dark, wood railing. It was early, but Hattie and Robert—Hoo-hoo and Pop-pop—were at the breakfast table in the alcove of the dining room, which looked out on a closely mowed lawn that seemed as big as Central Park. I recognized the artist of the shimmering oil over the sideboard. It had to be a Claude Monet.

They greeted me with a welcoming "Good morning" and "How did you sleep?" I don't remember the details, but the conversation could easily have gone something like this:

"What would you like for breakfast?" asked Hoo-hoo. "How about some rye toast?" She rang a silver bell and Ella arrived in her crisp, black uniform with a white apron for my order of scrambled eggs, bacon, and the toast.

"We get the rye bread from Toledo," Pop-pop said. "It's the best outside of New York. Try some of the jam." He passed me a cut-glass jar with a silver lid. "I think it's quite special." They bought the jam by the case from a woman in Charlevoix, Michigan, where the Lazaruses spent part of the summer.

Pop-pop was about to go downtown to the store, where he was called "Mr. Robert" by all the associates—people who worked at Lazarus were not employees; they were associates. But he didn't leave without making sure I'd had enough to eat.

"You need a little more sody for your ice cream," he said and then explained. "You've run out of jam but still have toast. It's like an ice cream soda where you need more soda water to make the rest of the ice cream taste as good. After that, of course, you need more ice cream for your sody."

I carefully took another piece of toast and enjoyed the rest of my raspberry jam, full of seeds and flavor.

I was too overwhelmed at the moment to pay attention to these strangers. I had to concentrate on not saying something dumb or spilling red jam down my polo shirt. The rye toast was crisp with abundant sour seeds; white bread was Belle's standard. The jam was raspberry; grape jelly was the norm at home. I was awed. I had classmates at Hewitt's whose families had fancy stuff, but they lived in apartments. I wasn't in New York anymore, and if this was Columbus, wow. Even better, Hoo-hoo and Pop-pop were captivating. If I had to get new grandparents, I was in luck.

❧

Robert Lazarus Sr.—Pop-pop—was one of four brothers in the third generation of a family of department store magnates. (I will refer to him as Robert when I need to distinguish him from his son Bob and grandson Bobby, as well as other grandsons named for him.) The "store" was Lazarus, which at the time dominated retailing in Columbus. Robert was a small, thin man of sixty-eight years when I met him. He held a Phi Beta Kappa key in political science from Ohio State and, in his rimless spectacles, looked best suited to be a scholar. That was not to be; in his generation, the men went into retailing. An unabridged dictionary lay open on a stand in the library of the Fair Avenue house so Robert could readily explore the outer penumbra of a word's meaning, which he did frequently. The library was stocked with a vast assortment of books, stacked up from waist high to the ceiling, including a strong collection of limited editions of classics. A few years later, my grandparents allowed me to reorganize the library, a labor that took weeks and resulted in an array that made bibliographical sense but left several shelves looking like ski slopes or ragged EKG printouts.

Hattie Weiler Lazarus—Hoo-hoo—came from Swissvale, Pennsylvania, a town near Pittsburgh. As a teenager, she read about Wellesley College in a book, liked the way it sounded, and headed there at the age of sixteen. Years later she would laugh about what she started: all her daughters, her daughter-in-law, and several granddaughters, including me, matriculated at Wellesley. Hattie loved golf, bridge, and mah-jongg. By the time I knew her, she was wobbly on her feet but would still do a few steps of the Charleston when urged. Like Char, she was a fanatic when she supported something. She was dedicated to fair play and rooted for the underdog.

Char was already in her bathing suit when she came down to breakfast that first morning. She always owned half a dozen, often custom-made because she had a consequential chest for her height and a nearly flat tush, as if weight that should have been low in the aft had somehow migrated to the upper deck of the prow.

"Go put on a suit," she told me. Feeling dumb for not knowing to start my day in a bathing suit, I ran upstairs to comply. Babsie still wasn't up.

Char led me out of the house, through the kitchen, and across the driveway to a stairway hidden in the midst of bushes and trees. She held on to the railing and worked her way carefully down the weathered stone steps to the swimming pool, where she fiddled with the key to unlock the gate. It was one of those locks you needed to be on good terms with.

We stepped into a private space, another sort of new world. It felt like the secret garden in the book, full of possibilities.

An ample supply of plastic chairs, rockers, and lounge chairs dotted the sides of the long, rectangular pool, calm and smooth in the morning light. The far end had a diving board, and behind it was a wide cabana with comfortable chairs, a sofa, and a ceiling fan. On each side, a large changing room faced out toward the pool. One had an *M* and the other a *W* embedded in large, opaque-glass circles. A small bathroom, which I quickly learned was a haven for spiders, opened in the back of the seating area on the right. On the left a room the same size stored floats and toys. It had another lock. The combination was easy for the grown-ups to remember: President Franklin Delano Roosevelt's birthday.

For decades after my introduction to the family pool, I considered it the center of my existence, like my rock in Central Park but with grown-ups as well as kids and a chance to learn what adults talked about.

On that first trip to Columbus, only my immediate family must have been visiting, at least at the beginning. Babsie and I would otherwise never have been billeted in Char and Big Babs's room. Mary Lazarus, Bob's wife, would have come over with three children—Tripper, Molly, and Jerry. Susan, the youngest, was not yet born. Bob was "Mr. Bob" at the store and

"Unkie" to me and the other grandchildren. The Robert Jrs. would soon be building a midcentury modern house on Hoo-hoo and Pop-pop's property up the hill on the far side of the swimming pool, off Parkhill Drive.

Dick was usually playing golf or tennis. When he came to the pool, he did his best to avoid swimming. He found the water too cold, which I thought was ridiculous. These days I feel exactly the same way as Dick did then about swimming pools. They're almost always too cold for me, and as I stand grimly on the edge of one, trying to figure out a way to avoid going in, I remember my father doing the same.

It was the first of many years that we kids—Babsie, Donnie, Bobby, and I, as well as friends and cousins—played endlessly in the warm summer water. We floated on plastic rafts and banged into each other and tried to knock each other off, sometimes coming up from below like sharks after a rowboat. We threw pennies in and went after them. We dove down to touch the dark, nasty drain at the lowest point of the deep end. We played catch with brightly striped beach balls large and small and made do with tennis balls if all the beach balls had deflated from hard use.

We threw ourselves into endless games of Marco Polo, which is like blindman's bluff, only in water.

"Marco," the kid who was "It" would call, swimming or walking in the shallow end with eyes firmly closed, except when someone cheated just a little bit and opened his or her eyes a crack.

"Polo," we would all yell back from spots around the pool.

"It" would try to zone in on someone close and call again, "Marco."

"Polo." The closest victim would be in trouble, unless he or she cheated and swam under "It."

As wild and waterworthy as dolphins, we cavorted until Char told us we had to take a break, often because our lips were turning blue. Red-eyed and stinking of chlorine, we shivered under our towels and admired the skin of our fingers, wrinkled like peach pits.

Char might also want the kids beached so she could swim herself. She was an inveterate lap swimmer. She only did the breaststroke, keeping her head out of water so her hairdo would not be spoiled. A child who splashed her hair was a child who got an evil eye and a time-out.

At one o'clock, lunch was brought down from the house, and we ate under the cabana, turning on the ceiling fan and spreading towels on the furniture to absorb our dampness. I wolfed down the wilted lettuce salad—called "wilted" because of the warm dressing made with bacon fat—or other unfamiliar dishes prepared by Dorothy Goins, the cook. There were pitchers of iced tea and lemonade and oatmeal cookies that were soft but grainy, sweet with a hint of tartness, and disappeared far too quickly. Those oatmeal cookies were so well loved that a family friend had one bronzed.[1]

In the afternoon, we swam again as the tall trees between the house and the pool began to block the sun. The adults moved their chairs from time to time to keep ahead of the encroaching shadows. The core group that summer was Hattie, Char, and Mary, who always had plenty to talk about. Other friends and relatives would join them. They read the *New York Times*. Char did the crossword puzzle, soliciting advice on the toughies. They talked. And talked.

In the summer of 1958, the adult women would have lamented the constant testing of nuclear bombs by the United States, as well as Great Britain and the Soviet Union. They would have worried about the Soviet lead in space exploration. The first Sputnik satellite had been launched the previous year. The third one shot into space, carrying two dogs, the day I arrived in Columbus that summer.

Char would have been happy because the Yankees were on their way to winning the pennant and the World Series under Casey Stengel. Many more baseball games were played in the afternoon then, so she might be listening to one on the radio as the shadows claimed the far side of the pool and left only a shrinking corner for the women's chairs. It wouldn't have been a Yankees game. She could get those only at night.

Vladimir Nabokov's *Lolita* had just come out, and Hattie or Mary or both had probably already read it and were tut-tutting over the scandalous sexiness.

Of course, the women talked about Columbus and their significant projects for Planned Parenthood and the many nonprofits they worked hard to support. Hattie was a founder of the Planned Parenthood clinic in Columbus. And of course, it wasn't all highbrow. They gossiped about the people of Bexley, with humor but not meanness. At least in front of me, they introduced no material that would have excited Mr. Nabokov, but I could see that life in Bexley was far more interesting than anyone could have imagined. At the time I thought Belle and her canasta crew must be comparative dullards, though now that I think about it, they must have had plenty to gossip about too.

That first summer, I didn't sit still. Over the next few, I perched with the grown-ups like a parrot trying to learn to talk. I studied their inflections, what they laughed at, their body language, and all their strange ways in silent fascination. Eventually I could chime in a bit, commenting on a book I had read, as had they, or the political crisis of the moment. When I managed to say something, they welcomed it and treated me as a member of the group.

The following August, the whole family visited. The house on Fair Avenue was packed to capacity, and I stayed in an unused maid's room over the garage. Besides the five of us, Char's younger sisters and their children were in residence: Babs Lazarus Rosenstiel and her three sons and one daughter, and Jean Lazarus Hoffman with her daughter and two sons. Lunch was served at a long table up the hill and near the house rather than in the shade of the cabana.

On August 29, 1959, we took a long enough break from the pool for a professional black-and-white photograph on the lawn of the house at Fair Avenue. Hattie and Robert are seated in the middle, their four children and their offspring surrounding them. The total number of grandchildren that year was fourteen.

Everyone could see the humor in a family-planning advocate with such a large brood. Char wrote lyrics for the situation:

> *Though Hattie vies for centers in each United State,*
> *If Lazari were mentors, we'd overpopulate.*
>
> . . .
>
> *We justly can demand—are all these children planned?*

The title of the song is "Sing Ho for the Fertile Loins of Lazarus," and it is sung to the tune of Noel Coward's "Stately Homes of England."

Somehow the photographer managed to group and stack us artfully, and, no doubt with parental urging, all the children are captured looking at the camera. I am seated on the ground in the front row at Hattie's feet, wearing shorts, with Char, in a floral-print bathing suit, close by in the middle of the three rows. Babsie (who today calls herself Babette) wears what looks like an Alpine hat with a white band and a couple of feathers. Donnie is behind me. Dick, in a plaid shirt, stands in the top row, not quite smiling but not too serious either. Bob Lazarus, who we grandchildren called Unkie, is to Dick's right, with Mary and their children in front of him. Bobby, the oldest grandchild, is also in the top row.

Filling out the back row are Dave and Robbie Rosenstiel, Babs's oldest sons. Babs sits in front of them, along with her other two kids, Nancy and Billie. Jean Lazarus Hoffman is on the far right of the picture with Prue, who is wearing the same hat as Babsie, and Ricky and Michael, a skinny boy in trunks. Like Char, Big Babs and Jean wear floral bathing suits.

The picture includes five Roberts—Robert, Bob, Bobby, Robbie (the one who wouldn't swim and lay on the drain until Char pulled him out of the pool), and Tripper. Robert Lazarus III was called Tripper from infancy, and today Trip Lazarus is the name on his checking account. The picture has only one Hattie, but there is a child in it named after Hoo-hoo. Pop-pop called his wife "Bill" as a pet name because she never liked the name Hattie, and Billy Rosenstiel was named for her.

The grainy imprint is over half a century old now, so it is not surprising that many of the people in it are absent. Even then, it was missing family. That short back row is filled out with boys instead of men. Babs's husband, David Rosenstiel, had died. Jean's husband, Junie, rarely visited Columbus. The story I was told was that he did not get along with Pop-pop and stayed away even though they lived only two hours north, in Cleveland.

Only a year later, Big Babs remarried, and Hattie and Robert welcomed new people into the family. Howard Sirak had two children, Catherine and Biller. Howard was determined to be a father to Babs's children. Not only Babs, but her four Rosenstiel children took the name Sirak. With Susan Lazarus, born in 1960, and John Sirak, Babs and Howard's son, in 1961, the number of grandchildren maxed out at eighteen.

The 1959 photograph is my archetypal family picture, the one where I know exactly where I belong. It shows me at my grandmother's feet, in the front of the picture and almost the center. All of a sudden, I had parents, siblings, and cousins—the whole crazy, wild shebang that I had longed for.

⤨

Not surprisingly, given my shyness, the whole shebang was more than I would be able to handle at dinner on Fair Avenue, when the younger children ate in the kitchen under Dorothy's demesne. She needed an iron hand, if not an iron skillet. On at least one occasion, Dorothy was reduced to chasing Donnie around the kitchen table, wielding a flyswatter.

"Twelve is the cutoff," Dick told me. That meant it had been decided that I was old enough to join Bobby and Davey Rosenstiel with the dozen or so adults in the dining room. I suspect they chose twelve not as a firm rule but because they didn't believe I would fit in with the rowdy crowd in the kitchen.

Hoo-hoo sat at one end of the table and Pop-pop at the other. Bobby always sat to Hoo-hoo's left. Since she was served first, she filled his plate as well so he would not have to wait forever. Ella's hands shook badly as a result of a car accident when she and Dorothy were on vacation. The tremor wasn't too bad for carrying platters of chicken Marengo, pot roast, or sweet-and-sour tongue. When it was time for coffee, however, the entire table held its breath. A cup in each hand, Ella advanced slowly, the cups clicking against their saucers like maracas. It made Pop-pop exceedingly nervous— and the rest of us nervous because he was and because it was nip and tuck whether Ella would indeed have a spill. Despite her tremors, only a few drops of coffee made their way onto the saucers before they were served.

Dorothy was born on Valentine's Day in 1900 and lived to be 106. She was still cooking past the age of 100. The day Dorothy arrived at the house on Fair Avenue, sometime in the 1940s, was a special one for Bob Lazarus. He said that he, Char, Babs, and Jean were told their new cook worked at a restaurant where she served the "blue-plate special." He waited in great anticipation for whatever that was. Would lunch be on a blue plate? Would the food be blue? He was disappointed to find himself with a plate of mere chicken salad, until he tasted it and, with a wild surmise, realized that anything Dorothy cooked would be special on any plate and in any color.

Dorothy and Hattie sat down together at the beginning of each week to plan lunches and dinners, Dorothy writing out the menus in a beautiful, swirling longhand on yellow legal pads. As far as I could tell, guests arrived almost every night. Columbus had few restaurants, and take-out was not yet normal except for Chinese food. Meals were eaten at home, though of course few families had a cook. I believe many of the recipes came from the Jewish *Settlement Cookbook*, but others were Dorothy's alone.

Those wonderful summers I would be ravenous after a day of swimming, but I disciplined myself to single helpings, though not necessarily small ones. The first night Dorothy made almond soufflé for dessert, and I wished I could go on eating forever. Ella brought it around to my left in a huge, round, silver bowl, a bowl I have inherited. The soufflé was a delicate brown and scented with almonds. I ladled up a scoop, the light crust giving way to a poufy center.

"That's not very much. Have a *bissel* more," said Pop-pop.

I took a second scoop. A silver pitcher was passed with sailor's duff sauce, made with raw eggs and rum. I poured on plenty and ate the confection slowly with the large silver dessert spoon, marveling at the taste and texture and digging out the last tiny bits from the edge of the plate. I felt like Edmund in the Narnia books, consuming the magic Turkish delight that you always want to eat more of.

"You're a clean-plater," said Dick.

No kidding. If I hadn't been in a formal dining room with a chandelier, impressionist paintings, and a bunch of grown-ups, I would have licked it.

Many years later, I borrowed Dorothy's two hundred-some pages of recipes and Xeroxed them. A twenty-first-century nutritionist would be aghast at the collection, and not only because of the use of raw eggs in sauces. It could be a how-to for expanding waistlines, hypertension, and diabetes. Michelle Obama would ban it. Even the spinach recipe calls for sugar, cream, butter, and plenty of salt. Measurements are often archaic or inexact. Dorothy wrote them down for herself in the shorthand of someone who already knew how to cook, and ingredients were often listed in the amounts in which they were packaged in the mid-twentieth century.

I can vouch for the recipe below because Jack and I have replicated it many times.

For the almond soufflé you will need:
A buttered and sugared soufflé dish
3½ ounces slivered almonds
4 egg yolks
5 egg whites
½ teaspoon cream of tartar
3 tablespoons butter
2 tablespoons flour
½ cup sugar
1 cup milk
1 teaspoon vanilla

Melt the butter in a double boiler with the flour, sugar, milk, and vanilla. Cook until thick over medium to high heat. Grind up the almonds. Take the mixture off the heat and add half the ground almonds. Add the egg yolks to the mixture. Beat the egg whites separately until stiff. Add the cream of tartar while beating. Mix the egg yolk mixture into the whites. Pour into the prepared dish and sprinkle the remaining almonds on top. Set the dish in a pan of water in a 350–375-degree oven. Turn the oven down to 325 degrees after 25 minutes. If the nuts brown too much, turn the oven down a bit more. Total baking time is about one hour.

For the sailor's duff sauce: Beat one egg yolk with one cup of powdered sugar. Beat ½ pint whipping cream, adding ¼ cup of sherry to the cream as you beat. Add the egg yolk mixture to the whipped cream and mix. Serve with the soufflé.

I hope the next generations of my family enjoy many almond soufflés. This recipe makes soufflés less airy than some, though far from the horrid puddings that are sometimes passed off as soufflés. Because it is not superinflated, Dorothy's creation is also less ephemeral. It rises beautifully in the oven and stays puffed afterward. Have some for dessert and try to hold on to a portion for the next morning. There's nothing like almond soufflé with sailor's duff sauce for breakfast.

6

POP-POP'S FINAL LETTER

The family called it "the store," as if it were the corner hardware dive. In this case, the store was the heart and perhaps even the soul of downtown Columbus, Ohio. At its height, F&R Lazarus and its branches represented one-third of the city's retail, more than any store in any other US city, according to *Look to Lazarus*, a history.[1] The F&R referred to the original Fred and Ralph Lazarus brothers, sons of Simon Lazarus, the Lazarus who opened the store in 1851. A hundred years later, no department store in the United States more thoroughly dominated its market.

In those first summers I spent in Columbus, a rainy day was the signal for Char to break the swimming pool routine to shop and have lunch at the store. The plan might be simply to pick up a skirt for me and a dress or two for Char. But shopping with Char was always a spree.

She would park in one of the Lazarus garages, inching her way into a space and making tiny, jerky, successive approximations with the steering wheel while I held my breath hoping she would not hit a pillar or ding an adjoining car. She never did. We walked into the store on the Front Street level, passed the TV sets, and stepped on the escalator, always amused at the "Up to Basement" sign. The store sold everything from "notions," meaning little stuff like needles and thread, to big stuff like mink coats.

We passed all of it by to head to the juniors' department on the third floor, where we picked out skirts and blouses for me to try on. It went something like this:

"Not that one," said Char. "The color's too yellow for your complexion. No muddy colors."

My skin tone wasn't her only concern. She felt I was too dour and detached already.

"Maybe this one," she said, "if you wear plenty of lipstick."

We ended up with a definite yes for three skirts and four blouses and a maybe for two more skirts and one blouse.

"Oh, we'll just take them all," Char told the salesperson with a shake of her head that meant, "What the heck." The skirts had to be shortened, so the seamstress was called.

The Wedgewood Room, where Char selected her clothes, was on the third floor too. If she found a style she liked, she bought it in three different patterns. The seamstress was called, who carefully placed dozens of pins in each acquisition at back and shoulders, under the arms, and at the hem.

By that time we would be running late for lunch in the Chintz Room on the fifth floor. We'd had no time to browse the book department on the way in, and I would have to visit the pet department on the sixth floor on my own time.

Hattie and other female family members would be waiting in the Chintz Room at a table for six or eight. I faced the next major decision of the day—whether to order the Lazarus chicken salad, with a dressing heavy on milk and egg yolks, or the hidden sandwich, so called because it was completely covered with Russian dressing.[2] Apple pie with cinnamon ice cream or a pecan ball—vanilla ice cream inundated with nuts and chocolate sauce—were my main alternatives for dessert. The executive dining room where the menfolk ate (and almost all Lazarus executives were men) was next door to the Chintz Room, so Mr. Robert, Mr. Bob, or Robert's nephew Mr. Charles might stop by to see how we were getting on.

The Lazarus women were not encouraged to join their brothers in running the store, though many were capable. I bet that Char, of all of them, would have been most likely to rise to the highest level. Her brother, Bob, certainly thought so. She would have had to learn organizational politics and ways to choose her battles, which she would have hated. But she had the mind and the guts to run the business.

My cousin John Lazarus tells of the leader of a major competing retailer remarking about Char, "You're missing a bet with that one."

On another rainy day, Robbie Sirak, Donnie, and I were awarded the special treat of being driven downtown to go to the movies by ourselves. Outside the theater, Donnie had a better idea.

"Why don't we keep the money and go to the store?"

I could see the advantages of holding on to my dollar, as could Robbie. We agreed.

"Let's go see Pop-pop," said Donnie, and we went to his office.

Though the visit was an unexpected interruption, Pop-pop used the occasion to take us on a tour of the inner workings of the store. We saw where the extra stock was kept and where the advertising group put together displays for the *Columbus Dispatch* and the *Citizen Journal*. He showed us the associates' cafeteria and introduced us to cooks, floor managers, and dolly pushers, all of whom he knew. It was a look at the routines behind the show on the sales floors, the operations of the business that made our lives so easy and full of promise.

Char was deeply aware of how lucky we all were. I never heard her ruminate on how her role, instead of high-level executive, was family fan. She loved the part and played it like a diva. She wrote this song, sung to the tune of "Thank Heaven for Little Girls," in praise of the store:

> *Thank heaven for F&R.*
> *The merchants sing its praises pole to pole.*
> *Thank heaven for F&R,*
> *Emporium that keeps us off the dole.*
> *It trains the men for stores across the nation.*
> *That's how our dividends have kept up with inflation.*
> *Thank heaven for F&R.*
> *Our blessings on the block that's bound by State, Front, Town, and High,*
> *The cradle of the clan Lazari.*
> *Thank heaven.*
> *Thank heaven.*
> *Thank heaven for F&R.*

My father had two jokes about Uncle Fred, Pop-pop's older brother. The first was that it was a good thing he hadn't decided to become a watchmaker. When we were introduced I understood why.

"I'm so glad to meet you, my dear," he said, his round face full of warmth and his eyes twinkling behind his even rounder glasses. It was about 1959, and we were at a family lunch in Cincinnati. Fred Lazarus Jr. was in the midst of lifting a fork to his mouth, and his hand was shaking. He had a lifelong palsy that would have made unpacking and refitting the tiny screws, pins, springs, and gears of mechanical wristwatches an unlikely career.

It's been written that Uncle Fred's palsy was a remnant of childhood disease. I think it was likely a genetic problem. Uncle Fred was supposed to have shot out a light bulb during his ROTC training for World War I,[3] which reminded me of Char, her wiggly eyes, and her story about being required to take archery at summer camp.

"She shot the counselor," Dick said.

I don't believe she impaled a camp counselor to a tree or even grazed her whistle. But Char knocking arrow to bow and aiming it somewhere was a terrible thing to contemplate.

The second joke, which Dick would deliver with mock sadness, his lips turned down and his eyes sparkling with conspiracy, was that Uncle Fred might have made something of himself if only he had gone to college.

Fred Lazarus Jr. was the most famous of the Lazarus clan of Columbus and Cincinnati as the head of Federated Department Stores and didn't give up the reins until 1966 at the age of eighty-one.[4] At that time the group of stores had sales of over a billion dollars, had major stores in twelve cities, and was the department store stock most widely held by mutual funds.

The progenitor of the Columbus clan, Simon Lazarus, arrived from Bavaria in 1851. Even then, retailing was an excellent venue for Jewish men to make a living. Over the next century, some made fortunes. It was necessity: they were blocked from other vocations. The best colleges, the ones Uncle

Fred didn't bother to apply to, had quotas for Jewish applicants. Ditto for medical schools and law schools. The Lazarus family, along with other Jewish families in innumerable cities and towns, found a way to do well.

Every Jewish family who settled in Columbus before 1855 went into the clothing business.[5] The original Fred and Ralph, Simon's sons, started by selling ready-to-wear suits to veterans returning from the Civil War, exactly where the demand was. The company grew through customer care, business innovation, and nurturing a growing community.

"A good store is like a big circus," said my great-uncle Fred.[6] He brought in an alligator to live in the store's basement. He hired a blimp to announce a change in hours.

A customer once telephoned Robert at home to ask how to serve tea properly. He carefully explained as best he could. I can imagine how tickled he was to be consulted. A customer called Bob Lazarus at home to complain that a monogrammed Easter egg had not been delivered. Bob personally delivered it to the man's home.

Uncle Fred briefly had his own perfume, like fashion designers do these days. At the end of a season when a bunch of different colognes and eaux de toilettes were sitting around unsold, he had them combined and put a label on the bottles that said "Frelajr"—vaguely Scandinavian with that *j*, as if it should be pronounced "Fraylar." Customers asked for it for years after the supply ran out.

If the store wasn't the first to use an invention, it was among the earliest adopters of novel business practices. Lazarus installed an "air door" that replaced glass with a wall of air on the High Street entrance, barring heat from crossing the air barrier in the summer and cold in the winter. Bob Levy Sr., a good friend of Robert's and owner of the Union department store across the street, complained, "They already have ninety percent of the customers. Now they're sucking them in."

During a time when it wasn't illegal to drink alcohol in Ohio Stadium unless you became a pest, one story has it that the stadium police removed a fan who was thoroughly inebriated. "Get me fifty dollars and a Lazarus!" the fellow cried as he was being hauled off.

The Lazarus family understood that their fate was tied to the community. If Columbus grew, more people could buy more goods. They loved Columbus, saw its promise, and contributed to making a town in the cornfields become a thriving city. In the flood of 1913, the one James Thurber lovingly mocked in his autobiography,[7] Simon Lazarus headed up the relief committee. The store's entire stock of canoes was dedicated to rescuing west-side residents from high floodwaters.[8]

The Lazaruses (informally called "Lazari") knew a customer when they saw one and never discriminated against African Americans. In the 1960s, a time of crisis in race relations, Lazari worked behind the scenes to cool tempers and make change. They checked on the employment practices of their suppliers to make sure they were not discriminating.[9]

Char was fervent about racial equality. She was on the board of the Urban League and a newly formed Columbus Community Relations Commission and loved making friends with leaders in the African American community. One of them was a registrar for a driver's license bureau. He made sure that when Char needed to take the eye test to renew her license, she wasn't hassled.

In the 1920s, Hattie joined the birth-control movement led by Margaret Sanger. It was a controversial cause; Sanger was arrested and jailed for her ideas. To become openly, actively involved, Hattie needed the blessing of the family.

The Lazarus men met to discuss the matter. On the one hand, Lazarus would lose customers. On the other hand, they believed access to birth control would improve the lives of women and their families. According to Bob Lazarus, "They decided not to let the business control them. They would do as they believed."[10]

The Lazarus family's decision to support Hattie was brave and foresighted. It also made business sense. If families had fewer children, they would have more income to spend on extras like clothes.

Much of what the Lazaruses did for Columbus was behind the scenes—in fact, as much as possible. Robert Sr. drove a Buick, not a Cadillac, because Caddies were too flashy; of course, in later years it was a Buick driven by the houseman. They quietly supported innumerable causes, with racks of money and shelves full of hard-earned influence. Innumerable social services and arts organizations have benefitted from Lazarus generosity over the years. The Hattie and Robert Lazarus Fund still sponsors *Washington Week* on PBS Friday nights.

The story we bring out annually about Uncle Fred is how he changed the date of Thanksgiving. This is how we tell it to our children and our children's children:

Times were hard. It was the Great Depression, and millions of people were out of work. President Franklin D. Roosevelt was trying everything he could to stimulate the economy. He wanted to know how to encourage consumers to shop more, so he called Uncle Fred into his office and asked for his advice.

"Mr. President," said Mr. Lazarus, "if Thanksgiving were a week earlier, there would be more days in the Christmas shopping season. That would mean bigger sales and more work for seasonal employees."

"That's a great idea," the president said and saw to it that Thanksgiving was moved up a week.

As with any good story, there are qualifiers. To be precise, Fred proposed designating the fourth Thursday as Thanksgiving. In 1939, when Fred talked to FDR, there were six days between the last Thursday in November—then designated as Thanksgiving—and the fourth Thursday. And of course other people were involved in the request to the president. The Ohio Retail Merchant Federation, the *Cincinnati Enquirer*, and the Ohio Newspaper Association did considerable legwork.[11]

Nor was the idea universally well received. Calendars, railroad timetables, and almanacs would have to be amended. Worst of all, it meant changes to the Ohio State football schedule, which was fixed for several years ahead. For Columbus, changing that schedule was like switching from the Julian to the Gregorian calendar. Fred's brothers were furious.

"What damn fool got the president to do that?" asked Simon.

"You're looking at him," Fred answered.[12]

On December 29, 1941, Congress passed a law making the fourth Thursday in November the day we give thanks for all our blessings, including the amazing luck of being associated with Fred Lazarus and the other Lazari.

By 1966, Federated was so big that the Federal Trade Commission concluded it was a threat to competition in retailing and forbade any more mergers for five years. That prompted Char to write, to the tune of "The Buckeye Battle Cry":

> *Fed-er-at-ed can't buy stores for five whole years, how sad.*
> *FTC has handcuffed Fred. He's feeling mighty bad.*
> *Down in Cincinnati they mourn.*
> *Life is strange when no stores are born.*
> *Wail, wail, poor Federated no more can proliferate.*
> *Safe is Macy's! Safe is Hudson's!*
> *Relax, relax. Expansion's ceased.*

Perhaps the FTC decision was not the beginning of the end, but it was a harbinger. The business was so large it was harder to add the personal touches that made the store so loved and trusted. In Columbus, Lazarus leadership fought expansion into suburban malls for as long as possible. The argument was that a mall store could not provide the full-service experience of the downtown circus. That was true as far as it went. The underlying problem was that downtown urban areas were in decline. Shoppers wanted to go elsewhere, and they would. Federated went through a series of grueling transitions. It took over Macy's in 1994, forming the world's largest aggregation of department stores. Many people think it was the reverse—Macy's took over Federated and Lazarus. Not true. The Macy's name just had better recognition nationally.

The Lazarus legacy lives on. For several years after the name change, the hair salon at the Easton Macy's kept their curtains with "Lazarus" stitched in the traditional block letters. I liked to look at the remnant of past fame as I got my hair clipped, recalling shopping with Char and Pop-pop's pleasure at serving customers.

When Fred Lazarus visited Boston in 1965, I was one of those who received a telegram ahead of time, typed in capital letters, printed on onionskin, and signed "Uncle Fred," saying he wanted to take younger members of the family in the area to dinner at Loche-Ober. College sophomores didn't eat out, much less at fine restaurants, unless a relative came to town. Courtesy of my gentle, powerful great-uncle, I consumed a lobster with several cousins and my brother, Bobby, who was at the Harvard Business School. It was thrilling to be a Lazarus.

By 1958, when Dick married Char, Gladys's family (the Butlers) had petered out except for a first cousin of Gladys's who lived in Monte Carlo. I was deeply ashamed of Gladys and wanted to wish her away. I thought I was the last Witkind, since Dick's brother, Lloyd, was a confirmed bachelor and to our knowledge had no children. Rumors persisted of a Witkind or two in Colorado, but if they existed, they were not in touch.[13]

By the time I was in college, we had moved away from New York, so I could easily exclude Belle's relatives from my picture of myself. I banished my second-rate past. I didn't like being a stepchild. That seemed second rate too.

But was it really second rate? All families are blended ones, after all, except in some far corners of West Virginia. Spouses have to come from different families, or the genes get extremely messed up. The Lazarus family today includes all kinds of people. For example, not a single member of my generation of descendants of Hattie and Robert has married in the Jewish faith.

Thinking about it in recent years, I've found things to like in my genetic makeup. It isn't all bad.

My third child, Charlotte, was born in 1986, joining Joshua (Josh) and Babette (Babsie when she was young and now going by Wit). When Charlie, as we called her to avoid confusion, was three years old, Char took a good look at her and said, "She has real style, that kid."

Shoot, I thought, remembering a time I went shopping with Belle and Gladys. "Doesn't Mommy have good taste?" Belle had asked as Gladys sized up a bright print blouse. I'd had no idea.

Char's message was clear: whatever else I have, I don't have style. Charlotte does; the kid is a throwback to a good thing about Gladys. After college, Charlotte acquired a master's degree from Parsons School of Design in fashion studies. She really does have style, whatever that is.

Like Gladys, Charlotte exudes sophistication, a handy thing to have. She can even turn on a snooty air like Gladys could.

"I talked myself into the King David Hotel in Jerusalem," she reported proudly to Jack and me. She and her mates needed a place to stay. One of them had her mom's credit card, so they could pay for anywhere for a night and split it six ways. Two of the young men went in to ask for a room. The guy behind the counter took a look at the scruffy Americans and said nothing was available. Then Charlotte went in and gave them the patrician accent and air of entitlement. They sold her a room.

Char used to laugh at how Dick and I looked from behind when we walked—the same shape of calves and the same gait, except I was a foot shorter. In Salt Lake City in 1996, I took Wit to dinner with some of her fellow AmeriCorps volunteers. Walking back to her dorm from the restaurant, Wit and I several feet in front of the others, we heard multiple peals of laughter. "The two of you walk exactly the same," explained one of her friends. It felt good.

My oldest child, Joshua, is adopted. We look nothing alike. For one thing, he is extremely tall. When Jack and I brought him home as an infant, I was surprised to find that babies came as long as ours. Charlotte is into style. Wit is our scientist. Josh, like me, is a writer. The others *can* write. Josh and I write because that's what we are when we don't have to do anything else, except that he has more stamina than me and is up until three in the morning churning out craft and art. His genre is science fiction, which I know as much about as how to dress stylishly. But we share ideas. A recent lunch conversation turned to a discussion of a novel.

"He has a sentence that supposedly goes on for a whole chapter," said Josh.

"He can get away with it. He's a great writer."

"But does it work? Can the reader follow it?"

"It gives the feeling of the parrot flying high over San Francisco," I said.

"But he uses punctuation. It's not really a sentence that goes on for a whole chapter. It's just a different way of writing sentences, only harder to read."

The conversation was going nowhere. I was annoyed at Josh. And proud of him.

The Butlers had died out. The Witkind name appeared played out. I was, however, tied to another family—the Speyer line of Belle, my grandmother. Unlike Lazarus, the name Speyer had a life of merely two generations. Belle's father, whose original name was Shapiro, had four daughters and one son. He delegated the son, Archibald (Archie), to choose a better name after they emigrated from Lithuania, and Archie chose Speyer. The son had two daughters. The daughters married. Nobody would carry on the name.

Archie intended the new name to sound less Jewish, and later changes carried on that ancestry-muddling family tradition. One of Belle's sisters married a guy named Shapero (with an e). His sons changed their surname to Marwell to sound more American. Another married a Jew named Cooper. Their firstborn was Moisha Velvel. A grade-school teacher Anglicized and reversed the name to William Morris. He was plain old Bill Cooper by the time I knew him.

In 2007, after Char and Dick were both gone, I decided to follow up on the Speyer line. Chuck Cooper, Bill's son, and one of Archie's descendants with the surname Zichterman, helped me start a family tree. When I brought several cousins together for cocktails in our suite at the Algonquin that year, I was stunned to find that some of my Speyer cousins had never met each other. I knew all the grandchildren of Belle's sisters because I visited their homes when I was a kid, often for weekends and once for a trip to Washington. Amazingly, Stuart Marwell and Tommy Wacht shook hands and introduced themselves at the suite's entryway. It was only then, after more than fifty years, that I realized Belle must have farmed me out to her sisters' children to give herself a break.

The Lazaruses had other advantages besides the ability to pass down a name. They arrived in the United States thirty years before the Speyers, a head start. They settled in a smaller town than the Speyers did and could thus make more of an impact. Along the way, they have had their own historians to keep the family story alive. Char was a cheerleader for the family and knew how every cousin was related. My sister, Babette, took the next step and made sure there was a written record. It is she who organizes the family reunions. There has never been a Speyer reunion.

Many families have hotshots. They don't talk as much about the duds or sad stories. Stuart Marwell did genealogical research that showed his wife is descended, if you weave through the family branches, to Roger Williams, the founder of the state of Rhode Island. Then there's Belle's brother, Archie, who likely died by his own hand, which held a gun.

If you bob through the Lazarus family tree, you will find my second cousin once removed, so distant I never heard of her before reading a lurid account, who is imprisoned for life. She fed her husband a sedative-laced milkshake, bludgeoned him to death with a sculpture, rolled him up in a carpet, and had the servants in her Hong Kong apartment help her carry the wrapped body to the storage room in the basement. Several days passed before the smell led police to the body and the murderess.[14] Obviously not a real family member.

None of the above takes away from the fact that Fred Lazarus Jr. was a genius. Together with his brilliant brothers, he forged a retailing empire. The Speyers had their chance. My uncle Nat Shapero was in the fur business, for example. I remember him, especially, because he brought me a coonskin cap with a snap-on tail at the time of the movie *Davy Crockett*, when every child in America wanted to wear one. He couldn't turn them out fast enough. No Shapero, Shapiro, Wacht, Marwell, or Cooper became a brand name like Lazarus.

However, blockbuster success in one generation doesn't guarantee a thing for the next one. Statistically, the opposite is more likely. My generation of Lazaruses, the fifth from the arrival of Simon in Columbus, is highly successful. Only a couple are retailers. The most sizable group works in nonprofit organizations. One was director of a Baltimore arts museum. One

Lazarus works for the federal government in counterterrorism, definitely a modern calling. A couple of my Lazarus cousins, though, have had troubles.

My generation of Speyers (though nobody else uses that shorthand) includes Stuart Marwell, president of a technology company; Tommy Wacht, a Yale law graduate and successful New York corporate lawyer; and Joshua Marwell, executive director of the Museum of Jewish Heritage in New York. Every single Speyer descendant up to this point is well educated and successful.

And what about the next generation of Lazaruses and Speyers? Like their fathers and mothers, they are highly educated, motivated, and headed for success, by which I mean careers where they make an impact, mates who are right for them, contributions to their communities, friendships, and times of happiness.

Loving family relationships are created from shared experience and values. Those almond soufflés count. My Lazarus family taught me the most essential value, that of loving-kindness. Love was not absent before I joined the family, but it came with a lot of noise, like a radio you couldn't tune to a station. Important things need to be said out loud every once in a while.

One bleak winter week in 1973, after Hoo-hoo died, Pop-pop stopped short on his way to his regular afternoon gin game. His head had gone fuzzy. He'd had a stroke. He declined rapidly, and by Sunday morning the family gathered at the house knowing he was on his way out. Jack and I went upstairs to say good-bye. Pop-pop was in Char and Babs's room, the one where I stayed on my first visit to Columbus. He was lying in that same bed.

His eyes were closed as we said hello.

"It's Vivian."

"And Jack."

"Vivian Louise?" he asked.

I don't know who that might have been.

"Have you done something kind for somebody today, Vivian?" asked my grandfather.

He left a letter to be opened and read after his death. Dated June 24, 1966, with a couple of small later amendments, the letter requested cremation and a small service at Temple Israel ("easy on the Hebrew") and specified that Char should inherit the impressionist painting by Claude Monet. Then followed, in his delicate handwriting, "one and only one word of advice":

"Keep the family communications open. As a big family gets bigger, there are bound to be friction and annoyances. It takes determination and restraint to see that the closeness of brother and sisters is not lost."

After the funeral service, Char shepherded Bobby, Donnie, Babsie, and me into her library and made sure we knew the "one word of advice" applied to us too.

"Stick together," she said.

People arrive in the world with idiosyncrasies and grow apart from there. My siblings and I are not immune to bickering and one-upmanship. Bobby and Donnie like to brag about bargains they have nailed. Bobby finds deals on eBay, like a gorgeous shirt for half off. So he buys a dozen. How many shirts can a guy wear? He turns over cars every year or so but always gets a great price. Right now he's looking at a used Bentley. If he buys it, it will be a steal. A steal on a Bentley is different than on a Hyundai. I don't know all the peeves Jack and I inspire, though I'm sure our fabulous trips to places like Southeast Asia and Africa have been pooh-poohed for the price. I don't particularly care. My siblings stick to the United States and Europe for travel, and that is their preference.

There have been bigger challenges. When Babette married an obstreperous Scotsman, Char and the rest of us dutifully included him in family doings. We kept our lips buttoned and were relieved when Babette divorced him. Babette now says the definition of divorce is getting rid of the guy roaming around your house telling you how messed up you are. "Messed up" is not the exact phrasing she uses.

As Pop-pop wrote, sticking together means communicating. Jealousy and grievances grow in silence. Goodwill and empathy arrive by coming together and talking and bitching openly about each other's foibles and then laughing. My siblings and I all live in Columbus, which makes it easier to celebrate birthdays and holidays together—not Jewish holidays, of course. It's shocking that twenty people jam into our house, and they're only Char and Dick's descendants.[15]

"Sing ho for the fertile loins," Char would say.

Jack and I have a bang-up Fourth of July picnic with all the family we can pull in. On Christmas evening we go to Donnie and Lisal's house ten minutes away, where she cooks a magnificent dinner and we exchange gifts. Lisal has taken charge of the rotation of the one-on-one exchange among the adults. Bobby and Linda are usually at their house in Hilton Head, South Carolina, at Christmastime. Thanksgiving has become the chanciest for family camaraderie. Wit and Charlotte are too busy and far away to come home for a couple of days. Josh and Lorraine and my nephews and nieces have in-laws and other family. They have to divide their time.

The bottom half of the genealogical X is starting to spread out from the individuals in my generation.

For many years, Jack and I sat across the field from Bob and Mary Lazarus, my aunt and uncle, at Ohio State home football games until Bob died in December 2013. We checked on each other with field glasses and compared notes on the game afterward.

I missed a game in the fall of 2013. I'm sure I had a good excuse. "Where were you?" they asked. So did a nephew who sat in an entirely different section. It was a family scandal.

At a quiet French restaurant in the Short North in 2013, Bob swore he could remember all the words from "The Begat," a song from his favorite musical, *Finian's Rainbow*. He set out to prove it—and did—as I accompanied as well as I could. Sotto voce so as not to disturb the other patrons, we sang over our beet and Roquefort salads about what Adam and Eve started:

> *They begat Cain, and they begat Abel,*
> *Who begat the rabble at the tower of Babel.*
> *They begat the Cohens, and they begat the O'Rourkes,*
> *And they begat the people who believe in storks.*
>
> . . .
>
> *So bless them all who go to bat,*
> *And heed the call, of the begats.*

7

A KENNEDY HALF-DOLLAR COIN

Washington and New York were bitterly chilly. The squirrels in Central Park limped through icy shards of grass, and the pigeons in the crannies of the Capitol huddled tight, puffing out their built-in parkas. I watched the inauguration of John F. Kennedy on the black-and-white TV at the foot of my bed that Monday, January 20, 1961. I was in tenth grade at Miss Hewitt's Classes in New York and must have been home sick to be sitting cross-legged in fleece pajamas instead of studying ancient and medieval history or Romantic poets a few blocks away.

We had finished with American history in eighth grade and would not touch it again. At Hewitt's, only European history counted. America was a young country, we were told, and raw. Not much of interest had happened there so far. In that eighth-grade class, the school year dribbled out around Woodrow Wilson and the League of Nations. We never made it to the chapter in the textbook on World War II. Never mind that in the 1950s, the United States was a superpower in military and economic might and that we viewed our country as the bastion of democracy and capitalism in Manichean opposition to the communist, totalitarian Union of Soviet Socialist Republics.

From the podium at the Capitol, Robert Frost read a poem from a piece of paper that flapped in the flurrying snow and threatened to slip from his hand. "The land was ours before we were the land's," the poet said and had to pause. I was sure he was wishing he could recite the thing from memory because he could hardly see in the sharp, white light. The young president himself stood up to steady the paper.

Kennedy gave a speech that day so strong, graceful, and uplifting that it inspired a generation, my burgeoning generation of postwar baby boomers.

"Ask not what your country can do for you. Ask what you can do for your country," he declaimed in his Boston accent.

We were the children of the soldiers, sailors, airmen, and factory workers who defeated Hitler, as well as of those who could only stand and wait. We knew we were lucky and affluent and had missed the miseries of the Depression and the war, though on the downside, the potential for nuclear attack was always at the back of our minds.

The president was bare headed, in stark contrast to the hatted generation of the men behind him. I was smitten.

The call to service stuck. For me, the message was that democratic government is a tool for social and economic progress. Others interpreted it differently. I cannot say that I chose a career that instant. I could not see further ahead than college, which was a looming prospect. But I heard clearly when the president said public service is a high calling and even a moral obligation.

I would graduate in June 1963 and expected life would go on as usual for the next couple of years. I would live with Belle and see Char and Dick and my siblings a couple of times a week.

Things only stayed the same until the fall of 1962.

☙

The musical *Camelot* hit Broadway and immediately became a metaphor for the Kennedy White House, the nation, and the simple folk like us. I went to the show with my parents, bought the original cast's long-playing, 33⅓ rpm recording, and played it until I knew all the words. I'd gently pick up the diamond needle from the turntable and move it back to the last blank space between the grooves to start the same song again until I had it down.

"The winter is forbidden till December and exits March the second on the dot." March the second. Got it.

And singing along with Julie Andrews, "Where are the simple joys of maidenhood?...Where's the knight pining so for me, he leaps to death in woe for me?"

I remember my first three years of high school as Camelot, which shows what memory does—makes you simple. It was adolescence, after all.

Char and Dick hounded me to be "outgoing."

"You hide behind your glasses," said Dick. He took me to Madison Avenue opticians, as if the latest French frames would change my personality. He bought me contact lenses, but at four feet and eleven and three-quarters inches, I was still able to disappear under the pressure of adult eyes, or so I believed.

"You're like the girl in *The Fantasticks*," said Char and quoted: "I'm special. I *am* special. Please, God, please, don't let me be normal."

I would have to be more like another girl in my class, Midge, they said. Midge wasn't a great student, but she was a bubbly, happy person.

"Midge it," said my father. Considering my height, it was a poor choice of words.

"Think of the other guy, not just yourself," said Char. "You have to try to become an 'effective person.'" Then, maybe needing something reassuring to add, she'd tell me how bright I was.

There was truth in all of it. Some of it was an unfortunate gift from Gladys—the gift of built-in fearfulness. That could be moderated over time by the hard work of learning empathy, learning where I fit in, and accepting myself as special in some ways and ordinary in others. "'Tis a gift to be simple...to come down where you ought to be." Char considered it a defect to be a person who looks inward for her strength. She did her thinking by talking and was most herself surrounded by other people. Thinking takes quiet time for me, and I tire of company. Char convinced me that this was all wrong.

"Don't contemplate your own navel," she said.

She was right insofar as brooding leads nowhere. She was incorrect, I believe, in applying her philosophy to all and sundry, and perhaps she would have done well to practice some systematic introspection herself from time to time. I was in no position to see that. She was my mentor.

In the meantime, I determined that I would have to take on a role, a façade, and play the part to the hilt if I was to look normal. I would have to resist the urge to hide like a turtle and instead stick my head out of my shell.

If high school was like Camelot, it was because of the turtle-shell of a school that I professed to despise. Frosso Iossifoglu, Georgia Kingson,

Lynn Mooney, and I considered ourselves the intelligentsia of the Hewitt's class of 1963. We were highly impressed with ourselves. Some of the fourteen other girls in our class may have considered us the social leftovers. They were the ones who went to "the club," even on school nights, where there were drinks, cigarettes, and boys. The older sister of one classmate was dating Cary Grant, the actor, and a black limousine would come by after school to pick her up. It was a closed car, and the windows were smoky. However slowly we walked by and however carefully we directed a quick glance, we could not get a glimpse into the back seat.

My group studied hard and talked for hours over our pink princess telephones. Belle sprang for the phone, but I had to pay for usage out of my weekly allowance. Charges were by the number of calls, not the length of time on the phone. If I needed to stop talking to Georgia about Byron or quadratic equations, I put the receiver down, perhaps for an hour or so, and picked it up again to continue. The conversations got inane as the evening wore on.

"The mountains look on Marathon, and Marathon looks on the muddy Mississippi," Georgia declaimed, and we giggled maniacally.

Well protected from the world, we practiced what we considered rebellion. Frosso, Lynn, Georgia, and I took pleasure in the idea that we were ahead of our time compared with the teachers. I suppose that meant we were closer than they to being of our own time, though we knew nothing of how teenagers lived in the rest of the country or even in the Bronx. We didn't know about the ones for whom school was an irrelevant diversion from the business of life, the ones who were working to support their parents, the ones who already had babies.

We adored Mrs. Delman, an English teacher with an orotund voice and rotund figure who sounded as British as she could as she acquainted us with the true literary canon. It was a supreme act of defiance for the four of us to stage *Le Malentendu* by Albert Camus under the auspices of Mme. Geno, our young Vietnamese French teacher.

The Misunderstanding is an existentialist work in which a mother and daughters in cold, dark, rainy northern France murder their long-lost and unrecognized son/brother for his money so they can move south. Frosso played the son, and I the mother. Lynn and Georgia were my daughters. We put on a single performance of the play in English. The Upper School was packed into the oak library, which had a stage and doubled as the school's auditorium.

I was delighted to see Mrs. Delman in the front row, her gray hair in a tight bun and her arms crossed over her *poitrine* as I blasted my child in the heart with a pistol and she collapsed dead in a dramatic heap. Unfortunately my lips began to quiver with laughter, causing Frosso an uncontrollable postmortem fit. There she was, writhing unconvincingly in some final death throes as Mrs. Delman's lips turned down in a stiff, red-lipped frown against her porcelain, oval face. She disapproved of Camus and his play because it was not "an affirmation of life." For us, in that one brief moment, she was dead wrong. We were affirmed. Death wasn't something we took seriously, after all.

The afternoon of Friday, November, 2, 1962, the fall of my senior year in high school, I arrived home outside the apartment building on Seventy-First Street and saw Dick's car parked at an abrupt angle to the curb. I rode the elevator to the second floor. The front door to our apartment had a sign that read "Do not ring bell." It was unlocked. I heard male voices. Dick, Char, and Lloyd, Dick's brother, were there. Medics were taking Belle to the hospital. She gave me a little wave and a smile that I suppose was meant to be reassuring. It was a heart attack.

My dog and I spent the night at the Ninety-Sixth Street apartment where my parents and siblings lived. The next morning, I woke up early and headed home down Madison Avenue with the dog, a miniature schnauzer named Val. Somewhere in the Eighties, Dick's car pulled up. He knew where I'd be going.

"Grandma took a big turn for the worse during the night," he told me when I got in the car. He meant she was dead.

I did not cry at the service at Frank E. Campbell funeral home Sunday. Dick did, and Char held his hand. I had what my diary calls "a thinking attack" that night and paced the creaking floor enough that Char woke up. She got me hot chocolate and a Nembutal, a barbiturate type of sleeping pill. Char talked and quietly recited poetry for a while as she went through several cigarettes. Then she turned on a radio for me and left. I still could not sleep.

I sleepwalked through the next day in school, botching a physics experiment, which was probably typical. Aside from a generalized sadness that I expressed in my diary in melancholy quotations from the Romantic poets and the numbness where my heart should have been, I felt relief. I was going to start a new life in college next year and could put boring Belle behind me as if she were a teacher like Mrs. Delman. Burying the impact of losing my grandmother and my caretaker from kindergarten on was a huge mistake. I would pay for it in my sophomore year of college by way of severe sadness and loneliness.

After years of successful resistance, I had to move into Char and Dick's apartment. Char put up her long-planned wall in the already tiny dining room to make a bedroom for me. While the bedroom was being built, Babsie and I shared the room she and Donnie had always had. Bobby had started college at the University of Michigan, and Donnie now had his own room. My new bedroom was cramped, what with me, Val, and Felix the parakeet, named after Supreme Court justice Felix Frankfurter. I liked the new room. The smaller, the safer.

Char, Dick, Donnie, Babsie, and I went to Columbus for Thanksgiving, meeting Bobby there as well as the rest of the family, and returned home to Ninety-Sixth Street to find a thin letter with Wellesley College in blue letters as the return address. I knew it contained a rejection and I would have to start thinking of other schools. I had applied to Wellesley under the early-decision plan, and they took a tiny percentage of their applicants early. Maybe I had a chance in the spring, but even then it was unlikely. The words from Wellesley to my headmistress, summarizing my interview, were "young and scared."

The letter wasn't a rejection. The fools were taking me. It had to be because of all the brilliant Lazarus women who got me into the legacy pool. I was certain I was doomed to failure. I learned much later that a large percentage of my classmates felt as I did when they got their acceptance letters—they were certain they were admitted by mistake.

In the winter of 1963, Char started talking about moving from the Ninety-Sixth Street apartment. It had seemed cramped before, and with me there it was like a rush-hour subway car. The street was on the boundary between the white, upper-middle-class Upper East Side and the poverty of Harlem. We were robbed regularly, partly because, with Char's approval, nobody kept the front door of the apartment locked. The building had a doorman who was supposed to safeguard the premises. The last time we were robbed, the doorman helped the burglar carry the TV set to a waiting cab. Bobby, who wore a jacket and tie day and night, even as a boy, had to give up his wallet twice on the street. Donnie, who didn't look as though he had a dime to his name, was never robbed, though he took the same route home after school.

Char wanted to decamp to the suburbs. Not a New York suburb, but Bexley, Ohio. It was only recently that I learned from Babsie that the idea was already in the wind a year before, but Char decided to wait until I graduated from Hewitt's.

Dick resisted moving. He argued that although the apartment was less and less pleasant, a move to Riverdale would take care of that. The Midwest was where midwesterners lived, and their place was on a lower rung of the evolutionary ladder. He was rooted to New York, but Char was a class-five hurricane when she wanted something. She was worried about her aging parents and wanted to be closer to them. She wanted Babsie to attend the Columbus School for Girls, where she had gone, and Donnie, the Columbus Academy. Char ranted. She cried. Dick was reduced to lying on his back in their bed with his pillow over his eyes and one arm over the pillow like a beech tree whose roots were wide, but not deep enough, and had been felled by a storm.

My parents would move, but Dick would commute to his job in New York, presumably for a few months. The few months turned into years and anonymous fame. *Future Shock*, a 1970 best seller about emerging trends, begins a chapter titled "The New Nomads" with an account of the Friday afternoon commute of one Bruce Robe, "a tall, graying Wall Street executive." The executive walks to the Wall Street heliport to take a helicopter to Kennedy airport, then flies TWA to Columbus, Ohio, where a car is waiting for him at the airport.[1] It had to be Dick coming home after four nights at the Cornell Club in the city. Char was the one waiting in the car.

Alvin Toffler, the author, puts a positive face on the long distance between work and home: "Claiming the best of two worlds, a job in the frenetic financial center of America and a family life in the comparatively tranquil Midwest countryside, he shuttles back and forth some 50,000 miles a year."[2] The reality was more that Dick was asserting a life of his own rather than one as an annex to Char. It would be forty years or so before telecommuting would become feasible, and he was bouncing between cities rather than be subsumed. That was one way to look at it. Another was that at heart he was a nomad in the sense of a guy who wouldn't accept all the obligations of marriage. Either way, the conflict between Char and Dick continued and got worse before eventually abating.

The perfect house was available: 256 South Columbia Avenue, at the southeast corner of Dale and Columbia in Bexley, about a half mile away from my grandparents' house on Fair Avenue and much like theirs both inside and out. The master bedroom alone was as large as our Ninety-Sixth Street apartment. I would have the adjacent bedroom for times when I was home. The house had a name—Melrose—carved on one of the stone pillars that leads up the curved driveway. It derived from Melrose Abbey in Scotland, though we never learned why.

The summer of 1963, after my high school graduation, we lived at Hoo-hoo and Pop-pop's house while Melrose was being renovated. If I'd been able to look inside myself, I would have found fear and emptiness. To fill up, I got up early to walk Val, the schnauzer, and stuff myself from my grandparents' refrigerator. It was an industrial refrigerator that spanned an entire wall like a tick-tack-toe board with multiple white porcelain doors and heavy stainless-steel hinges and handles. Behind each door was something delicious left over from Dorothy's cooking the days before. One and a half peach pies, for example: I would eat half of the half, then open another door. Creamed spinach: I helped myself to as much as I could without, I thought, it being noticeable. Later in the day, I would bike through Bexley for hours, trying to work off the calories, which was not successful.

Pop-pop was headed for Boston on business the weekend I had to leave Char and Dick's new home for Wellesley to begin freshman year and, I assumed, the process of flunking out. Maurice (Mogey) Lazarus, the president of Filene's in Boston, met us at Logan airport when we arrived around eight o'clock at night and drove out to the campus in the evening. I had only one suitcase, but it was enormous and packed to the bursting point. I was packed to the bursting point myself. After a summer of popping open the levered doors of Hoo-hoo and Pop-pop's restaurant-size refrigerator, my clothes were too tight. Pop-pop said afterward that it was lucky Mogey was along because he could never have hauled the suitcase into the lobby of Claflin Hall, where I would be spending the year. It was dark and quiet on the first-floor hallway. I dragged the suitcase to my room.

I was seventeen. At bottom, the thing I least believed, among Char and Dick's perorations to change my personality, was that I was bright. They pushed it as an advantage, but in truth I was not as intelligent as I thought I was supposed to be. Math was a weakness, and it showed up starkly in my SAT scores. Since I knew I wasn't smart enough for one of the best women's colleges in the country, I would have to work all day, every day, and be in the library until it closed at night. I would have to stay quiet in class so the teachers would not find out how stupid I was. Meanwhile, I would take notes constantly so I could figure out what they meant afterward and how the whole thing fit together for the tests and papers.

I would allow myself to go out Friday and Saturday nights. After years of Hewitt's, I wasn't going to deny myself the opportunity to meet men. But that was it.

My strategy turned out to be adequate for getting by and even acquiring the valuable skill of synthesizing information. It's not a good strategy for generating new questions, gaining fluency in the give and take of live argument, becoming a leader, or what Char called becoming an effective person. If anything, it was a recipe to retard that effort.

I signed up for courses. Freshman English was mandatory. Psychology did not emphasize mathematics, and I thought I could get through it as one of the two required science courses, with geology to follow in sophomore year if I made it that far. The other three courses were political science, Philosophy 101 on Plato and Aristotle, and first-year Spanish. I figured I'd had enough French.

Physical education was required, so I signed up for field hockey. That was a mistake. All the other young women were eight-foot-tall Amazons and had played for years in East Coast prep schools. They were tall and strong and carried sticks. The coach assigned me to right wing so I wouldn't interfere with play. That was fine, because when the women went after the hockey ball as a group, they were dangerous. Since I was dieting by denying myself breakfast or lunch, I wasn't as fast as even my usual self by late afternoon, when we practiced. I spent the hour or so of violence dragging myself up and down the battlefield in the right-wing lane. The actively engaged players would dash down the middle of the field, their sticks smashing air and ground for purposes that were unclear. I followed in my outside lane, getting about halfway to them by the time they turned and headed for the other end of the field. I swiveled and got about halfway before they turned again.

Spanish was not hard for one determined to study. Senora Concha Breton taught us *"el buen Castellano."* Senora Breton carried herself like royalty and looked like it too, with an aquiline nose and high hairdo. I believe she took refuge in the United States after the Spanish Civil War, having been on the wrong side of Generalissimo Franco.

From the first lecture, I loved psychology. The professor, Miss Zimmerman, started us off by asking us to write an answer to the question, "Why do people continue to do things that are bad for them?" The results represented all the current schools of psychology, from Freud to what was then the dominant approach, behaviorism. I loved it the way a lemming loves a cliff. But I knew I could not major in psych, no matter how much I was attracted to it. If I did, I would have to think about Gladys. And myself. I would implode.

In philosophy we started with Plato, and I was lost. I could read the dialogues, but my mind did not engage. There did not seem to be right answers. The lecturer, whose name I cannot recall, was young. It was her first time in front of a class, or close to it. Tall and Valkyrian in build, she stalked back and forth in front of the blackboard. I sat in the front row on the far right, close enough to try to pick up every nuance of the lecture but not risk eye contact. I was also closest to the door—able to zip out the minute the bell rang without talking to anyone.

Miss Philosophy casually asked us one day to draw a picture of what Plato's world looked like to hand in at the next class meeting. I obediently did one, but it turned out nobody else had, so I sat at my desk to wait out the class.

The lecturer spotted my penciled work. "Somebody's done it. And three-dimensional," she said. "Come on. Put it on the board."

The blackboard was high, and I looked up at it, chalk in hand.

"Here," said the prof. She pulled over a wastebasket, flipped it upside down, and gestured for me to stand on top to reach the higher parts of the board. I obeyed, feeling like a circus elephant. I froze and could not draw. The lecturer realized I was terror-stricken and bade me descend.

That was nothing compared with freshman English, especially since I came to college thinking I was good at it. In philosophy I felt like one of Plato's ignoramuses trapped in a cave, barely able to discern the shadows of real things. In English I felt like Icarus, who thought that, by dressing himself in feathers, he could fly to the sun and instead fell to earth while the rest of the world went on with their lives. I had read most of the major novels of the previous two centuries by the time I arrived at Wellesley. They were a fine means of escape. My freshman English professor, Miss Craig, was an enthralling lecturer. Mrs. Delman had told me I was one of the best English students she had ever had.

That fall we read *The Dubliners*. I had no idea what Stephen Dedalus was feeling or thinking. We read *Return of the Native*. Miss Craig got more out of two pages than I did out of the whole book.

Miss Craig told us to go to a lecture by a famous Gestalt psychologist and write it up. I think she meant it as a journalism effort, but I took it as a literary one and wrote about how ancient the lecturer was. It was a particularly juvenile perspective. I came to Miss Craig's office to pick up my paper. D– was written large in red. I began to sob, and I could not talk because my throat was locked in a spasm. I hadn't cried when my grandmother died, and now the tears streamed down my cheeks. Miss Craig looked annoyed. I crept out of her office. I would not be an English major. The study of literature is a humanist endeavor, and I was way behind on understanding the human condition.

That left political science. Mr. Stratton, the professor of the yearlong introductory course, was married to Miss Zimmerman, the psychology professor. The latter had been a classmate of Mary Lazarus, and the union was quite a surprise to the class of 1950, perhaps something of a scandal.

In the first semester, we studied the Soviet Union. I already had an interest in the country beyond the stereotype of a monolithic enemy. Along with our venture into French existentialism in high school, Frosso, Lynn, Georgia, and I had organized an extra noncredit seminar on the Russian revolution. We were taking advantage of the knowledge of our physics teacher, a recent Bryn Mawr graduate in Russian history. The mother of one of my classmates, Lynn Outhwaite, was an expatriate Russian ballet dancer and teacher. She arranged for our class to visit Alexander Kerensky, once upon a nanosecond the leader of all the Russias. Kerensky was in his eighties and living as a guest at a brownstone on East Ninety-First Street.

We met him in his upstairs library, where books reached to the ceiling on three sides, with a tall window on the fourth. He sat sadly, an old man with a crew cut and dim eyes. He was almost blind by that time. He was a forgotten man then, had been for forty years or so, and will no doubt stay forgotten. I was spellbound at his account of the revolution. Basically, his story was that the people around him stymied his attempt to establish a republic. I don't think he told us all would be well if only he could return to Russia, though that had been his argument for many decades before, like the caged canary with one song.[3] I was struck by how much of history was chance and how politics and violence trumped ideology.

I was primed to learn more about the Soviet Union. It was exciting to go beyond the allegory of evil presented to Americans. I liked Mr. Stratton. His background was in public administration, and he was more interested in public policy than in theory. He had a way of talking about something grand and abstract and then leaning back in his chair and saying, "Well, I don't know; maybe that would work, or maybe it wouldn't." I did all the required reading and the suggested reading. The fundamental logic of political science made sense. It was about power—who gets what, when, and why. And it was about policy—effective ways of making things better for large groups of people.

The first midterm test came back with a grade of B and a note from Mr. Stratton: "You are obviously in possession of a great deal of information, most of which is relevant to the question." My blind dedication to taking notes on everything and then trying to figure out what it meant was going to pay off, at least for a while.

By November, three months through the first semester of freshman year, I can't say I was thriving, but I was hanging on. And I was learning a tremendous amount, which felt good. I felt stronger, braver, and more fulfilled in spite of myself. The second semester of freshman year, my grade in English went up substantially. And in a second philosophy class, I earned a top grade. Much later, when I was teaching public policy analysis to college students, I learned what it was like to try to reach exceptionally quiet students. I wanted them to ask questions. It makes it more interesting for the professor. They were not as bad, however, as the ones who took constant notes, then raised their hands to ask, "Will that be on the test?"

⟿

Friday, November 22, 1963, was chilly, rainy, and headed toward a dull evening. We listened to Miss Philosophy as she paced nervously and authoritatively back and forth. It was toward the end of the course, so she would have been talking about Aristotle.

An administrative minion of the college appeared at the door and stood next to my front-row seat.

"The president has been shot," she said and quickly disappeared to go to the next classroom, high heels clacking on the stone floor.

This was stranger than anything in Miss Philosophy's lecture notes. She did not know what to say. She tried to carry on with her lecture.

I heard the tapping of high heels in the hall again. The administrator came in, stood next to my desk, and talked over me to the teacher and the rest of the class.

"The president is dead."

"Well, that's it, I guess," said the professor, turning to us and shrugging her shoulders in a *c'est-la-vie* motion. "I suppose you're dismissed."

I slung my green canvas Cliffie bag,[4] loaded with the suddenly irrelevant wisdom of the eons, over my shoulder and headed back to my dorm. The sun was halfway set, and on the hill leading to the chapel, a dark moving line was etched against the bloody red. The seniors in their black gowns were seeking song and prayer.

In my dorm, we huddled in front of the TV set, the only one in the building, a thick-set flickering thing with rabbit ears for an antenna. I don't think we left it for the entire weekend and into Monday.

My president had been riding in an uncovered limousine in Dallas, Texas. Conspiracy theories bubbled up later, but I was convinced then and now that the official investigation got it right, and a lone gunman, Lee Harvey Oswald, shot Kennedy from a nearby book depository. He zeroed in on the exposed head of the leader of the free world with a high-powered rifle and good aim. The bullet pierced the right side of the skull. I think that may be why Kennedy half dollars, like the one minted in 1974 that I keep in my jewelry box, show his left profile.

Yes, it was happening, but absorbing the information from the small screen was like watching *The Twilight Zone*. We saw Lyndon Johnson take the oath of office on Air Force One. We saw Oswald captured, and before our eyes we saw Jack Ruby kill Oswald. We saw the echoing funeral service in the Capitol dome and worried as we looked at ancient John McCormack, speaker of the House, the next in line of succession. We saw tiny John-John, the president's son, saluting his father's coffin. Students around me wept, though tears couldn't thaw the frost. I felt behind, as if I hadn't done the reading for the course.

Camelot was over.

❧

A couple of years earlier, on a hot September day in 1961, the fire-drill alarm had sounded, and all of Miss Hewitt's Classes had headed for the stairs excitedly—several hundred girls. Once on Seventy-Fifth Street, we walked according to class the half block to Park Avenue. It was a reprieve from school, which had started just a few days before, and from the stultifying, un-air-conditioned classroom, where I was probably dressed in back-to-school clothes way too warm for late summer. It was early in the year for a drill. It wasn't a drill; it was because the school had reason to expect the morning would yield an educational experience: a presidential motorcade.

We lined the avenue waiting, listening for police sirens, wondering whether the president had yet left the Hotel Carlyle around the corner on Madison. Then came the procession of cars. I couldn't see him, and even if I'd been taller or better positioned, the entourage was moving fast. I have not been able to confirm the date. My diary for that time is a dull account of a teenager's insulated worries. I believe it was September 25, 1961, and President Kennedy was on his way to the United Nations. Soviet President Nikita Khrushchev had given an ultimatum: Western armed forces must be withdrawn from Berlin. Kennedy would stand firm, telling the UN General Assembly that Western powers would not abandon Berlin and warning of nuclear war if the Soviets didn't back down and engage in negotiations "rooted in mutual respect."[5] The crisis culminated in the Soviets erecting the Berlin wall, dividing the eastern and western sectors of the city, a wall that stood until the beginning of the collapse of the Soviet Union in 1989.

On that hot, bright morning, we cheered for our country. We waved in the direction of our leader. Then we went back to class, the music room, the library, or the gym, which was on the roof of the school with a fenced wall and roof. The lower-school kids could slip off their light-blue tunics and be ready for kickball in their bloomers and blouses with the Peter Pan collars. The seniors could have a smoke in the lunchroom, one of their class privileges. My diary says I got a paper back from Mrs. Delman.

Frosso remembers a crowd and the open car. Lynn remembers how tan Kennedy looked. Georgia doesn't remember the incident at all, but does remember Mrs. Delman telling us, "Down, beasts," when we were unruly.

We never talked about whether it was odd that a schedule for the president's trip downtown was publicly available, nor that his head was exposed.

8

A GLASS BONG

"How come you keep a bong in your vanity drawer?" asked Josh.

"How come you know it's a bong?" I asked him.

My teenage son didn't answer, and I didn't press him. Josh was conscientious and conservative. Still, I suppose I should have followed up.

The bong is buried in the middle drawer of the antique cherry vanity table I inherited from my grandmother Hoo-hoo. It's an odd place for a treasure that represents rebellion against my ancestors' mores. The vanity has a stool covered with flowery fabric on which a lady may perch as she applies layers of makeup while looking into the tall, three-part mirror in the light of a pair of delicate glass lamps on either corner. I keep perfume on the tabletop—Femme, Char's favorite; Chanel No. 5, Gladys's favorite; Desert Queen, to remind me of La Quinta, California, where I have spent many winters; and Diorissimo. The Diorissimo is too young a fragrance for me, but Belle loved the scent of lilies of the valley. She would buy a tiny pot of bulbs each spring, and a half dozen sprigs would push up and unfold into a bouquet of white flowers and sweet aroma.

The bong shares its drawer with a jumble of silk scarves, nestled safely in the bright prints. Hand-blown by hippies in Chicago, it is as exquisite in its way as the antique piece of furniture. My cossetted marijuana-delivery system is an open-ended, clear glass tube that swells to a bulb midway, with an indentation in the bottom for a thumb. Within, a fanged glass snake aims a venomous tongue toward the smoker's mouth. The smoke from the pungent, hand-rolled weed cigarette would arrive on the palate with a sting.

I've always been curious about World War II, the multinational cataclysm that ended with a nuclear bomb the year before I was born. When I asked my middle child, Wit, née Babette, what she was curious about that happened before she was born, she said the sixties. Our wedding pictures alone made Josh, Wit, and Charlotte curious before they recognized the bong in the vanity for what it was. Even their father had long hair, though he was not in blue jeans. Jack has never in my memory owned a pair of jeans, and he routinely dons serious button-down shirts where other men choose more relaxed polos. And their uncle Donnie looked like a biblical hermit dragged into civilization after twenty years meditating and starving in the desert without a change of clothes, a pair of scissors, or a comb.

My kids' American history textbooks probably had a chapter called something like "The Sixties: A Time of Turmoil." The chapter would tell how, with brave, determined, nonviolent struggle, blacks gained simple rights, such as being able to sit in restaurants or on buses with white people. It would tell how in the 1960s the United States sent Americans to war in Vietnam, how more and more Americans, including in the leadership, figured out it was a lousy war but couldn't get out of it. It would tell how women figured out they were oppressed by male dominance and rose up to do something about it. It would tell how the adolescents of the time, the baby boomers, my generation, a huge cohort of energy-charged youth who some would say hadn't heard the word no often enough, decided their elders had cheated them out of their ideals. We started a counterculture where young men looked like Donnie and flaunted radicalism to our antediluvian parents. I could understand my kids' curiosity.

Yes, I was there. How I remember joining the endless teach-ins on the Vietnam War. Storming the college administration building. Marching on Washington singing "We Shall Overcome." How I remember the summer of 1967 when the straight-of-way seemed lost, and I drove to San Francisco on a wandering route, listening to psychedelic rock. It was the summer of love, and I went with flowers in my hair. I didn't wear a bra. I didn't even pack a bra. I wore ragged jeans, a tie-dyed shirt, and filthy earth shoes. I crashed in Haight-Ashbury, the heart of the counterculture. How I remember heeding the call to the Fillmore, the heart of the Haight, for a concert by the Doors, the epitome of rebellious anger. I smoked sweet marijuana, watching sunsets that turned into high drama as the THC fuzzed up my brain. And the LSD. I don't know how I ever came down from that three-week high. Then there was the trouble with the lawman. He nabbed me red-handed at the end of that summer. No wonder my kids thought I was concealing a reckless period of high drama.

Small problem with this story: I didn't do it. It wasn't like that. I did not smoke marijuana that summer. I have never tried LSD or anything harder than Mary Jane because it seemed too dangerous. The last thing I wanted was to be lost in a psychotic state. I did not march, storm, or sit in. I largely missed the culture of the sixties.

On the other hand, it is true that my political position was anti–Vietnam War and pro–civil rights. I did go to liberal lectures and campaign for liberal Democrats.

And it is true that I drove with friends across the country to San Francisco the summer of 1967. I did sleep on the floor of an apartment in Haight-Ashbury and went to a Doors concert. I even did my laundry in the Haight. And had an ice cream cone.

I am sorry to admit as well that I did indeed have a run-in with the law.

I'm not the only one in my generation to look back and wonder what I lived through. Tom Brokaw, the NBC newsman and author, in the introduction to *Boom: Voices of the Sixties*, asks himself, "What was it all about?"

"Have you cracked the code yet?" he quotes a 1969 college graduate asking him while he was writing the book. From the context, it could have been Hillary Clinton, one of his interviewees for the book. If *they* weren't clear on the past, how can I be?[1] What was it all about?

As I revisited history that I was supposedly part of, sometimes I felt like I was researching the Peloponnesian War. The first thing I figured out was that the sixties took place over more than ten years. It was a fifteen-year period, or maybe twelve, but not a mere decade. Perhaps it did indeed start in 1960 with the presidential campaign that pitted the old guard (we thought) of Richard Nixon against an upstart young Catholic. Or maybe the sixties began in 1963 when Kennedy was assassinated and hopes were dashed. Either way, the poignancy of enduring the worst of times on the heels of the best of times is imprinted on those of us who lived it. My Wellesley class of 1967 graduated before the collapse of confidence in our government. It was two years later when Hillary's class graduated and in her commencement address, she passionately called on our generation to live up to ideals of social justice.[2]

Whichever year you choose as a starting point, the sixties were not over when the ball dropped in Times Square at midnight December 31, 1969. The US invasion of Cambodia had yet to come. That was in 1970, and the Wellesley campus, along with many others, closed down. The Watergate break-in had yet to happen. The president of the United States feeling compelled to tell us he was not a crook had yet to occur. I think of

1975 as the close of the era in my country and my life. On April 23, 1975, President Gerald Ford, whom I trusted as an honest, decent leader, was able to declare that the Vietnam War was over. More importantly, Josh, our first child, was born in June. It was a time of beginning.

To understand what it was like to be fully involved in the sixties, read Carl Oglesby's *Ravens in the Storm*. Oglesby, an early president of Students for a Democratic Society, a prime force in the antiwar movement, didn't keep a diary, as I did, to remind him of where he was when as he wrote his memoir. He didn't have to because the FBI documented his every move for him.[3]

In the middle of the sixties came 1967, when young people throughout the United States, the United Kingdom, and Europe gravitated to San Francisco, answering the siren call of hard rock and free love. I was tripping that summer, if you extend the meaning to include avoidance of life. It was a cross-country adventure after college graduation. I bought the bong in a hippie area of Chicago at the tail end of the road trip. The purchase seemed like the thing to do, as was much of that memorable summer.

My escape vehicle was not dope, but my car, a flame-red Oldsmobile 88 with a long hood and sweeping roofline. It looked like a car that would be going unusual places, probably faster than the speed limit. If a grandchild of mine needs to ask why it was red, their parents were remiss in passing down family tradition. As all my family members had better know, when Hoo-hoo and Pop-pop were ready to give Char an automobile in the late 1930s, they wondered aloud what color she might like.

"I think she'd like a red one," said her brother, Bob. She did, and since then, any car that Char had a say in and any car I have some say in will be as red as the top stripe on an American flag. This tradition has not prevented Jack from purchasing a Mercedes that he tried to tell me was red but was in fact aubergine. In principle, however, there is only one right color for an automobile.

Char and Dick bought me the Olds in Columbus for my twenty-first birthday in February, celebrated in La Quinta, and they drove it east to Wellesley after spring break. I hardly said hello to them before clumping as fast as I could manage out of Freeman Hall to where it was parked.

"We should have gotten her new boots instead," Char said to Dick. After a Massachusetts winter, my snow boots were caving in, one sole half off.

The state of my boots reflected the state of my mind that winter and into the spring. I was worn out, and it showed in my work, or lack of it. The last few steps of my senior honors thesis in political science were a slog.

The game of choice on the fourth floor of Freeman was charades. We played deep into the night and woke in the morning to the charade of our last semester and the necessity of finding something to do the following year. I wanted college to be over, yet was terrified because I didn't know what was next. The way out for a couple of my friends was marriage. I had an ardent boyfriend at Penn, but his interest in me was as an alternative to a girl who wanted him to make a long-term commitment. He was on the nervous side, and I disliked him for that, while pursuing my own version of flightiness. We broke up on my initiative.

For college seniors hard up against the real world, graduate school is one method of postponing the unknown. Several of my dorm mates were going to grad school with long-term plans in mind. In my heart I was not at all sure I wanted to continue in international politics, but I was admitted to the Fletcher School of Law and Diplomacy at Tufts, so at least that was settled. Fletcher was the available path to avoid standing still, make my parents happy, and demonstrate to myself that I was headed somewhere.

I can read my desperation in a diary entry the winter of 1967 before I got the word from Fletcher: "I think that Snoopy, the *Peanuts* dog, is more of a hero to American students than Batman, the Beatles, Allen Ginsberg, or Martin Luther King. Snoopy's Walter-Mitty-like battle with the Red Baron is, if not more of an issue than Vietnam, attracting more attention than wire-tapping, open housing and the trial of the Boston Strangler. The last year there seems to have been a movement away from protest marches and sit-ins and toward a more personal kind of questioning. I go around saying 'a bowl of potato soup and I'll be on my way' all the time."

Snoopy imagined himself as a World War I pilot fighting the evil Red Baron in his Sopwith Camel. Between raids he would enjoy a helping of earthy soup on the fields of France. Reading the entry, I know it was facetious, yet I see a longing to be a child again, reading the comics on my bed in the Seventy-First Street apartment. Was I truly engaged in personal questioning that winter? Or was I pleading for escape to cartoons?

I named my car the Red Baron, which seemed aesthetically correct, although the historical Red Baron was neither enemy nor machine.

A girl with a car is a girl with friends. It wasn't long after the Baron arrived that my classmates Ann Hill and Cathy Miller appeared in my dorm room with an idea. Ann and Cathy were political science majors like me, and we had roomed together as Washington interns the summer before. Ann had a full scholarship at Wellesley and was headed to Germany on a Fulbright scholarship that fall. She got a free ride at Yale law school beginning the year after she returned from Germany.[4]

Ann had applied her reasoning skills to her summer plans. She wanted to see the sun set on the West Coast. She would have to do that cheaply.

Vivian had a car. With Vivian's car, she could get to the West Coast cheaply. The sun would set at least once while she was there.

What Ann did not explain, and what I should have guessed, was that she felt she would be an ambassador for the United States while in Germany. People would expect her to know something about the country, and she had never been west of Harrisburg, Pennsylvania. The trip was already well outlined. Cathy would summer at her parents' home in Reno, Nevada, so that would be one of the places we could stay. Other classmates they named could be persuaded to provide way stations as well. Where we didn't have someone to visit, we would camp in a national park. Sue Austin from Colorado would join us for a good part of the trip. Sue had a brother in San Francisco. We could stay with him. It was a plan with dates, people, and places.

It was not quite a fait accompli, but I am reminded of the power of a well-fleshed-out first draft in law and in life. Come to someone with a venture that is thought through, and you are halfway there. I proposed a summer on the road to Char and Dick, and they bought into it. It was a good time in my life to see the country.

We commenced our postcollege lives on June 3, 1967, among the blooming rhododendrons on Severance Green. The school required white clothing for the graduation ceremonies, and I wore a tennis dress under my black robes as we sang "America the Beautiful," written by Katherine Lee Bates of the class of 1880, and listened to the speaker, Sol Linowitz, the US representative to the Organization for American States. We tittered when he included health among our youthful advantages. We knew we were healthy and always would be.

Back home in Columbus, I was surrounded by activity, though none of it was yet mine. Bobby had been sucked into Vietnam War service. A year out of Harvard with his MBA, he was off to the quartermaster corps at Fort Sam Houston in Texas. He left wearing a cap from the Greenbrier, a venerable resort in West Virginia, and a sports shirt, driving his new red Mercedes with the Ohio license plate ZEUS. He looked like someone heading for a round of golf rather than the army. Ethel, the cook, equipped him with four sandwiches made from lunch meats like tongue and hard salami bought from Thurn's on Greenlawn Avenue. Char threw in some Callard and Bowser butterscotch from the Chinese porcelain candy dish in the living room. Babsie was off to Seascape, a summer camp for losing weight. Donnie, finished with his sophomore year at Ohio University, arrived home looking, as Char put it, "like an insane fundamentalist." His matted hair was shoulder length, and he had a mustache that drooped down below his lips, making him look dour. He was jealous of me heading west.

"He wants to make a pilgrimage to the Haight-Ashbury district of San Francisco, the center of the cult," I wrote in disgust. Freshly hatched from college and filled with academic language, I wrote that I was attracted to the utopian, antimaterialist aspects of the hippie movement but complained that its doctrine was based on an amorphous concept of love and togetherness.

Looking back, I can see that although Bobby and Donnie were only four years apart in age, they were in different generations. At twenty-one that year, I was in the middle. Vietnam divided the generation of those who endured World War II from those born afterward. By the mid-1960s it had divided youth from youth. I was on board with the politics of my generation but hadn't given up on the national elite. My own pack was not yet on a fully mobilized antiwar footing. Less than a year later, the atmosphere had changed. Even I had to rebel against authority, though within the political system. And new habits already adopted by those a bit younger than me or based at more radical campuses began to filter into my cohort.

~◆~

Ann arrived at the Columbus airport to begin our western sojourn wearing a sweatshirt that read "Curse You Red Baron" and a necklace made of pop-tops from soda cans. (The pop-tops came right off the cans at that time. It was later that they were attached to reduce the waste.) We bought supplies, including a tent and a snakebite kit. The tent was a heavy canvas monster with long ropes and wooden pegs to hold it in place. We practiced putting it up. With the help of Leroy Hawkins, Char and Dick's houseman, it took an hour and a half. We would have to get better at it. Leroy often played old songs for us on the grand piano in the living room after dinner. In his earlier years, he had been a jazz pianist. He played with professional proficiency despite having two fingers halfway missing on one hand.

"You do the best you can with the tools you got," Leroy liked to say.

That would apply to the tent.

Donnie, with his hair falling into his eyes, showed us how to change a tire, then made us do it ourselves to be sure we understood. To guide us we had a TripTik from AAA, an ingenious custom-made spiral notebook. Each page showed a bird's-eye view of a segment of the trip, with our route highlighted in yellow. For major cities there were extra pages with closeup views.

It seemed impossible that we would get everything into the trunk of the car, especially since we had some of Sue Austin's stuff to carry as well. And eventually Sue herself would join us. On the first try, the lantern and air mattresses were left over. It was going to take a Phi Beta Kappa to solve the puzzle. Luckily one was available: Ann made everything fit.

The morning of our departure, July 15, Ethel served a leisurely breakfast of scrambled eggs with cheese, bacon, rye toast, raspberry jam, coffee, and orange juice. We diddled around, searching for a couple of last-minute things, then figured out where to squeeze them in the back seat.

"I hate long Jewish farewells," Char said as the morning went on.

"Maybe you should take it easy and have lunch at the Maramor," Dick said, speaking of a restaurant all the way downtown.

I was excited. The first car I ever drove was Dick's boxy, green MG sports car with bug-eyed headlights that he shared with his brother, Lloyd. I was six, and my father sat me on his lap with his arms around me and his hands, as well as mine, on the steering wheel. It was a Sunday in Central Park long before they closed off roads to car traffic. The wheel was a compass rose in my hands—a circle endlessly divided into choices of direction. Puttering in the sweet spring air, my father's feet controlling the speed and brakes, I felt all of New York was mine.

Actually steering a car when I was old enough that my feet could reach the pedals had been a different experience. As a New Yorker, I walked everywhere, unless public transportation sufficed or Dick was driving us somewhere far. I practiced driving in Hoo-hoo and Pop-pop's stone-paved courtyard, circling around and around the tree in the middle. From that I graduated to Preston Road, a tree-lined street with minuscule amounts of traffic, accompanied by a bored adult.

"I don't think she's ever going to get out of first gear," Dick had told Char.

I failed my driving test in Columbus the first time, though I passed the parallel parking part. I managed to pass the driving section on the second try.

The compass rose showed west, where Americans headed for adventure. Ann and I would take turns at the wheel of my very own automobile. The whole country was about to become mine.

At 11:10 a.m. we pulled out of the driveway of 256 South Columbia. An hour or two later, we made it to West Broad Street, the other side of town. (The freeways through and around Columbus had yet to be built, so this was not quite as bad as it sounds.) Something was clunking that might have been the car. Worried, I pulled over. The clunking was from my Cliffie bag. It contained the tent pegs and a bottle of Dubonnet. Char had sent us off with two bottles and a load of butterscotch. I found a payphone and called home with the news that there had been a weird noise, but the car was OK, sending Char and Dick into stitches.

"They're never going to get out of Columbus," they said to each other when they caught their breath. "How can they get to the West Coast?"

We made good time thereafter. The speed limit was sixty-five, and my red car wanted to test out seventy-five, so I did. We overnighted in a motel in Terre Haute, Indiana, almost to the Illinois border.

"Turn left," said Ann the next morning. She was the passenger and had the TripTik in hand. I dutifully turned onto a large road out of Terre Haute. I flipped down the visor because the sun was glaring into my eyes.

"I'm not so sure this is the right direction," said Ann, still studying the map.

The next road sign said "Indianapolis."

"Vivian," Ann said in her quietest voice as she flipped back a page. We were going east. I turned around. I wondered what Char and Dick would think if we arrived home for lunch.

Besides getting to know her country and seeing the sun set over the Pacific Ocean, Ann had a third goal—to acquire a forest ranger's hat. (All the rangers were men then; it was a man's job.) Ann could talk a bull terrier off a meat truck, but I did wonder whether she could talk the hat off a forest ranger. It remained to be seen.

I'm not sure I thought about it then, but I do now question Ann's methods of meeting guys. The summer before, Ann and Cathy decided that we should take in laundry, specifically the shirts, for male summer interns in Washington. Like Lazarus customers at Christmas, men would come to our door, and we would talk to them as we handed them their freshly pressed shirts and took their money at twenty-five cents an item. The plan possessed a key flaw, but it wasn't lack of customers—we couldn't keep up. We had long day jobs, and entertaining options arose for our evenings. Boys showed up at the door with bulging laundry bags. We stowed the bags safely in the closets of our residential hotel room. We trundled downstairs to the laundry room when we could. I had never done my own laundry, much less a man's cotton dress shirt. Even in college I used a service. It was a simpler process than when Char was at Wellesley in the 1940s; she sent her laundry home to Columbus by train, and it arrived back the next week, fresh and folded with a carton of cigarettes embedded in the clean clothes.

Ironing a single shirt took me half an hour the first few weeks, sweating in the un-air-conditioned basement. They were either too damp or too dry, and when I sprinkled water on a shirt, it would be too much or too little. My finished products had wrinkles that I had ironed in myself, especially the collars.

Cathy was wearing a metal and plastic neck brace that summer because of an undefined nerve injury. One evening when she was in our basement sweatshop wielding the iron, an older resident took pity.

"Poor dear," she said. "Let me help with your husband's things."

She took over, but quit when she started work on a seventeen-inch collar with a thirty-eight-inch sleeve immediately after a fifteen and a half/thirty-two-inch shirt.

The men continued to come to the door, but it was not to ask us on dates. They complained. They pleaded. One boy, who we disdainfully called "Princeton," yelled at us.

"He's treating us like laundry women," Cathy said.

The boy was probably interning for a major committee on the Hill in dirty shirts, the only ones he had left. There he'd be, delivering a fresh amendment to a bill to the hands of Mike Mansfield, chair of the Foreign Affairs Committee, who was busy grilling Secretary of State Rusk on requests for additional manpower in Southeast Asia, and Senator Mansfield would catch a whiff of the boy's shirt and think, "I'll make sure nobody ever hires that kid."

Other boys were more polite, but their opinions of our competence were clear. One time we made a batch of chocolate chip cookies. Only one was left when a guy stopped by the apartment to pick up shirts. He spotted it on a large plate.

"I see you baked a cookie," he said, probably wondering how many days it had taken us.[5]

Once we were headed in the right direction, Ann and I made good time in our red getaway car through Hannibal, Missouri, then Saint Louis, Kansas City, and Colorado Springs, acquiring experiential knowledge of geography. On a map Kansas looks as if it stops eventually. It does not. Kansas is a never-ending Möbius loop where you drive by the same cornfields, cows, and water towers over and over again forever. I don't know how we escaped, but I credit the Red Baron, which must have made a desperate eighty-mile-an-hour leap to cross the Colorado border.

We arrived in Evergreen, Colorado, on July 20 to pick up Sue Austin. Sue met us in her car at the beginning of the dirt road leading to the Elbert-Austin ranch, her family's country home, figuring we could get lost otherwise. I was at the wheel and had to keep up with her, though my instinct was to go more slowly on the bumpy path. Rocks were not good for the Baron, I thought, and I felt the car's pain as we bounced along at thirty miles per hour through pine woods with no end or even middle ground in sight, only dust and wheel ruts.

When we finally pulled into a dirt driveway, the first things I saw were huge pairs of antlers hanging over each front window of the low, two-story, pine house built to nestle into the countryside. It was a cozy house, with comfortable old chairs, a stone fireplace blackened by many toasty fires, faded Native American rugs on the wood floors, and a supply of wooden jigsaw puzzles in bold patterns that looked like 1950s advertisements.

Best of all for those few days was the stable, where friendly bay geldings put their heads over their stall entrances, asking, "Do you have carrots?" We took long trail rides, getting shifting views of Mount Evans.

The Baron was now loaded like a circus clown act. Three young women were squeezed in with camping gear and clothes for city and country. One extra tent peg would have popped all the doors open.

We headed to the Grand Canyon. There, on July 25, Ann got her first big chance to try to winkle a hat away from a forest ranger. He looked like a nice young man and had to be pleased to chat with a willowy, soft-spoken, young blonde as her two traveling companions looked on. I have no record of the conversation, but perhaps it went something like this:

"I like your hat," said Ann.

"Oh, yeah," said the ranger, taking it off and fingering the indentations.

"How long have you been a forest ranger?"

"A couple of years."

"Have you ever had to fight a forest fire?" Ann was in fact not batting her eyes, but she was doing the Southern-belle routine.

"I'm not that kind of ranger. I just help the tourists find their way."

"Oh, how cool. What trail would you recommend we take to the bottom of the canyon? Can I try on your hat, by the way?"

"Bright Angel Trail is a good one," he said and handed her the hat. "It'll be about an hour to the bottom. A mile and a half. Harder coming back."

"Ann, that looks fine on you," said Sue. "I have to take your picture."

She cocked the lever, took the photo, and wound the film ahead.

"It's such a neat hat," Ann said to the ranger, smiling her sweet smile. "May I have it?"

The ranger looked embarrassed.

"It's regulations," he said and reached out for his property, frowning uncomfortably.

On the Bright Angel Trail the following morning, we comforted Ann, saying she was bound to get another chance.

San Francisco beckoned. On July 29 we arrived at the house where Sue's brother lived on Ashbury Street, two blocks above the Haight. The apartment was exactly the mess you'd expect of a young man who was out most of the time as a medical resident in radiology. We cleaned it for him. (Sue told me recently that these days her brother has a wife and a cleaning lady and is much neater.) Sue's brother volunteered at a free health clinic serving the hippies, where he dealt with drug abuse, sexually transmitted diseases, hepatitis, and alcohol abuse. The kids in the Haight were treated like outcasts at San Francisco General Hospital. The free clinics were emergency rooms for them and became more than that over time. Sue's brother may have been the closest to a radical we met on the whole trip, since it was considered abetting the crazies to treat them.

That night we went to Berkeley to see *Don Giovanni* in an English translation with a black man playing the lead, which was considered avant-garde. We went to dinner at a Chinese restaurant where Edsel Ford Fong, famous for his rudeness to customers, was the server. "Sit down and shut up," he told us as we entered.

Even with our air mattresses, sleeping on the hard floor of Sue's brother's apartment was less than restful. It was better than many of the experiences the couple of weeks before, however. At least we were not shivering in our flimsy blankets in the canvas tent.

Above left: Gladys Butler Witkind, probably late 1930s. *Above right:* William H. Butler, early 1900s. *Below:* The *Forget-Me-Not*, William Butler's yacht.

Clockwise from youngest: Frances (Frankie), Goldie, Isabelle (Belle— the author's grandmother), and Ethel Speyer, c. 1903.

From left: Lloyd Myron Witkind and Richard Jules
Witkind, c. 1941. Photo by Fabian Bachrach.

Above left: The author with the MG sports car owned by Dick and Lloyd Witkind, early 1950s. *Above right:* Belle Witkind in Atlantic City, 1957. *Below right:* Dick Witkind and the author, Miami, Florida, 1952.

Family of Robert Lazarus Sr., 1959. *Back row, from left:* Robert Lazarus Jr., Dick
Witkind, David Rosenstiel, Robbie Rosenstiel. *Middle row:* Trip Lazarus, Mary
Lazarus, Jerry Lazarus (on Mary's lap), Molly Lazarus, Char Witkind, Babette
Gorman (Babsie), Hattie Lazarus, Robert Lazarus Sr., Billie Rosenstiel, Babette
Rosenstiel, Michael Hoffman, and Jean Hoffman. *Front row:* Bobby Gorman, Donnie
Gorman, the author, Nancy Rosenstiel, Ricky Hoffman, and Prue Hoffman. All the
Rosenstiels changed their name to Sirak after Babs married Howard Sirak in 1961.

Above left: Char Witkind at a tailgate picnic, 1965. *Above right:* Char, 1958. *Below:* Char, Babs Sirak, and Leroy Hawkins singing old-time favorites, Thanksgiving, 1969.

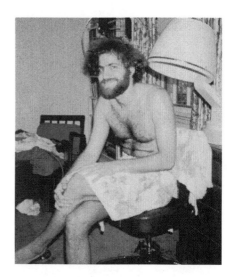

Above left: Sue Austin, the author, and Ann Hill headed for dinner at a restaurant to celebrate the Red Baron reaching ten thousand miles, Grand Teton National Park, 1967. *Above right:* Donnie Gorman in his hirsute period, 1969. *Below right:* Mark Shields, 1970. Photograph by Chuck Riesz.

Above: Chuck Riesz, Florence, Italy, 1970; *Below*: Hugo Black, golden-crowned conure, c. 1970. Photograph of Hugo by Chuck Riesz.

Above: Babette Witkind Davis and the author in George Steinbrenner's office at Yankee Stadium, 1990. *Below:* Char and Dick Witkind on the top deck of a double-decker bus in the 1999 New York Yankees victory parade, New York City.

Wedding photo of John Richard Davis (Jack) and the author, 1972.

We had tickets to see the Doors at the Fillmore Auditorium on Sunday, July 30, but that day we were treated to our first exposure to the relaxed life of the left coast during a visit to a patch of blue water we found beyond Half Moon Beach. A young man who was a friend of Ann's brother escorted us to San Gregorio. The purpose was to dip our toes into the Pacific, since it was too cold to swim, and for the boy to entertain us with an acoustic guitar. Our wet feet were quickly covered in sand, and the cold wind seared us. The beach smelled dank and wild, much different than Jones Beach. The cold and wind were not stopping a couple of adult men who revealed to me that this was a nude beach. We could tell it was not the usual mode of beach fashion for these guys because their behinds were brilliantly sunburned. They were accompanied by a small boy with more intelligence. He wore trunks.

The Fillmore was pulsing when we arrived that evening. It was a barn of a place, a huge dance hall packed with youth who were the beating heart of the counterculture. The cool kids danced inventive, spine-bending dances. The walls were covered in rhythmically moving projections of kaleidoscopic colors interspersed with photographs of real people or, surprisingly, medieval illuminations. My imagination had no place for the effect of the strobe lights, but the dancers' imaginations did, and they exaggerated the disjunction of vision by waving brightly colored scarves or pieces of yarn that stopped and started in the dark, stuttering light. I saw several people licking lollipops and wondered what was in them. A guy passed out on the floor. Another was trying to get his sandals on and couldn't manage it.

"Come on, baby, light my fire," Jim Morrison wailed at the decibel level of an airplane on takeoff. He seemed continuously to be on the edge of an impossible-to-finalize ejaculation. I swayed to his desire, though it was the strobe lights that were getting to me more than the music.

"If you had been the least bit high, the whole thing would have grabbed you," I wrote. "As it was, it only affected my balance, so I felt like the room was swaying. I felt nauseous. It was a relief to leave."

They handed out free posters of the Doors as we left. I picked up one for Donnie.

Ann felt we should observe more of the hippie culture, so she, Sue, and I walked back to the Haight the next day carrying four bags of laundry (our own laundry). That gave us plenty of time to be anthropologists, especially at the Hippie Dippy Ice Cream Store, where we enjoyed large cones. There's no high like ice cream on a warm day. My immediate concentration went into licking the edges off quickly before they dropped to the linoleum floor. That done, I could use my tongue like an icing spatula to smooth the coldness into smaller and smaller orbs until I had no choice but to bite into the cone.

Ann had secured her view of a sunset. The getaway car was waiting.

The three of us headed to Reno, where Cathy and her family were in a dither because Cathy had decided to marry her boyfriend. From there it was on to Redfish Lake, Yellow Bay, and, at high speed along the Going to the Sun Highway, across the Continental Divide to Glacier National Park. We met rangers in Glacier, but they would not give up their hats. Next came Yellowstone, the Tetons, the Bighorn National Forest, the Black Hills, and Pierre, South Dakota, where we stopped to do laundry. Laundry seems to be a consistency in my friendship with Ann.

It was close to the end of the trip when Ann, Sue, and I pulled into Lac qui Parle, a Minnesota state park. We were the only campers in the green wood. The lake was green too, but that was because it was stagnant, so we did not swim. We cooked a grocery store Chinese dinner over a wood fire.

As we were eating, a forest ranger showed up in full uniform with a pistol on his belt. The man of the law wanted to collect $50 for our use of the campground. This was a ridiculous sum. We had paid $14 for a two-room motel suite in Pierre the night before. We were used to sleeping in parks for free.

"Would you like some dinner?" asked Ann. The hat issue was off the table. His hat was out of the question. She would have to concentrate her effort on avoiding paying the money.

The ranger was of Norwegian descent and not inclined to contribute to conversation. Nor did he eat. Perhaps it was the meal, with rice that was still on the brittle side and canned bamboo shoots smelling like their drainage water. We offered him Dubonnet, but he declined. We talked our own ears off, cheery hostesses eager to please, until it started to rain. The ranger drove us to a nearby shelter and left us with a vroom of his official car. We congratulated ourselves on avoiding coughing up the camping fee. When the rain abated, we walked back to the campsite to clean up.

It was still early, and we had spotted a drive-in movie theater on the way to the campground. We hopped into the Baron. Nine other cars were parked at the theater. *Hombre* was showing, with Paul Newman battling Apaches in Arizona.

We thrilled at the familiar scenery. Much of the trip, the first things on our minds were finding our way to somewhere by dusk, hammering tent pegs into barely yielding dry ground, traipsing through brush to get enough firewood to cook our dinner, and freezing as we pulled ourselves out of our warm sleeping bags when the first light hit our eyes. Now the images came back that were already memories: descending the depths of the Grand Canyon, with its Linzertorte layers of pastel sedimentary rock; a Montana glacier forbiddingly high above our campground and an icy, perfectly smooth lake below. I thought about the warm-nosed horses at Evergreen, a huge moose appearing in early morning light around a bend of the Snake River, and Jim Morrison's feral cry.

An eleventh automobile pulled in beside us with a vroom and a sharp brake.

"So you thought you could avoid the long arm of the law," said the Norwegian forest ranger. We forked up the $50 for the sticker to allow us to stay in the park and left, chastened. That was my brush with the law in the summer of 1967. I said I had a run-in, and that was it.

It wasn't only the ranger experience that was disheartening in Lac qui Parle. A Kamikaze squirrel found its way into our already crowded tent that night. It pattered into Ann's side of the tent, scaring her into a scream as it ran over her. Ann took a squirrel-like leap into the cooking gear with a clatter and an "ouch." The three of us scrambled for our flashlights, and in their crisscrossing, strobe-like light engineered an escape for the squirrel among the scattered clothes and equipment.

Ann, Sue, and I piled into the Red Baron extra early the next morning, eager for a room with walls and a thermostat far away from Écureuil qui Saute.

ᙍ

We stopped in Minneapolis to revel in the comfort of a classmate's house, then journeyed on to Chicago. We paused in Wisconsin for Ann to have a glass of milk in honor of the state and drown her sorrow at failing to cop a forest ranger's hat.

The last night of the trip, Ann and Sue took me to dinner at Topper's, an old-fashioned restaurant in Old Town, the Haight-Ashbury of the windy city, to thank me for providing the Red Baron.

If the car had not been broken in going to Wellesley from Columbus, ferrying my friends around Boston, and heading back to Columbus, it was now not just broken in but weathered. The wild drive to Evergreen had been far from the only road test. Ann and I almost lost the car in Saint Louis. We went to a Cardinals–Mets game and could not find the very red car in the parking garage afterward. We searched every row and every level before realizing an identical garage stood on the other side of the stadium. Going up Pike's Peak, we had decided the car was supposed to be in a different gear for an uphill climb. I put it in low. Only when it started gasping did we figure out we had that wrong. Another time, much to my dismay, I returned to the San Francisco airport's parking lot after dropping someone off to find a dent that was more than a ding on the driver's side. Removal of the dent cost twenty dollars. The car was so dirty at one point that we wrote with our fingers on the sides and trunk, "We love you Red Baron" and "Snoopy and our gang." The car and I were both more experienced than when we began our summer journey.

After dinner at Topper's, the three of us shopped in the hippie district. At a store with a head-turning assortment of handmade jewelry, tie-dyed T-shirts, feather headbands, and other artifacts, I found my bong.

The next day we turned to the last page of the TripTik. Leaving Columbus had been harder than expected. The leg home from the city outskirts to Bexley was challenging too. We passed Delaware, Ohio, on Route 23 after dark. Coming in from the north, I had no idea where we were. Somehow we segued onto Route 33 along the Scioto River, not quite where we should have been. The road was intermittently lit and seemed as wide and unfamiliar as Kansas. Finally we found Broad Street. I pulled the dusty Red Baron into the driveway at South Columbia late in the evening, happy to see the lights of home.

Char and Dick had returned from Europe that day, August 20, Char's birthday. Dick roused himself enough to ask me, "Where are you going to pitch your tent?" He went back to sleep.

Char was awake. We told her about Route 33, and she told us how Air France served caviar in first class on their flight.

"Today is my wife's birthday," Dick had said to the stewardess. "And she loves caviar."

The stewardess gave her a second helping, and that incident was added forever to Char's repertoire of stories.

Char and Dick were home from France. No more mountain ranges and western sunsets for me. Babsie had escaped from Seascape looking sylphlike. The camp sounded like a minimum-security prison with the counselors on guard and the campers endlessly battling to obtain controlled substances like Snickers Bars and Charleston Chews. Bobby had endured basic training in San Antonio, including having to crawl under live machine-gun fire, something his MBA did not prepare him for. He came through unscalped and had traded the Mercedes for a Porsche.

Donnie was the one who had been home all summer by himself. Alone with his friends, that is, and avoiding the army. He was ultimately successful in that endeavor and always credited Dorothy for frying him bacon by the pound so that he managed to develop symptoms of gallbladder disease. I have never since heard Donnie complain about gallbladder problems.

I gave him the Doors poster.

"I have some marijuana," Donnie said.

"Where?"

"In my room. An ounce."

Donnie needed a cigarette-rolling machine, and I drove him to Smoker's Haven, a mainstream store selling cigars and pipes, to buy one. It was a simple device, not like the machines invented in the late 1800s that revolutionized the tobacco industry and gave my grandfather William Butler a start. Marijuana was a do-it-yourself drug.

The satisfyingly rounded ending for this story would be to say I went all the way to the West Coast, watched the sunset, and returned home to find what I wanted was right there all along. But no, I didn't pull out my newly acquired souvenir of hippiedom and join my brother then and there to see what all the excitement was about.

That does not explain the nasty residue below the hole in the bong where the cigarette was inserted, nor the brown tail of ash visible all the way up the tube. It was a couple of years later that I first used the bong. By that time my own friends were into it. When Jack and I married in 1972, we incorporated marijuana into our weekly dinner parties. We experimented with Julia Child and with weed: a pot of beef Bourguignon, accompanied by wine, followed by a bit of pot and more wine.

The bong's long tube softened the smoke as I pulled it through the snake's fangs and found an expansive, lucid world in which I had thoughts that seemed so coherent and beautiful they could win me a Pulitzer. Smoking was good. The mistake I once made was eating what turned out to be an extra-strength marijuana cookie. There is no way to tell how much you have ingested when the weed is a food ingredient. I was poisoned and came close to passing out.

When Charlotte, my youngest, was a teenager and asked to go out overnight with friends, I posed a series of questions, as parents are bound to do. Who would she be with? Where was she going? Would the girl's parents be home?

"Mom, don't you trust me?" she asked. It was a joking, warmhearted question.

"I trust you, but I don't trust the situations teenagers get themselves into," I told her.

You only get one brain. High doses of pleasure have a way of becoming distinctly unpleasant.

Daredevil "experience," like going over the guardrail at the Grand Canyon, is stupid. Moderation in all things is the ticket.

The sixties in me requires that I rephrase this good advice: moderation in all things, including slavish moderation.

9

A School Sweatshirt Emblazoned "Illegitimus Non Carburundum Est"

The year the republic came closer to falling apart than any time since the Civil War, I was a graduate student at the Fletcher School of Law and Diplomacy, a bastion of traditional education in US foreign policy. Even someone as personally conservative and loyal as I was could see that the power elite in the United States had lost its compass and was trying to hand my generation one with a rigged needle and engraved "trust us" on the back. Going west in the Red Baron had been a snap. This was going to be tougher.

"I know even less than last year what direction I'm heading in," I wrote in my diary January 3, 1968.

I faced a career choice.

From the time I was in elementary school, Dick had made it clear that I had to be able to support myself. This is a good rule for daughters, as well as sons, but I realize now that it was unusual for a man at that time to be so certain that his female offspring must work. I wanted to work. I wanted to be a brilliant success in some field or other. The Foreign Service was Dick's idea of a good career for me. It had high social status in his time and would ensure I would make a living and see something of the world. I couldn't fully admit it to myself in 1968, but the Foreign Service sounded like exile. My father supported the Vietnam War because that's what good citizens did. We were in a cold war with the Soviet Union, and if Southeast Asia was where that enmity was being played out, so be it. Young men should go into the army, and young women should support them. I wanted to please Dick, but I was furious at him about Vietnam.

I faced a daughter's choice.

Dick made no suggestions about marriage and family. In those days it was common for women to marry right out of college. Some of my friends were already hitching up. I knew I wasn't ready.

"I've taken to thinking of marriage as an antidote to loneliness. I'll have to grow up more before I take such a gigantic step," I wrote in the diary. The husband choice could wait. It's cheering to find a fragment of self-knowledge in my younger self, although I have to allow for the possibility that I didn't fully believe what I wrote. It sounded like the result of a late-night talk with Char in which we came to a sensible conclusion that would be shakier in the morning.

I remember the biting anxiety at the years yawning ahead of me. Fletcher was an ideal way to evade the inevitable draft into adult responsibility. As it turned out, Fletcher was summer camp all over again, except for the homework. I had a blast, with no strings and no rings.

Dick's other plan for me, college teaching, was a bad idea at the time. I would have to prepare lectures constantly and then stand in front of a class and give them. I didn't speak up in the classes where I was a student. How could I run a classroom?

Fletcher, in Medford, Massachusetts, outside of Boston, was ideal for buying time at my parents' expense. It was operated by Tufts University, with cross-registration for some courses with Harvard. The most valuable Harvard tie for me was a Coop Card—membership in the cooperative bookstore—that and the library card. Dick, however, was thrilled with the Harvard connection.

Signing up for one more year of education had its drawbacks. Deadlines for papers gave me the shivers, and a written exam made me feel like a heroine dispatched to the bottom of the sea to kill a multiheaded monster. It's been a long time now since I took a test, but I still dream about them. In my dreams, it's the end of the semester, and I can't find the examination room and realize that I didn't show up for a single lecture. It's way too late to drop the course. I have the textbook and another hour before the test starts, so maybe I can cram. But the book is about advanced econometric methods. It's all quantitative and cannot be skimmed. Where the equations have letters, they're in Greek. Where there are words, they're in Urdu.

It didn't bother me that I was wasting my parents' money and my own time. In retrospect, maybe it would have been smarter to stop for a year and work or travel. Then again, I think of Emerson's essay "Self-Reliance," in which he rails against getting locked into a career you hate rather than trying out a number of possibilities. I gave foreign policy a good shot. It didn't work out, but the next forays did, in a stop-and-go sort of way.

My college had an "in" at Fletcher—it accepted a Wellesley student almost every year. Wellesley's political science department did a good job of turning out women schooled in international politics, so Fletcher wasn't simply being lazy. Madeleine Albright, class of 1960, became the first woman secretary of state; Hillary Clinton, class of 1969, followed soon after. (Neither of them went to Fletcher.) I became the annual Wellesley student at the second-best graduate school of international relations in the country. The best at that time was considered to be the Woodrow Wilson School at Princeton. Princeton did not accept women. As with my acceptance at Wellesley, I was sure I would be faking it at Fletcher—I was not smart enough.

In fact, another Wellesley student was in my class. Mary von Briesen had been out of school long enough to be back from serving in the Peace Corps in Nepal. In addition to the two of us, my class had six women and ninety-two men. Two of the other women were French, and one was Canadian. A substantial minority of the class came from countries other than the United States, sent by their governments to learn diplomacy in English, the lingua franca of that dark art.

The US political climate was already more turbulent than in my undergraduate years. More people with power were questioning the war. It was easy for me to cringe at Dick's beliefs. Moderate commentators were weighing in, saying the war was dragging us down. The war's opponents could no longer be viewed as a bunch of spoiled boys trying to avoid the draft.

Arthur Schlesinger Jr., for example, a historian and former member of the Kennedy administration, spoke at Wellesley in Alumnae Hall on May 8, 1967. He had been opposed to negotiating an end to the war until a few months before that. Now he was saying how "incredibly depressing" the war was and how it was estranging the country's youth: "The young men and women who at the start of the sixties were beginning to look on the United States as the hope of the world; exactly those today who watch our course in Vietnam with perplexity, loathing, and despair."[1] Three of Schlesinger's children were in college at the time and one in VISTA (Volunteers in Service to America). All opposed the war.

Char and others in the Columbus branch of my family opposed Vietnam. Federated president Ralph Lazarus predicted at a press conference in May 1967, speaking in his capacity as chair of the economic committee of the Business Council, that the war would cost $5 billion more than the official estimate for fiscal 1968.[2] He was transmitting the estimates of Business Council economists. According to John Lazarus, Ralph's son and my second cousin, Ralph really thought the cost would be closer to $15 billion. Much of that would be deficit spending. Today a deficit of a few billion seems like nothing, but at the time it was big bucks. Abe Fortas immediately called Ralph to say President Johnson was asking if he could lower his number. Fortas was a friend of Ralph's who had been on the Federated board and was also a close advisor to the president. Johnson would later elevate Fortas to the Supreme Court. Ralph would not budge, but, as a compromise, he did make a public statement that his figures were based on estimates by Business Council economists independently of any input from the government. The war's actual cost was more than Ralph's estimate.[3]

No matter what was happening outside the self-contained Fletcher campus, I had to get through the year. I couldn't do that without studying like an army grunt. As in college, my strategy was to memorize and synthesize received wisdom and avoid puzzling anything through myself if I could help it. I'm not sure I even realized I was ignoring that extra step of analyzing for myself. I'd done well in several college classes where the professors didn't notice I was acting as the amanuensis for their lectures, writing as fast as I could in my backward-leaning script and covering the test booklet to deliver their words back to them. The more I wrote, the better my answer was. Right?

The Fletcher faculty was world class. Some of them would be hard to fool. Not Professor Ruhl Bartlett, however, who had taught the history of US foreign policy for many decades. He was more than ready to retire. An alumnus offered a tremendous gift to the school if he would teach one more year. I don't know what he was like when he was younger, but in 1968 Dr.

Bartlett's classroom manner was saturated with sorrow, perhaps because of the Vietnam War or perhaps because he would rather have been on the Cape writing his memoir. Bartlett's knowledge was encyclopedic, and I in turn tried to memorize the textbook assertions of underlying causes, proximate causes, dates, and outcomes of every tiff that ever vexed our sovereign shores, plus the dates and provisions of all the treaties that brought them to a close.

My international economics professor, Dr. Halm, started his lecture the minute he was at the podium, always at exactly the spot where he left off the time before. One day he began talking as he advanced on the class from the back of the room: "Another measure of the height of the tariff wall—and this applies to revenue tariffs rather than those blatantly aimed at protection—is to take the ratio..."

My pencil began to move at the sound of his voice. We were off on the chase, like rum runners slipping through a blockade. By the time Dr. Halm got to the blackboard and picked up a piece of chalk, it would be too late to understand what he had already said as fuzzy, white numbers and swooping lines accumulated.

The liveliest, most engaging course was a seminar on nationalism in the second semester, led by Professor Karl Deutsch at Harvard. He started with a few lectures, but they were highly interactive (except for me, of course—I maintained silence). The dialogue moved at warp speed. When students began delivering seminar papers, the class became even more exciting. The ideal of the nation-state gave way on close inspection to a norm of racial and ethnic conflicts. What countries could be blown apart by them? Eastern Europe, under the iron heel of the Soviet Union, was the obvious cauldron of ethnic disunity. One of my Fletcher classmates, a Muslim Indian from Tanzania, presented an eye-opening paper on his country, where I had no prior idea of the fault lines.

Dr. Leo Gross, the international law professor, prided himself on humiliating those of us he could. "How many are in your class?" a potential student from the Air Force Academy asked him midway into the year. The student was with a group visiting Professors Gross and Bartlett.

"Thirty-six first semester," said Professor Gross. "And twenty-four this semester," he added with a grim-reaper smile.

"It's lucky you don't have a third semester," said Bartlett.

Dr. Gross would call on people in class to explain cases, a normal practice in law schools. As small as I am, I tried to hide behind a tall guy who sat in front of me. Gross lamentably held an attendance list in his hand.

"I can't see Miss Witkind," he said one February morning when he got to my name. The class roared with laughter. They knew me well by that time. At the next session, the boy in front of me was absent.

"I can see you today, Miss Witkind," Dr. Gross said and grilled me on a case called *United States v. Pink* for several minutes, until *Pink* was picked clean.

My diary gives no details about *Pink*, and I don't care to Google it. The only international law case that has continued to interest me over the years concerns migratory birds. That's because I know that no matter how much my neighbors hate the Canada geese that land on our pond in Ohio, they are prohibited from killing them. When I recently looked up the US Supreme Court ruling on migratory-goose laws, I could once again see Professor Gross intoning in delight the lines from the final paragraph, which reads, "Here a national interest of very nearly the first magnitude is involved [meaning the geese]. It can be protected only by national action in concert with that of another power. The subject-matter is only transitorily within the State and has no permanent habitat therein. But for the treaty and the statute there soon might be no birds for any powers to deal with."[4]

If Dr. Gross was the professor who enjoyed playing sadist, Dr. Bartlett was the one who went out of his way to avoid inflicting wounds. My name being at the end of the alphabet in my class, I got my tests back close to last, long after Robin Christopher, a Brit (try saying the last name first). I was the last to leave the classroom one day when I was exulting in a high grade and had to reread the professor's comments to taste the victory over again. I headed for the door as he did.

"Is it all right?" asked Dr. Bartlett.

"Yes."

"Good." He put his arm around me as we walked. "Can you hear all right at the back of the room?"

"Yes."

"Good. Sometimes I wonder."

❧

I'd never been in school with men before, and we all lived on campus. The co-ed campus presented new opportunities for entertainment and for slacking off on my studies. I was going out with a boy in Cambridge and one in Philadelphia, but I had no need to climb on the T and leave Medford. A Mexican guy in my Fletcher class sweetly whispered to me at a dance, "Quiero llegar a conocer tu mejor" ("I would like to get to know you better"). A Japanese guy cooked me a spectacular meal in his apartment and gave me his view of the origins of Pearl Harbor: the attack was a mistake, he said, but the United States pushed Japan into it.

Running in a Fletcher pack was at least as much fun as dating. Nowadays, it's normal experience for men and women to go out in groups.

In the 1960s, kids often acted like courting couples whether they were serious or not.

I quickly began to have fun and was forever putting off starting a paper, then staying up all night to finish it, because interruptions invited themselves in. I hadn't learned to start early, get a draft done, and use the draft as an unfinished model for the paper.

Char figured out what was going on—a co-ed playground after four years of single-sex Wellesley. "Camp Fletcher," she called it.

College and university logo wear was a rare commodity then. The Fletcher School had no sweatshirts or T-shirts, but a couple of entrepreneurs in the class custom-designed a sweatshirt. It displayed a shield with a dove in the upper right-hand corner and a martini glass, so essential to diplomacy, in the upper left. The martini had an olive in it, presumably bugged. The shirt was emblazoned with my class's motto, "*Illegitimus non carburundum est*," or "Don't let the bastards get you down." There were all kinds of bastards out there to get us down, from the president of the United States to certain professors inclined toward Teutonic methods of interrogation.

The Winter Olympics was perfect indoor entertainment for our multinational campground. It was broadcast live via satellite from Grenoble. We crowded around a single small, black-and-white TV set in the common room to cheer our countries on. The French students were especially excited because it was the year Jean-Claude Killy dominated the Alpine skiing. We watched every skier, luger, bobsledder, figure skater, and biathlon skier-shooter until all were done and the scores were in. We were transfixed day and night for two weeks.

One time a lecturer came to educate the budding diplomats on American wine. The idea was that we should be able to serve it abroad and promote the California wine industry. He brought samples, and we all listened studiously and did what was billed as a "laboratory experiment," otherwise known as a tasting. In Columbus, Char and Dick only approved of French wine. I assumed that the American samples were dreck. Maybe the samples weren't all that great in 1968, but that didn't stop several guys from hiding all the bottles they could in their coats for further tasting elsewhere.

⚘

It snowed that January. It snowed inches that became feet and feet that the plows piled into mountains. When it stopped and the winter sun turned the white world brilliant, we poured out of the dorms and began a spontaneous mass football game that turned into Red Rover. Another day the courtyard, bounded on three sides by the dormitories, became a battleground for a snowball fight that recalled the epic warfare we had learned about in Dr. Bartlett's class. It was the Battle of Quebec, a Revolutionary War confrontation that took place in a blinding snowstorm.

An arctic air mass slid into New England. The wind whistled through my corner room, whose window frames had long since warped. The radiator clanked and dripped mercilessly. I slept in pajamas, two pairs of socks, and my "bastards" sweatshirt. The weather wasn't going to get me down. The temperature hovered at zero. Boston schoolgirls came home with frostbitten knees. Frost nipped the ear of an unprepared Fletcher student from a warm country.

Deep into the next night, a megaphone shocked the air to announce, in a Boston accent, that all cars in the Cousens gym lot must be moved. I had parked the Red Baron there, on the main campus, when our own lot, close to the Fletcher complex, had to be plowed. I hadn't driven it for days. Mary, ViAnn Beedle, and I staggered from our rooms in antiarctic gear and headed across the courtyard. Mary and I thought we heard a muffled titter above us in a section of the men's dorm. ViAnn dismissed it; she was determined. We'd already had to move the cars once, so we were primed to do it again. ViAnn had matriculated at Grinnell, in Iowa, where perhaps musical cars was normal practice.

The Tufts campus is at the top of a steep hill. In fact, the campus is called "the Hill." Tufts students have the happy advantage of being *in* the city but not *of* it. Theirs is a community of scholars unless they choose to visit the lower realms. It was a starlit night, and from the top of the Hill, Boston was darker than I'd ever seen it. The low suburbs sprawled toward the city buildings. My face was already in pain from the subzero temperature and thirty-mile-an-hour winds. The view was bracing; the air, abrasive.

Curiously, we were the only ones in the parking lot. The Baron wouldn't start. My face was numb. I sat in ViAnn's car while she put antifreeze in Mary's and mine. My gloved fingers began to hurt as I waited. I could barely move them.

When we got back to the dorm, I called the campus police. No, they had not made an announcement. No, there was no necessity to move the cars.

"I bet Bruce Miller did it," said ViAnn.

Bruce admitted to being an accomplice but would not identify the idea man.

"Bruce," I said, "you know that proportionate reprisals are legal in international law. I'll bet that holds under other legal systems."

It appears that I did learn something that year.

When we weren't watching the Olympics or Batman on TV or out cavorting in the famous student life of Boston, our small remnant in the women's dorm played bridge, drinking Canadian Club and eating salty, sweet-smelling popcorn. Mary, ViAnn, the Canadian woman, and I cadged ice from a far-flung refrigerator and kept it on the windowsill through the long night. When the popcorn ran out, we carefully poured a thin layer of oil in the bottom of a saucepan, then a layer of corn kernels, put on the lid and turned up the hotplate, and waited for the rat-a-tat of a fresh batch to begin.

The board game Diplomacy was naturally a favorite at Fletcher. Six or so players formed and dropped alliances to achieve world domination. Turkey always had it tough, stuck between East and West. She could only win if the game went on into the next day and she knew when to switch sides.

The outside world was bearing down like the arctic weather. Our class took a field trip to Washington right after the first-semester exams to size up the agency career opportunities, and for them to size us up as well. The visit began badly, with an angry lecture from our dean in the inner sanctum of the operations control center at the State Department. Many of us had signed a petition protesting the war. I hadn't known where the petition was going and should have asked. I probably still would have signed it, but it was foolish simply to add my signature to a document. The petition was sent to everyone who would be addressing us. The undersecretary of defense canceled his talk.

Others didn't, so at State we heard from Averell Harriman, former New York governor and ambassador to the Soviet Union and Great Britain, and McGeorge Bundy, national security adviser to Presidents Kennedy and Johnson and a prime mover in escalation of the Vietnam War. A slew of visits followed over the next couple of days: to the US Information Agency, Agency for International Development, International Monetary Fund, and Department of Defense. At the DOD, the decidedly lower-level panel was evasive and patronizing, not surprising given our petition.

The National Press Club was a breath of fresh air. The panel there spoke honestly about Vietnam and other issues.

One evening we attended a cocktail party at the home of the Japanese ambassador. On another, we had hors d'oeuvres and cocktails on the eighth floor of the State Department, amid antique furniture and art collected during the earlier years of the republic. As I downed quiche lorraine and a martini without an olive, Dean Rusk came downstairs and circulated through the room. The secretary of state leaned down to shake my hand. I looked into his worn, unhappy eyes and was surprised by my feeling of empathic sorrow.

On February 1, at the Executive Offices, where Vice President Hubert Humphrey was based, we had to wait and then be searched before we could start our visit to the Bureau of the Budget. This was an era before routine scanning and searching at public buildings. While I'm sure an appointment was required, bags and pocket change did not go through a screening device, and visitors were not routinely questioned.

The problem was that the vice president's newspaper was missing, and all visitors were suspect. On the front page of the *New York Times* that day was the infamous photograph of a South Vietnamese man with his back to the camera putting a gun to the head of a Vietcong man, who faced the viewer in the moment before his execution. I wrote in my diary, "The figures were dark, in contrast to the white background, which gave the scene an aura of timelessness. If Goya could have had a camera, you'd say he took that photo."

At the Capitol, Senator Ted Kennedy, off the record like all the speakers on our trip, told us he did not plan to support Senator Eugene McCarthy for president. The antiwar senator was campaigning in New Hampshire, and many Boston college students were flocking to the state on weekends to stir up McCarthy votes.[5] It was widely known that Senator Kennedy's brother, Bobby Kennedy, did not get along with the cerebral McCarthy.

A student asked whether if "stronger leadership" emerged in the Democratic Party, Kennedy would support that person. The question was phrased to have a degree of subtlety, but everyone in the room knew what was meant: would his brother be a candidate for president?

"If Bobby runs, I'll back him," Kennedy grinned, a good, stock answer.

Another asked about the "credibility gap," the distance between the bloody American casualties in a seemingly endless conflict and the evasive rhetoric President Johnson and his cabinet used in the face of those facts.

"My father always used to say you could believe what a person does, but not what he says," Kennedy answered. "And that's the way to judge this administration or anybody. There are people, for instance, who say they're not candidates…" He broke off. We were shocked into silence because we knew whom he meant by "stronger leadership." He'd strayed from the stock answer. Everybody laughed, including Kennedy.

McCarthy won 42 percent of the vote in New Hampshire, badly shaking the president. Bobby Kennedy jumped into the race.

We knew things were getting worse. We had no idea how bad they could be. Early in the year, North Vietnam launched the Tet Offensive. Though we had almost five hundred thousand troops in Vietnam, it felt as though we were losing. At Fletcher, the only TV set was the black-and-white we used to watch the Olympics. I never watched the evening news. When I went home to Columbus for spring break, I could see what people meant when they lamented the corrosiveness of the six thirty network news constantly showing snippets of noisy, choppy, unintelligible combat, immediately followed by body-bag pictures that hit the brain so fast they seemed to bypass the optic nerve.

President Lyndon Johnson scheduled a speech March 31. Dick and I sat on the library couch, and Char, to see better, lay on the floor two feet from the set with her elbows holding up her head. I poked my tongue around my mouth to feel the edges of a couple of teeth chipped from crunching down on unpopped popcorn. My dentist appointment was the next morning. The president announced a unilateral de-escalation of the war. Most of North Vietnam would be off limits for bombing. He would offer peace talks with Ho Chi Minh. It was a huge surprise. Plenty for one evening.

Then he said something strange: "I am a free man, an American, president, and a member of my party, in that order." Char leaned on her left elbow and pointed her right eye toward me and Dick.

"Don't be ridiculous," I said. I knew what she was thinking.

Johnson meanwhile had looked off to the side at somebody not in the picture. We learned later it was the first lady. He turned back to the camera and told the nation he would not be a candidate for reelection.

The newsmen could barely put sentences together after the speech. Char had guessed right. I wrote in my diary: "Who would ever have believed that power-loving, egotistical LBJ would throw in the towel instead of his Stetson?"

The evening of April 4, 1968, Char, Dick, and I didn't have the television on. We were sitting in the library after dinner, thinking about going to the movies, when Leroy Hawkins, the African American houseman, appeared at the door.

"Did you hear Martin Luther King was shot?" he said.

Char leapt for the radio. King had been blasted in the head by a white man in Memphis and was taken to a hospital. As we listened, his death was announced. The country was in enough trouble already without an assassination of one of its finest, most reasonable leaders.

Dick and I still had the notion we would be going to the movies. Char was much more shaken. She went to the television and pressed the on button, finding the vice president at a banquet delivering an extemporaneous eulogy. Humphrey called for a clergyman to lead a prayer. "Where is the reverend?" asked Humphrey, and a huge man in tails popped up on the screen just behind him. It wasn't even the clergyman.

I collapsed in nervous laughter at the incongruity. Char laughed too, though not as hard. She was on the board of the Urban League at the time and had many friends in the Columbus African American community. That didn't mean, of course, that we invited Leroy in to sit down and watch TV with us. It's interesting that Char had a line to draw, or maybe she was considering Dick, who would have been horrified to have a black servant sit in his library.

Hundreds of thousands of people attended King's funeral in Atlanta. I'm not much for tears, but I cried when they sang "We Shall Overcome" and when Bobby Kennedy gave the eulogy. At least we still had Bobby.

Flaming riots erupted in Washington and other major cities. Our prophet of nonviolent change was dead. Whether the country would sink into chaos was a live question.

With May, a major paper came due for Karl Deutsch's class on nationalism. I stoically turned down a movie date with my Japanese friend so I could work, then relented and went to a wine-tasting party the next day and to a picnic in Duxbury with tennis and Frisbee on the beach the day after. A college friend came down from New Hampshire in her new blue buggy—a Volkswagen Beetle. We tootled around Cambridge in the buggy and alternated ice cream cones with jimmies (the Boston word for sprinkles) at Bailey's and Brigham's. I got the Baron washed and waxed. I caved in again and went to dinner at my Japanese friend's apartment.

I'd gone three weeks without writing by the time I managed to hit the Widener library, but despite the procrastination, I had the paper done, with bibliography, by six in the morning on May 22, the due date. I hadn't made a carbon copy and had to get it Xeroxed. We hadn't had a Xerox machine at Wellesley, but we did on the Tufts campus, thank goodness. Unfortunately, numerous other students had dashed off their works of wisdom the night before. The line was long. Worse, the machine, whose name was "Electric Gregory," was not feeling well. When coaxed it would lamely flash its lights, then stop. The sorter was jammed, or the machine was out of sorts. Students came in and out asking how Electric Gregory was feeling.

"Nobody's asked me about *my* health," grumbled the bearded boy operating the machine.

Electric Gregory finally vomited up two copies of my contribution to the literature on possible nationalistic tension between Australia and New Zealand with special attention to their rugby teams. I bought binders next door at the typewriter shop, one with a blue edge and one with green. The morning was shot, and I needed to be studying for exams.

Sleep was a stranger that spring, and when I did sleep, the nightmares slunk in: I should find the professor, say I know I'm going to get an F, and ask if there is anything he can do. But I don't know the course number or the professor's name or which classroom it's in. I look for a university schedule in my dorm room and realize I don't have one. Someone in the administration building would know, but I'm not sure where that is or how to get to it, except that it's on the main campus, which may be over that way, but could be more in the other direction. There's a lake in between and some tall buildings. There's supposedly a golf-cart service to the campus, but it only runs on the half hour.

I woke to a reality with way too much resemblance to the dream. The country might be dissolving, but I had to take exams anyway. Ninety-nine other Fletcher students were facing mass incarceration with pens and paper that could not be negotiated with Frisbees or beer. Bartlett's exam would come first. A student shared a chart she'd plotted of all the Pan-American treaties. Since I hadn't made the chart myself, it was hard to absorb.

Studying economics, Mary and I read an article on "Problems of a Key Currency" out loud, trying to internalize it. It was repetitive and whiny about the role of the United States. As we took turns, we waxed melodramatic.

"The world monetary system rests on US shoulders, and an ungrateful Europe yaps at her heels," read the article, or something like that. Mary wept and moaned her way through the passage, and I hummed a fortissimo dirge. It was loud, rousing a hall mate, who brought over a pineapple and a dull knife. All three of us worked through the article amid sprays of pungent pineapple juice.

The law exam looked hopeless, and I typed a paper for Mary while I waited for the urge to study for it, which never came, though I pushed some of my notes around on my desk. The major question on Dr. Gross's test was about the USS *Pueblo* incident, which had happened in January in the midst of everything else. An American naval intelligence ship was boarded and captured by North Koreans, who said the ship was in their territorial waters. I might have expected it. International lawyers adore the law of the sea. There was no easy answer. "Professor Gross forced us to think," I wrote, annoyed, in my journal.

Oral exams followed. How I passed mine, I do not know. Possibly my written work was enough to get me through. Mary and I laid down a string from the room where Bruce had his oral that led all the way to his dorm—and a waiting six-pack of beer.

The California primary was approaching, a deal-maker for the Democrats. I was for Kennedy rather than McCarthy. Kennedy could pull the country together. He would respond to the desperation in the urban ghettos, get us out of an evil war, and lead us to a world where youthful ideals became practice. He would make us a more just, more peaceful country. He would, in fact, be the reincarnation of his brother Jack that the United States needed.

The primary was on June 4, between exams and the Fletcher commencement. Mary von Briesen and I drove down to New York. She stayed with her mother, and I with Dick at the Cornell Club. (This was still the period when he spent the workweek in the city and flew home to Columbus on weekends.) We ate at the Toque Blanche and walked Mary and her mother back to their hotel, picking up a *Times* on the way. It was eleven o'clock or so, and the returns would be coming in soon from the California primary. The TV in my room had no picture, but I listened until CBS announced that according to their computer, Bobby Kennedy had won.

I went to sleep happy and hopeful.

Mary called early the next morning.

"Did you hear about Kennedy?"

"Yes. Fifty-one percent of the vote."

"You haven't heard."

Another one shot in the head.

Besides the recurring nightmare about exams, I have "wave dreams." In them I am near an ocean, or, scarily, the ocean arrives near me, with rollers that pour in, first gently, then with force, and rise up until they are walls of water so tall I can barely make out the fringes of foam on the top. They are poised to crash down over me. There is no way to run. I am supposed to dive through the waves, the way I did with rollers at Jones Beach when I was little. But these are far too big. I will drown. My father is not there to save me.

Now I was having a nightmare like the wave dream, only it was occurring in brutally wakeful, long June days when we students still had to go through the motions. Bobby Kennedy, the last hope for a country bent on self-destruction, was gone.

My parents arrived in Medford for commencement. The speaker at the dinner the night before was Senator Gale McGee of Wyoming, a war hawk. One of my radical American classmates took the opportunity to attack him verbally—a student dressing down a US senator.[6] McGee countered just as loudly and forcefully. Luckily, a diplomat intervened.

In the same impossibly incongruous juxtaposition that characterized that entire semester, McGee was followed by a fellow student whose speech's theme was that Fletcher was really a summer camp. He addressed the dean as he expounded on life at "Camp Fletcher" and ended by awarding him one of our don't-let-the-bastards-get-you-down sweatshirts, a safari hat, and a lanyard with a whistle. Char laughed. She had known about it all along. Professor Bartlett was made emeritus, allowing him finally to retire.

The funeral mass for Kennedy was at Saint Patrick's Cathedral the next day, June 8, and the body was transported by train from New York to Washington, with acres of silent people waiting at every station. In the dark, the train pulled into Washington to an enormous gathering. They took Robert Kennedy to his final resting place in Arlington National Cemetery, next to his brother.

Daniel Patrick Moynihan, senator, ambassador, gifted rhetorician, and a Fletcher graduate, was our commencement speaker. But it was John Kenneth Galbraith who made the greatest impression. He had been on the funeral train the day before. He talked about our loss and, in particular, the loss to the disadvantaged people of our country, deprived of their finest leaders.

I said good-bye to Camp Fletcher. Dick drove the Baron back to Columbus; Char and I took a plane.

"Security is June in Columbus," I wrote in my diary.

But there's no security in standing still. That's when the bastards get you down.

10

PETER HART'S PITH HELMET

My future career in 1968 was like a scrap of folded white paper to be picked out of a used army helmet. Not any piece of paper—I certainly wasn't cut out for medicine or carpentry.

I wanted to sail beyond the sunset—follow my dreams. The dreams were on the hazy side but had to do with good government, and the sixties demanded close engagement even from people who in general preferred to be in the bleachers with binoculars. Opportunity arrived for a brief, shining moment in the political fray.

"You get to be a player," said the ragged-edged scrap of paper. "A minor player, but this will be good."

❧

As a college senior, I had thought I might find a vocation teaching history, writing humorous newspaper editorials, or becoming ambassador to Greece or Australia. When I secured my MA from Fletcher in June 1968, the road to ambassador, or, realistically, consular officer or information officer, was open, but I wanted to close it. Perhaps Dick had thought of working overseas himself at one time. If so, I was not going to carry out his dream for him.

It took determined evasion to get out of a career in the Foreign Service or US Information Administration. I scored the highest in my Fletcher class on the written exam for the two agencies. Several students failed. Bruce Miller looked at me askance when he heard my results. I figured he was thinking, *How could this silent woman beat me out?* It was because the Foreign Service written test could have been stamped, "Designed for Vivian." The test contained no math, and half of it required synthesizing and summarizing information about hypothetical events in an imaginary country and writing them up into a dispatch. I didn't have to talk to anyone, go out in the field, or collect any information myself. It was what I'd been practicing for years—doing every line of the reading in my courses and spitting it back into the laps of my teachers.

I was thrilled with my score. Dick would be thrilled. (Char never cared much about test scores.) I had little faith in myself, and a score from an outside evaluator was a boost. Following through on the implications of the test was another matter. I would live forever in foreign lands, probably third-world foreign lands rather than somewhat familiar Western Europe. If I joined the USIA, I would learn the countries' politics, economy, social structure, and values in order to craft messages that would inform the foreign lands about the United States in a way that would make them like us better. I told myself I could not do it because I didn't trust the information my government was dishing out at home and certainly didn't want to be broadcasting falsity to the rest of the world.

I also was sure I would be perpetually lonely. I didn't know how I could meet a man to marry if I were lost in the wide, wide world. Let's face it. Seeing the world sounded to me more like wandering in the wilderness.

Unfortunately, I was eligible for the oral exam. I had two sensible choices: I could prepare for the exam and be energetic and outgoing when I took it, or I could admit to myself that I didn't want to follow through and tell my parents why. Instead I scheduled an interview in Cleveland. I didn't bring it to my waking consciousness, but my ploy was to prove that my abilities conflicted with Dick's expectations.

The exam was a waste of time for the four middle-aged gentlemen on the panel and for me. I'd been to a friend's wedding in Kansas City, a three-day lark, and flew to Cleveland after little sleep. I expect I looked catatonic at the interview. I acted as though I were being drafted, not as though I wanted a job. I arrived closemouthed, with a flattened affect that must have called into question my ability to relate to anyone, much less to project confidence in myself and my country. A little desperately perhaps, or very kindly, one interviewer asked if I knew any jokes. I remembered the previous day's *Peanuts* cartoon, which wasn't particularly funny, and stumbled trying to repeat it. After the test, a member of the panel gently told me I had failed, and I happily flew back to Columbus.

I look back on my ignoble retreat with regret and dismay. It was my own expectations I couldn't live up to as much as those of Dick and Char. I harbored a black hole deep inside where my love of self, or at least forgiveness of myself, should have been. I could blame the early bruising of one kind or another by Gladys, or being coddled afterward, or the built-in genetic code that carried on Gladys's sadness and fears and Dick's worship of elites, whatever envy and self-abnegation underlay that. Whatever the reasons, many twenty-two-year-olds have achieved serviceable self-knowledge, grace, and kindness. I had not.

The experience I would soon begin to accumulate in the working world would help enormously. Being mentored, working in a team, and taking stands in real-world conflict would impel maturity.

˹6˺

It was June, and life stretched ahead of me in a jungle of possibilities. I had to find something to do. I knew I'd be unhappy if I disappeared entirely into reading Agatha Christie books. My family had hopes for me. I hoped for something. But what?

I'd played the graduate-school card. I had no obvious way to go back to school again. Luckily, in your twenties, you have at least one more effective method to avoid making a long-term commitment: join a political campaign. In 1968 that was linked even more than usual with big dreams. The nation faced a history-making presidential campaign. It would pit Hubert Humphrey, an old-time New Deal–type of Democrat, against Richard Nixon, Eisenhower's vice president and already somebody I mistrusted. We were an angry country. Angry over Vietnam. Angry over race. Angry between generations and within generations.

Besides the national election, there were major state races. Those of us who did not want a revolution but did want tectonic policy shifts could direct our energies to Congress and the state capitols. In Ohio, a US Senate candidate emerged who had the ideals and golden tongue of Bobby Kennedy. He was even Irish. He was tall and handsome, with an aquiline nose and thick, carrot-colored hair.

John J. Gilligan grew up in Cincinnati, served in the US Navy in World War II, where he won a Silver Star, and came back home to teach English at Xavier University. He ran for city council in Cincinnati and won in 1952. Gilligan was never a back-slapping politician. He always retained something of the academic, which was one reason I admired him and others complained he was aloof. Yet he championed the weak and the poor, often in highly personal ways, and believed that government was an instrument of moral justice. At Gilligan's funeral in 2013, his children told moving stories about their father's lifelong devotion to making a better world through politics.[1] His daughter Kathleen Sibelius, who became governor of Kansas and US secretary of health and human services, said she was sixteen before she found out there could be a picnic or football game without a speaker.

When Cincinnati enacted a strict curfew in the 1950s and was enforcing the most minor violations by throwing young black men in jail, Councilman Gilligan would go to the courthouse late at night and demand second chances. After church on Sunday, Gilligan[2] lectured his family on how he would rewrite the sermon to strengthen it. His children's friends weren't always sure they wanted to be invited to dinner; it would start at seven, but the passionate argument about the Vietnam War would not be over until midnight. If hope existed in 1968 in Ohio, it was with Jack Gilligan.

My family in Columbus backed Gilligan in a big way. Howard and Babs Sirak, my uncle and aunt, had taken him to their bosoms, as did Bob, Mary, and Char. Howard attacked fund-raising for Gilligan the way he did everything—full tilt. Howard was an innovator in surgery on the heart. The instruments he needed for tiny children were not necessarily manufactured. So he crafted them, late into the night, in his basement. When Howard contracted hepatitis and was laid up for months, he educated himself in classical music, filling his enormous library with LP recordings. He had four or five different versions of the ballet *Sleeping Beauty*, for example, and listened assiduously to compare them section by section. When Howard dove into an interest in saltwater aquarium fish, he delegated Dick to transport tank loads of exotic creatures only available in New York. Babs and Howard's house soon gurgled with enormous fish tanks. He ended up giving the fish away to the Columbus Zoo, virtually making the zoo's collection.

Howard and Babs's grandest collection by far was impressionist, postimpressionist, and German expressionist paintings. You can see their acquisitions at the Columbus Museum of Art. They include Renoirs, Monets, Kandinskys, and a whole batch of Paul Klees that used to be on one wall in Babs's upstairs office. It is hard to believe that I sat at Thanksgiving dinner with Emil Nolde's spectacularly menacing sunflowers on the wall over the Sirak fireplace.[3]

Jack Gilligan was Howard's new hobby. It wasn't surprising he had a new hobby. It was surprising he would support a Democrat. That was not his party. His son John, who at six was trying to keep up, posed the question: "Daddy, how do you get to be first a doctor and then a Repelican?"

Char and I both had the answer to that one: "First you have to be a pelican."

One of Howard's prospects was Char, of course. As she wrote a check for $250, which was a lot as far as she was concerned, he looked over her shoulder and, disappointed, said, "I'll go see Dick."

"When Howard goes after somebody for money, they'd better do it," said Mark Shields, the one-time campaign manager who became a television pundit. "Otherwise, he'll cut their heart out."

Dick was also a "Repelican," but agreed to vote for Gilligan because the rest of the family was so involved. He said the only reason he wouldn't was that he hated the thought of Howard being such good friends with a senator and constantly advertising his closeness to power to everybody else in the family.

Later, after Howard retired from heart surgery, he mellowed some, but at that time he was opinionated, aggressive, and paternalistic. Maybe the stress of cutting into people was part of the problem. He and Char got along like a tea partier and a communist would, though their political positions were, in fact, similar. Dinners with both of them present were often stormy since Char was herself about an eight on the opinionated scale. One time Howard got up from the table, saying, "I can't take this anymore," and went home. For the sake of her sister, Char tried to choke down silent fury. One server confided in me that she considered pouring the contents of a casserole of prune whip over Howard's head because he treated her rudely. Babs and Dick were perpetually in peacekeeping mode.

Babs was as strong as Howard in her own less-provocative way, a tremendous force in Columbus organizations, such as Planned Parenthood. She had a superb eye for art and for people. Babs always saw the best in everyone, as did all the Lazarus women. She had a way of zeroing in on people's quirks and finding them amusing rather than annoying. Howard and Babs were one equal temper of heroic hearts, as the bard would have it.

No surprise: I was led to the right people about a volunteer job on the campaign and promised one beginning August 1. Why wait until August? They didn't need me until then? I suppose that could be true. The campaign wouldn't heat up for a while. It was also because I was going to France with Dick, Char, and Babsie in July. People my age were going the limit, risking everything for what they wanted changed, but I wasn't going to devote my life to it, even short term.

Finally, one morning in August, back from a delightful trip, I drove downtown to the Lincoln-Leveque Tower, then the tallest building in Columbus, to report to Peter Hart. Peter, the in-house pollster, was in his late twenties and barely starting out in life himself. But his path was well set. He would continue to support Democratic candidates for many decades and was well respected by the media. He still appears on TV every once in a while to comment on a political race.

The campaign office was an open floor with tall windows and perhaps a dozen scattered desks and tables, more like a newsroom than an office. It was tiny for a major Senate campaign, though of course in any campaign the main activity had better be in the field. Peter's workspace was distinguished by the olive-green helmet on his desk from his stint in the Army Reserves. I'm quite sure that reservists during the Vietnam era did not have to serve overseas, unlike the Iraq War of the 2000s. Peter was a tall guy whose eyes were already developing laugh wrinkles.

By now I was itching to get started. I hadn't considered that Peter would need to size me up, but of course he did. He said he needed to be certain of my "company loyalty." And he wanted to make sure I was genuinely willing to work. He was bringing me in as a relative of fund-raisers; he didn't want someone wandering around doing nothing and distracting the real workers, even if the person was costless. Deciding that I was OK, Peter introduced me to the small, determined staff, including Mark and Ann Shields. Mark was co–campaign manager. Today, Mark still appears on the *PBS NewsHour* show (formerly the *MacNeil/Lehrer Report*), balancing the *New York Times'* David Brooks's moderate, right-of-center opinions with his own moderate, left-of-center ones.

Peter assigned me to the speechwriter, a guy who reminded me in looks of Congressman Frog from the *Pogo* comics. He had bulgy eyes with bags under them and had acquired something of a corporation, though he was probably only in his late thirties. The speechwriter placed me at a table cattycorner to his and gave me something to read. He was working on a speech and asked me how to spell *choose*. He said his major problem with the campaign was deciding when to go to lunch.

My first assignment was to put together a profile of William Saxbe, the Republican opponent. It felt odd because Bill Saxbe's son Rocky and my brother Donnie were high school classmates and great friends. The Saxbe office was also at the Lincoln-Leveque building. Later that summer, on a day when the Saxbe campaign bus was parked on Broad Street and I was walking by, Rocky came out of the bus, shook my hand, and said, "Hi, Vivian, I just want to tell you to vote for Saxbe and buy at the Union" (the department store across the street from Lazarus).

The paid staff was overwhelmed and quickly figured out that if they threw scut work my way, it got done. I clipped newspaper articles, delivered stuff to field workers, helped with scheduling, and turned up to be part of a glowing audience on a TV campaign ad. Someone gave me a writing assignment that could do no harm—a position paper on the International Monetary Fund.

"She can write," said Dave Vienna, the press secretary.

They started giving me better writing jobs and sending me out to observe Saxbe surreptitiously at events and bring back notes. They asked me to write down some ideas on representative government for a speech. They liked it and gave me a whole speech to draft.

I was able to live on less than five dollars a week by parking the Baron at the Vets' Memorial lot, about half a mile away, for fifty cents a day. My only other big expense was a diet Pepsi with the lunch I'd brought from home. I bet I also charged my gasoline at the Dorsey-Reynolds gas station on the corner of Main and Parkview. Even so, I started to run out of money and said something within Pop-pop's earshot. I don't think I was deliberately making a request, but soon after, when I was their only guest for dinner, an envelope with a hundred-dollar bill was at my place.

"Why?" I asked.

"Because we like you," said Hoo-hoo.

❦

The Democrats met in Chicago for their convention the last week in August to solidify their platform and nominate a presidential candidate. Humphrey was the presumptive winner, but McCarthy was still in the race. Jack Gilligan was there, as were Peter and other campaign honchos. Gilligan coauthored a minority plank on Vietnam and defended it passionately, taking on staunch insider Senator Abe Ribicoff from the floor. The plank was defeated by a margin of 2–1.

At the convention, the New York delegation broke into "We Shall Overcome," but the official band quickly drowned them out. Mayor Richard Daley's police, faceless in their riot gear, beat protesters outside convention headquarters while we watched in Columbus, transfixed. The National Guard poured tear gas into the crowd. Char and I saw people trying to exercise their freedom to assemble; Dick saw a gang of dangerous thugs who should all be thrown in jail. We learned later that the gas wafted into the open window of Humphrey's suite on the top floor of the Hilton. The rioting was not only outside but in the convention hall itself. The chairman of the New Hampshire delegation was arrested. Dan Rather, the CBS news commentator, was bloodied trying to get an interview. On Thursday night, the convention and the rest of the world saw a heartrending, delegate-rousing film about Bobby Kennedy.

After the convention, I picked Peter up from the airport, and we all got back to the urgent work of electing somebody who would stand up to the Ribicoffs and Daleys of the world.

A long string of Kennedy associates, such as Frank Mankiewicz, came to town for press conferences, in which they unfailingly said how much Gilligan was like a Kennedy in looks, antiwar fervor, and caring for the weak, the poor, and the disenfranchised. Dan Rather visited the office and gave us a big boost with his coverage. Rather's story showed Saxbe as a slick, rich, tobacco-chewing idiot and Gilligan as Ohio's Kennedy.

A single candidates' debate was held, the traditional one at the Cleveland City Club. By this time I had made a notebook of all of Saxbe's positions and conflicting statements. There were plenty of those, plus a great quote to set them up with: "Anyone who changes his mind in an election year is crazy," Saxbe had said. The campaign was in full roll, and I helped the scheduler, who was also the candidate's driver, arrange events. Dave Vienna reviewed my work on Saxbe and had a bunch of questions. The candidate weighed in with more. New questions came up that should have been answered months before. Gilligan wanted a breakdown of the federal budget by category, for example. I struggled through piles of documents to get it for him. (There was no Internet to make it easy back then.)

The top office staff went up to Cleveland to prepare for the debate, calling Columbus with last-minute questions. What were Ohio's educational needs going to be in 1975? How much debt did Ohio have? I found answers. The rest of the staff left behind, mostly the women, huddled around a tiny radio for news. Our side had tried hard to have the debate broadcast on radio and TV, but the Saxbe campaign was successful in beating that back. They knew how good a rhetorician we had. They tried to keep us from making an audiotape of our own, but in that they were unsuccessful.

Immediately after the debate, the first news report called the face-off "a draw." The members of our staff, when they arrived back later, were ecstatic.

"We killed them," said Dave. "Slaughter. Massacre."

Mark agreed. "We won. No doubt about it."

Saxbe had taken the offensive from word one, accusing Gilligan of fomenting riots. The statement he cited was from several years before and supposed to be off the record. The gist of it, according to my diary, was that riots were inevitable if government was completely unresponsive to its citizens. In retrospect, this certainly sounds both inflammatory and easily used by the opposition to cast our candidate as a wild radical.

Gilligan responded to Saxbe's accusations by staying above the attack for most of the debate, emphasizing that the political system must respond to legitimate citizen protest. He talked about the problems facing the country and how they shouldn't be trivialized. Saxbe continued to pound, and Gilligan, in his summing up, decried the pettiness of much of Saxbe's contribution to the debate, saying, "I ask you, what is the difference between this appeal [Saxbe's] and the appeal of George Wallace?" It strikes me now as a bit on the petty side to compare Saxbe to the defiant southern segregationist governor, but we all loved the line. Babs Sirak said they were words that would go down in history. It shows how caught up in the battle we all were.

Dave Vienna came over to chat. "What are you doing after the election?"

"Looking for a job," I said.

"Why don't you go to Washington?"

"That'd be great if I could."

"Sure. There are a lot of lightweights in this office who are going to *go* after the election. Have you talked to anybody about it?"

I glowed with pride that Dave thought I was a middleweight, and I started to think about what Washington would be like. Dave was on loan from his own Washington job and would presumably be returning to it. He was telling me that some campaign staff would not be accompanying our new senator, but perhaps I would be considered. That was how I heard it. It didn't occur to me that we could lose. Washington was not impossibly far from Columbus, not like Indonesia or some other end-of-the-world jungle where I could be posted with the USIA.

The day before the election, nothing was left to do in the main campaign office, so I helped at a phone bank at the Southern Hotel. The candidate stopped by. Camera lights were on him as he asked everybody to hang up so he could talk to us. Slam, went all the phones, probably losing us votes. Gilligan thanked us and said that whatever happened we should be proud of being part of the biggest volunteer effort Ohio had ever seen.

Tuesday, Election Day, several of us sat in the campaign office forecasting the results. A betting pool seemed in order. Howard led with a bet of 53 percent, but Peter the pollster said it was a bad method of setting up the pool because Howard could be hedged: someone could take 52.5 percent and another 53.5 percent and bracket him. Peter marked pieces of paper with numbers ranging from 51 percent to 53 percent and put them in his pith helmet. I drew 52 percent. Howard drew 51.5 and traded with Dave, who had 53 percent. The room was bright with sunlight and confidence.

I headed to the voting booth, checking three times to make sure I'd pulled the lever for Gilligan. I packed and gassed up the Baron, then drove to Cincinnati, glad to be at the wheel because it made me feel I could control something. Peter's directions to the Sheraton-Gibson Hotel were easy to follow. The hotel was a huge old hulk whose major advantage was being cheap. At six thirty I entered an elevator, surprised that my eyes were level with the navels of the men already in it. The Chicago Bulls were in town to play basketball. I felt as big as a Chihuahua.

A scattering of people were already in the ballroom, but nobody I knew. Someone from the campaign staff spied me and led me to "Peter's Parlor" behind a Wizard of Oz sort of screen. There, Peter Hart put me to work monitoring CBS. I started watching Walter Cronkite, the anchor. Dan Rather was covering the Midwest. Peter was nervous, which I hadn't seen before. I could see he was keeping his hands from shaking. My own heart was beating too fast.

More people arrived. The room quickly became too crowded, too noisy, and too smoky. Supporters and hangers-on stopped by to ask how things were going.

"It's in the bag," Mark said to one and all.

Howard helped Peter. Babs monitored ABC. Dave took the paper county results out to the ballroom and wrote them on the blackboard.

Fred and Irma Lazarus from Cincinnati came by.

"It's in the bag," Mark told them.

At about eight o'clock that evening, figures came in showing Humphrey, the presidential candidate, doing better than Gilligan in Ohio. Peter loosened his tie. He said later that he and Mark knew then that it was all over. I was involved with CBS. I didn't look around. I heard Peter's calculator steadily clicking. Over the course of the evening, it slowed to a requiem.

I didn't get a good sense of what was happening by watching CBS, where hope was alive. It was when Dave came in, looking bleak and miserable and asking Peter what the hell was going on, that I got the message.

Dan Rather stuck with us until three o'clock in the morning. It was for the wrong reasons. He kept repeating that there were still votes to come in from Cuyahoga County, meaning Cleveland, which would be good for our guy. But the outstanding votes were in fact from Hamilton County, Cincinnati, which was conservative.

By six in the morning, almost nobody was left in Peter's Parlor. He'd given up on the calculator and was looking at the television with glazed eyes. The presidential election wasn't over. A couple of Gilligan's children were still watching, lying on the floor. The room smelled of stale smoke and yesterday's hamburgers. All I'd had to eat since lunch the day before was a large Coke. Desperate to pee, I went upstairs. I slept for a bit. At nine o'clock, Cronkite was still face-to-face with the nation, looking remarkably alert. Illinois put Nixon over the top.

As I drove home to Columbus, I turned up the radio as high as it would go when the hit song "Those Were the Days" came on:

> *Those were the days my friend,*
> *We thought they'd never end,*
> *We thought we'd live forever and a day.*
> *We'd live the life we choose.*
> *We'd fight and never lose. Those were the days.*
> *Oh, yes those were the days.*

When I got home, Char and I played Scrabble. "To bring us back to normal," she said.

Peter came back from Cincinnati. "Here we are with this stupid calculator," he said. "It told me fifty-two percent, but it didn't say for which guy." Peter came over to Melrose and played Scrabble with me and Char. He took me to lunch at the Ohio State student union before he left. I hadn't realized that his father was head of the English department at Berkeley. He gave me his helmet from the reserves. I took him to the airport. We shook hands and wished each other luck.

I wrote to Dave, who had already headed back to DC, and asked him to keep me in mind if he saw anything. He called the next day with a string of ideas. I was to phone him again on January 2.

It took a couple of months, but Dave came through.

"*Congressional Quarterly* is having a housecleaning," he said. "Come to Washington and show up there."

I knew what *Congressional Quarterly* was—a weekly magazine that tracked congressional action. The housecleaning wasn't voluntary. Several editors and writers were leaving to start a new magazine, *National Journal*. I showed up in a *CQ* editor's office in February 1969 to apply for a researcher-writer position.

"My wife went to Wellesley," the editor said and asked me to take a two-hour written test. Wellesley connection and written test were good signs. No oral exam. Waiting to hear back, I walked the halls of the Senate from top to bottom, knocking on doors to see if there were any job openings. The *CQ* editor called. I was hired.

Washington was a fork in the road, and I took it.

Jack Gilligan distributed an inscribed tile after the campaign. At the top was the campaign crest, a logo of the US Capitol slightly skewed, as if by a wind of change. The inscription, signed by Gilligan, was from Tennyson's "Ulysses" and read:

> *My purpose holds to sail beyond the sunset*
> *And the baths of all the western stars,*
> *Until I die.*

Abstract, romantic, optimistic. And when all the poetry was declaimed, the underlying image was opportunity. Other people already wanted Gilligan to run for governor in 1970 and almost immediately after the campaign started encouraging him.

"I feel like an early Christian down in the pit with the lions while the crowd cheers me on," he grumbled.

Babs and Howard were for it. Babs told Gilligan privately that she and Howard would have half a million raised before the gubernatorial campaign began. But when the three of them were at dinner, Howard, in his gruff, authoritative voice, announced to the once and possibly future candidate that if he ran again, he would raise $400,000 before the campaign even began.

"What happened to the other hundred thousand?" asked Gilligan. The "early Christian" was not completely opposed to being thrown to the lions. He was getting ready to see what he could pull out of the helmet next time.

11

A WORLD
SERIES RING

However much they adore their sports teams, most fans can't buy them. Even the few who have the wherewithal are unlikely ever to have a chance. Char did. Opportunity showed up like the crack of a bat in 1973 and saved a marriage that had threatened to become unstuck.

Char fell for the New York Yankees in 1950 when her sister Jean would come down from New Haven to meet friends for a game. Char was married to Warren Gorman then and new to the city. In between trips to the ballpark, she could listen to baseball on the radio, her perfect medium since it was aural. When a game was on, she would carry a transistor radio held to her ear wherever she went. Visiting her parents in Columbus in the summer, she would check the schedule. A night game meant she would be able to listen.

"You've got to think about the game," she would say, a line from the musical *Damn Yankees*. Then she would trundle out to the backyard and maneuver the radio with its tiny antenna until she picked up the signal.

"This sport is wonderful," she told an interviewer from the Columbus Jewish Historical Society late in life, "because it goes for six or seven months of the year, and it happens every day, and it's like this wonderful continued story."[1]

It's an especially wonderful story when your team dominates, and the Yankees were perennial winners. John Freund, one of our next-door neighbors in the apartment on Ninety-Sixth Street, recalled deciding to root for the New York Giants at the age of five. Char dressed him down. She made it simple:

"Why be a Giants fan?" she asked. "The Giants lose. Giants fans are sad people. The Yankees win. Their fans are happy people. You don't want to be a sad person."

When Dick married Char in 1958, he had to convert. Theology wasn't the issue. They were both nonpracticing Jews. It wasn't one of those cases where a spouse had to figure out catechisms or learn to recite prayers in Hebrew. Char's religion was New York Yankees baseball and Ohio State football, and he had better be in the game with her. Me too.

Not that Dick and I had much choice. The Giants and the Brooklyn Dodgers both moved to California in 1956, leaving only the Yankees. Dick was for the Giants. I don't think it made him sad. My first baseball game was at the Polo Grounds to see his team play. The activity on the field bored me, and Dick tried to keep me amused by buying one of each of the available snacks—a hot dog, Cracker Jack with a prize, popcorn, ice cream, and soda pop. The vanilla ice cream had a woody taste from the flat piece of plywood used as a spoon.

A pillar partially obstructed my view high up in Yankee Stadium on Saturday, October 8, 1960, where I perched with Char, Dick, Bobby and Donnie, but it couldn't stifle my excitement. Char had quickly made me a disciple of the right team, and I was thrilled to be at the World Series, tied at 1–1. The Pittsburgh Pirates had won the first game. The second was an example of the kind of game Char liked best, one where the Yankees took the lead and then slowly pulled away. The final score was 16–3. That team was stocked with some of the greatest baseball players of all time—Mickey Mantle, Roger Maris, Yogi Berra, Elston Howard, and more. The coach was Casey Stengel. I knew all the batting averages. Possibly to assert my independence from the usual thinking and especially to be different from my brother Donnie, my favorite player was Clete Boyer, the third baseman, who could really go to his right, sometimes leaping and stretching parallel to the field to snag a hard line drive or grab an erratic grounder. My other favorite was Bobbie Richardson, the second baseman, often called "little." His size made him look like an underdog, especially on that team, though he was the lead-off hitter and a superb fielder.

Whitey Ford was pitching. It was only the bottom of the first inning, but our guys batted around, bringing Richardson to the plate for his second at bat with the bases loaded. I saw his arms sweep wide and heard the solid thwack a split-second later along with the swelling roar from seventy thousand fans. I leaped to my feet and peered around the pillar as Mel Allen, the mellifluous Yankees broadcaster, told Char through her portable radio, "It's going, going. It's gone." Little Bobby Richardson, who hit one home run the entire regular season, had belted a grand slam.

By Monday the series was tied at two games apiece. Early in the afternoon, I sat on a bench in the lobby of Miss Hewitt's Classes trying to look nauseous. I kept my eyes on the book bag at my feet and hoped a passing teacher wouldn't detect the thrilled anticipation I was trying to make into fear of throwing up. It was a brash move to fake illness at lunchtime rather than skipping school entirely. Perhaps I had a test in the morning that I didn't want to miss. I would not be changing into sickroom pajamas at home but into a skirt and sweater suitable for a ball game. Not shorts or jeans, though I suppose it wasn't warm enough anyway. Denim was yet to be anytime clothing, and Dick said unless a woman was built like a model, shorts made her legs looked lumpy. I think he really meant her hips stuck out.

It seemed impossible, given the way the Yanks were hitting and pitching, but we lost that day. The series went back to Pittsburgh. We were tied 3–3 by Thursday, and I do not know how I managed to be at home at Belle's apartment for game seven, one of the more unforgettable of any season in the history of baseball. Did I have to fake illness again? My diary doesn't say.

Our pitching was off-kilter. The lead went back and forth. In the top of the ninth, the Yankees tied the game at a blazing nine runs apiece. Then Bill Mazeroski of the Pirates hit the first-ever game-winning home run in the ninth inning of a World Series. Mantle is said to have cried for the only time in his career. Richardson was named MVP, the first time that a player from a losing team earned that honor.

Char telephoned right away. She had watched at the Ninety-Sixth Street apartment and had a lot to say. We'd outscored them and outhit them. We'd outplayed, them, for God's sake. Sometimes even winners lose.

On a Saturday morning in January 1973, ten years after their move to Columbus, Dick read to Char from the *New York Times* about the plans of George Steinbrenner from Cleveland and several partners to buy the New York Yankees. Steinbrenner was a shipping magnate who had unsuccessfully bid for the Cleveland Indians.

I had run across Steinbrenner while working on Jack Gilligan's campaign for governor in 1970. He was one of the guys who would pop into the office for unclear reasons. Mark Shields likened Steinbrenner and

Marvin Warner, another magnate, to "big puppies who don't know what to do with themselves." Warner later got into big trouble in a national savings and loan scandal; Steinbrenner did better.

That Saturday night Char and Dick went to a dinner party at Jules and Judy Garel's house in Bexley that included Jack Gilligan, now the governor of Ohio. Char chatted with Peter Mykrantz, a friend who remarked that George Steinbrenner had been a classmate of his at Williams.

"It was as if something came down from the heavens and hit me in the head," Char said later. "And I said, 'How well do you know him?'"

"I don't know him very well. I don't know him anymore. But the governor knows him very well."

Char spotted Gilligan's red hair and crossed the room.

"I would love to be a part of that deal," Char said to the governor. It was a throwaway line. She wasn't imagining something would come of it.

Yes, Gilligan would be glad to call Steinbrenner and see if any room was left in the Yankees partnership.

On Monday, the telephone rang while Char and Dick were lunching in the dining room.

Leroy answered the phone in the back hall.

"The governor is on the line," he said.

"Tell the governor's office I'll call them back," said Char.

Leroy went back to the phone. He was murmuring in his most mellifluous baritone. He returned.

"It really is the governor," he said.

Gilligan had spoken to Steinbrenner about Char's inquiry.

"Call George," he said. "He's expecting it."

Char and Dick were going to her father's house for dinner that night. (Her mother had died in July 1971.) She was terrified to tell Pop-pop what she was doing.

"It sort of gave me the shivers because you see, I felt that I was being like a whimsical child, like a willful child," she said. "I really was worried about telling him that I had gone and done this crazy thing."[2]

Pop-pop didn't think it was crazy.

"Look, Char," he said. "If you're doing this to make money, don't. But if you're doing it to have fun, I think you'll have a ball."

She had a ball. So did Dick. From the first, Char was allowed to bring Dick to the business meetings. It was clear at the beginning that they would have no part in the area of the business called "baseball operations"—in other words, the team itself. Those decisions were all George's. They did get scouting reports, which I read on at least one occasion and found fascinating, partly because it was an inside look, but also because the writing was as amusingly stilted, concrete, and as full of baseball clichés as one would expect from baseball scouts. The limited partners had to throw a huge fuss to be allowed to be on the committee that dealt with taxes, which were their legitimate concern.

❧

I'm not sure Char and Dick's marriage would have survived without their mutual love of the Yankees. Though they had a tremendous amount in common, Dick refused to be a full family participant. It wore Char down. It drove me crazy because I worried that it threatened my relationship with Char, though she told me it did not.

The partnership in the Yankees renewed Char and Dick's own partnership. They started commuting to New York together. For many years they went to nearly all the home games at the old Yankee Stadium and many of the away ones. For their twenty-fifth anniversary Char gave Dick a piece of her share of the team.

Dick learned to love Columbus. He felt like a country gentleman, the master of an estate, with Ohio an undiscovered Greenwich, Connecticut. He had quick hands from playing lacrosse in college, and in the local Bexley matches on private tennis courts he was a hammer at the net. He had a smooth swing for golf and could drive the ball far down the fairway. He dressed in a suit and tie every day for lunch. He contemplated the difficult question of whether the gardener should put in more ground cover and was excited to discover the wonders of pachysandra. He was a charmer at dinner parties and a fan at Ohio State football games. Char and Dick kept a purple-inked ticker tape on the second floor of the house that clickety-clacked all day, spewing the thin paper on the floor. The carpet turned purple, despite Leroy's best efforts to keep it clean. Char would bring the tape up to a half-inch from her eyes to pore over it, threading it through her fingers and turning them purple. If the local Fourth of July parade had gone by their house instead of around the corner on Drexel Avenue, they could have made quite a contribution. The ability to track the market from Columbus eventually weaned Dick away from his commuting life.

When in New York, they stayed with Charm and Seelig Freund in their apartment on Park Avenue. Charm in particular became a huge fan herself, going to Yankee Stadium so often that the staff started to assume she was an owner too. Often before an evening game they ate at Elio's, on Second Avenue near Eighty-Fourth Street, accompanied by the Freunds or other friends or family. Normally Elio's is packed and noisy, but at six o'clock or so it was reasonably quiet. My parents had time to enjoy dry martinis made with Bombay gin served on the rocks in a wineglass with three olives, followed by excellent Italian meals. Dick was the only anchovy eater in the group, so he was likely to start with roast peppers and anchovies followed by veal Marsala; Char was more likely to have the mushroom salad and veal piccata. Well before the last bite, Char would start to worry about being late. She curled her fingers into fists anxiously.

"Get the check," she would mutter to Dick. In his polite, unrushed way, he did.

Dick and Char sometimes made the trip up to Yankee Stadium in a taxi, but often in the red car that they garaged in town for the baseball season. Early in their Yankee-ownership days, Dick got the idea that the car should have license plates that said DPL. That's short for "diplomat" in the city and gives the driver immunity from parking tickets. He reckoned the police wouldn't notice that the plates were also clearly labeled "Ohio." He eventually gave up that idea and changed the plate to "Yankees." They had plenty of time before "The Star Spangled Banner" to dock the car in the team parking lot, which had a highly unscalable fence. The lot abutted the stadium near the press and team offices entrance, where Char and Dick were headed, but it could be a tough slog for them. For big games during the season and for postseason games, the hardest part of the trip was negotiating the thick crowd of ticket holders jostling for position New York–style as Char and Dick headed to the gates. By the guarded press door, the fans were three deep, hoping for a glimpse of a star. Dick would shepherd Char, who not only had trouble with her sight, but looked a bit like an upside-down bowling pin that would be a cinch to tip over.

Both Char and Dick were as happy as they had ever been in their lives sitting in the owners' box in the old Yankee Stadium. On a deep fly, Char had to judge what was happening by the outfielders' moves, and Dick or the broadcasters would fill her in on the details. But she knew all the players' stats and strengths and reveled or suffered with the team.

"Your father seemed right in his element," my cousin Bea Cooper told me about being invited to Yankee Stadium. "He was such a good host and so cheerful." Bea and Chuck weren't big baseball fans, so I don't think they were as impressed as Dick wanted them to be.

"Close only counts in horseshoes," said Steinbrenner's Christmas card early in his reign. He wanted winning teams and would spend whatever it took to buy the best players on the market. There were deep troughs in the Yankees' record, but the World Series rings continued to accumulate, and when the players got their rings, the owners did too. The first time the Yankees won the series after Char and Dick became limited partners, Char was offered a pendant on the assumption that a woman wouldn't want to wear a ring about the size and weight of a baseball. She demanded a ring and got it. Eventually they had so many that she had a pair made into earrings and then lost them at a hairdresser's shop in Paris.

Char gave her 1978 ring to our older daughter Wit (then called Babs) for her twenty-first birthday, along with a note signed, "With special love, Char":

> *This gift makes it clear*
> *It takes away all mystery*
> *That Babs's birthday year*
> *Was the greatest comeback in history.*

Char would show off her rings at every chance. Jack joked that her message was, "You may kiss my ring," like an empress or queen. Most of the time, the response was gratifyingly gushy. Very rarely, the recipient of the offer to gaze at a ring did not know its meaning and was uninterested. Once in their last years, when Dick was undergoing surgery and Char and I were waiting at the hospital, she headed for the information desk with me trailing close behind carrying the oxygen tank she needed for pulmonary disease. She asked the volunteer for news. Unbidden, she offered a look at her bling-laden finger.

"How lovely," said the desk worker, looking behind Char at me with a smile that made me an accomplice to being kind to an old lady, instead of sharing admiration for my amazing mother.

Raising a family and working full-time kept me from paying as much attention to baseball as I had in my teen years, however much I did and do enjoy the connection. Jack and I still hoist a Yankees flag with the American one in our backyard for the summer, though we opted out of purchasing a piece of the team when Char and Dick died. Bobby, Donnie, and Babette carry on the tradition of Yankees ownership. It wasn't only the money that deterred Jack and me—and the foregone income from investing in something that pays no dividends. The opportunity cost in time was too great for us. We would have felt obliged to pay considerable attention to baseball and travel to New York more than we wanted.

We did make it to New York for games with Char and Dick infrequently. Even better was when Jack and I lived in Delray Beach, Florida, in the late 1980s, and the Yankees held spring training in Fort Lauderdale. When my parents visited, we sat behind the home team dugout, about ten feet away from famous and aspiring players. The guys on the way up were even more interesting than the established team members. It gave you a mental edge on the regular season to know who was trying to make it in the bigs because you'd seen him chalk up singles in the grapefruit league.

One evening we took our friends Bruce and Jenny McKinney to a spring game. Char and Dick had gotten me a parking pass, and when I pulled into a preferred section a few feet away from the ballpark entrance, Bruce said, "Well, I'm impressed."

"Me too," I said. I was embarrassed.

It was Wit who got in trouble for the sin of pride, however. On the first day of fifth grade at Gulf Stream School in Florida, a stuffy, Waspish place, the teacher asked her to introduce herself. She proudly told the class that she was Jewish and her grandmother owned the New York Yankees. Thus she was branded as a liar, a braggart, and a Hebrew. Three strikes against her. Everyone knew that George Steinbrenner owned the Yankees. The limited partners were rarely mentioned.

"There's nothing in life quite so limited as being a limited partner of George Steinbrenner," one of them, John McMullen, said.[3]

Wit was and is the biggest Yankees fan in our immediate family. In fact, she was a fan of all of baseball and had collected cards from all teams. She was amazed that at one time I had the Topps cards for the 1960 Yankees but threw them away. I've often dug in my basement to see if by some chance they are still there among the playbills and silver oddities. I found trading cards, but worthless ones of horses, dogs, and flowers. Wit not only knew the names and statistics for all the players in the major leagues but at one time had the hundred best minor league prospects memorized as well. She didn't share that with Char and Dick, feeling they would think it was a bit crazy.

When Wit was twelve, Char and Dick decided to invite her to a weekend in New York to see the Yankees play. They couldn't figure out how she would get to and from La Guardia, however. So they invited me too. I would be the nanny. We sat in the owners' box adjacent to Steinbrenner's office. We all gaped at the memorabilia in the office, where we took a photo of Wit in an enormous chair shaped like a baseball mitt. A Yankees executive escorted Wit to the broadcasting booth to meet Phil Rizzuto and secure his autograph. While she was there, the scoreboard flashed "Yankees Welcome Babs Davis." My daughter arrived back in our box floating in ecstasy.

"If everyone is famous for fifteen minutes," I told her, "You have about fourteen minutes and forty-six seconds to go."

These days, the teams have figured out they can make a few bucks by scrolling long lists of welcomes, birthdays, and anniversaries. For Wit, it took Char talking to the right person.

Asked about her relationship with George in the 1999 interview with the Jewish Historical Society, Char responded, "It is said, though I don't believe it, that I'm the only one he's scared of."

"Because you speak your piece?" asked the interviewer.

"Occasionally. Every couple of times I have…well, you know."

She had indeed. I have an example from 1987 that followed conference calls with the limited partners. Char wrote to George:

"Most of the partners were seriously upset by the unbusinesslike and almost frivolous way that Dan solicited our approval of an open-ended, ongoing payment of very large and unknown amounts of money. He acted as if the partners were willful and ungrateful children for withholding our instant and unreserved agreement during these two, unorganized, disorderly conference calls."[4]

Char used to say that George liked Dick more than he did her. Dick didn't speak his piece. When Dick turned seventy-five in 1995, Jack and I flew to New York to see a couple of Yankees games and to celebrate. A game had been rained out, so Saturday, September 23, was a twi-night double header. Steinbrenner worried about whether the kids in the owners' box were getting enough to eat. He arranged to have pizzas brought in for all of them.

George sat down next to Char to chat.

"Where are you guys going to dinner?" he asked.

"Lutèce," she told him.

"What time are the reservations?" asked the Boss.

"Eight," she said. "I'm sorry we'll have to miss the second game."

We arrived at Lutèce, meeting David and Ruth Sussman, and were shown to a table on the second floor.

"Drinks?" asked Dick to the table at large as the waiter arrived.

"Mr. Witkind, Mr. Steinbrenner has sent you champagne," the waiter said. He brought a bottle of Taittinger Kristal.

The meal was wonderful, and with the Sussmans present, Dick and Char had a great time. David was chief operating officer and general counsel of the Yankees, and Ruth a federal court judge. Both were lively talkers and enthusiastic about many things. They were fun, and I was pleased that my father was enjoying the evening. The glasses emptied quickly, and Dick ordered a second bottle of champagne. Then a third.

The bill came. Dick gave it a look and called the waiter back.

"This doesn't have any champagne on it."

"Mr. Steinbrenner said you should have all the champagne you could drink," he said.

Dick computed afterward that we had managed $750 worth.

On May 17, 2003, the day before Char died, Jack and I went over to visit. Char and Dick were both flat on their backs on their beds upstairs. We pointed out that the Yankees were playing, and Char, who at that point did not have the strength to brush her own hair, said, "A ballgame. I have to see that," and made her way slowly to the stairs, down the chairlift and into the library, where we turned on the TV set.

You've got to think about the game.

12

A PHOTOGRAPH OF HUGO BLACK

"What I need to do is marry someone who wants to settle in Columbus, get myself a Ph.D. at OSU and teach at Capital," I wrote in March 1969. Finding love and work are a twentysomething's routine problems. I added a personal constraint that a more adventurous person would eschew: Capital University was down the street from my parents' house in Bexley. Grown women were supposed to leave home. I liked where I was.

In the late 1960s, the women's movement had begun but not fully taken hold. Many of my classmates were already married, happily, I thought, though that did not always turn out to be true. I laughed when Daisy Mae sang in *Li'l Abner*, "I'm past my prime…Seventeen last spring, still without a wedding ring." Seventeen and married was what they did in Appalachia. Twenty-three years old and still ringless was different. It was not a laughing matter.

Within two years I had it all: work, location, and love.

But before there was Jack, there was Chuck. Then Chuck and Jack. Or Jack and Chuck. It was confusing until I married one of them.

❦

While I waited for Dave Vienna to call about possible work, Bob Lazarus, my uncle, got me a job at the store in the planning department. Department stores give as little room as possible to back-office tasks. Planning and research had an office about as big as a kindergarten cubbyhole, hidden on the seventh floor along with merchandise that rumbled in, sat in ghostly rows for a bit, and rumbled out to the store floor. I would be paid $1.75 an hour, an increase from my part-time summer jobs in sales at the store. Those had been on the sixth floor, the highest one open to the public, as an "extra" salesperson at back-to-school time and Christmas.

The jobs had been educational. Reporting to work the first summer, I had asked to be assigned to pets.

"You'll go where I need you," said the floor manager.

First lesson: the supervisor decides. I raced to help hordes of families from as far as West Virginia and Mansfield, Ohio, who came in to stock up on preteen girls' clothes. I planned to spend my earnings on fall clothes for myself. I skipped breaks, probably earning resentment from salespeople who thought I was a rate-buster. I learned how to avoid the conversation-freezing "May I help you?" I outsold all the other extras in the department. When the summer was over, I only had enough money for a couple of drab dresses from the basement. That was lesson two: you can't earn a living as a department store extra.

At Christmas I worked in preteen boys. We ran out of bathrobes, and I had the sickening experience of having to tell grandmothers that we did not have what they were looking for. Lesson three: plan ahead. If you don't have inventory, you can't sell. On the other hand, many grandsons were spared fluffy bathrobes.

Now, as I worked at the store after the campaign, and February 1969 approached, flocks of caged canaries rumbled into the seventh floor, flinging their fullhearted songs against the bleak surroundings. They would soon be distributed throughout the first floor to encourage customers to think about spring. I sat at my simple wooden desk amid a cacophony of birdsong, assembling the "Lazarus Growth Plan" from documents submitted by the department managers. It was the first year they were putting together a plan that way. One manager expected to "grow the bathing-suit business to ten months a year," which made me imagine the bathing suits themselves growing.

When Dave called and asked me to come to Washington, my boss at Lazarus offered me a full-time job in response. I turned it down, and he said if I changed my mind in a couple of months, I could still have it. Working at Lazarus would keep me in Columbus, but I was interested in politics and government, not business. If I worked at the store, I could easily fail right in front of the disappointed eyes of my family. I could end up in something like the Boy Scouts department, where one family member had already been stowed because it was the most he could handle. In Boy Scouts, the problems are limited to inventory. The uniform is what it is.

"If you don't enjoy it, you shouldn't hesitate to come home," Char said. I would be welcome any weekend, and she would spring for the airfare. A round-trip ticket to Columbus cost about fifty bucks at the time. I would be earning $105 a week.

"Don't make an endurance contest out of it," she said. "Don't get feeling trapped. Don't feel you have to separate yourself from the people you are closest to."

Dick concurred. He was still commuting between Columbus and New York. We were both being pushed and pulled. We loved Char and Columbus.

"Nice advice from Char that I will follow," I wrote as I prepared to head east. "But I also have to make my own life. I can't always be leaning on my parents. I get restless and irritable, and they can't enjoy that any more than I do. I have to stand up and do my own thing."

With a teddy bear in my suitcase, I checked into the Washington, DC, YWCA on March 2. Lonely and in a strange place, I had second thoughts.

"It's self-imposed exile," I wrote.

It was not clear that I would give *Congressional Quarterly* a chance.

The next morning I reported to work.

"You're going to be a transportation expert," the managing editor told me and assigned me to a bare desk with a typewriter in the immense, open newsroom populated by writers busily knocking out prose amid piles of paper.

Wow. I was going to become an expert. Within a couple of days, I figured out how I got the assignment—nobody wanted it. Highway aid appropriations were the top story. The experienced writers considered transportation legislation as exciting as traffic out of DC on a Friday afternoon.

I found a place to live in Georgetown. I would have two roommates I didn't find especially interesting, but the room was great. It was on the second floor of a brownstone off Wisconsin Avenue and had a door with a board nailed over it that led nowhere except into a tree. But I had a view.

The first few stories I wrote weren't on transportation at all. Eyeing the scared-looking cub reporter at her empty desk with nothing to do but read up on the percentage of highway bridges in need of repair, other staff saw a way to dump the scum at the bottom of their in-baskets, such as "House action on a bill to create a commission on national observances and holidays." Despite the bland description, it was interesting. The bill was defeated because some House members saw the commission as a sneaky path to making Martin Luther King Jr.'s birthday a national holiday. The editor minced my prose as if it were a fat yellow onion.

My first paycheck arrived. It was a glorious feeling to have real money I'd earned myself: $210.68 for two weeks. I could pay my rent. Barely. I was worth something in the real world—unless they figured out I was faking it and fired me.

I watched from afar as a bald editor in thick glasses, Marlyn Aycock, approached another recent hire. They had a conversation that included a lot of nodding by the writer. The next day he was gone and his desk as clean as if he'd never existed.

Congressional Quarterly at the time had little competition as a source of trusted, high-quality coverage of Washington. Contrary to the name, the magazine came out once a week. It went to bed on Thursday in order to be on the doorsteps of subscribers on Monday morning. Congressmen and their staff looked for it to help them see the big picture of action on Capitol Hill. Newspapers across the country used it for data on the affairs of the federal government and ran op-ed pieces we provided. *CQ* covered not only Congress, but executive-branch actions and the Supreme Court. It was considered an excellent training ground for journalists. My parents could brag about my job to their friends.

My next assignment was House action on increasing travel allowances for federal employees "and for other purposes," a phrase all the bills seemed to have. What the other purposes could be was a perpetual mystery.

I watched from a distance as Marlyn held my latest work in his left hand and a scissors the size of a scimitar in his right. Without looking over at me he cut it to pieces and put it back together with Scotch tape.

Another editor returned a story with red marks that almost obscured the black ones. The thing had been eviscerated. As a transportation piece, it was roadkill.

"Not bad for a first story," he said encouragingly.

"It's my fourth."

By May I was writing four or five pieces a week on congressional committee hearings, many on such unexciting topics as maritime appropriations, but some more interesting. The editors were no longer treating my stories like manatees that had met up with the working ends of motor boats. *CQ* gave me a raise, for which Pop-pop sent me a bottle of champagne.

I took on an in-depth piece on air traffic control. The air traffic controllers and the Federal Aviation Administration were at war. The controllers said they were desperately understaffed and underpaid for the highly skilled, nerve-racking work of keeping planes moving without accident. I interviewed FAA managers, who said the controllers were complaining over nothing: aviation accidents were extremely rare, they pointed out. I interviewed air traffic controllers who recounted details of near misses in the air: Piper cubs coming within feet of Boeings, screaming passengers, and air traffic controllers who twitched uncontrollably afterward. Near misses were increasing rapidly, they told me and then produced the statistics to prove it.

The technology for directing plane traffic still relied on black-and-white radar monitors from World War II. Since the monitors only showed two dimensions, the controllers used small tabs of paper to write down the planes' altitudes and Scotch-taped them to the monitor screens. When an altitude changed, they'd pull off the old tab and write the new number in pencil. It would have been a higher tech system if Post-it notes had been invented. I had no knowledge of radar or aviation, but it seemed to me that the people making sure that planes did not bump into each other and spill the human contents to earth like leaflets should be able to do it in three dimensions.

Full of nerves and terrified by the deadline, I dosed myself on coffee for days—and, on the last night, Edrisal, an amphetamine Char had enjoined me to use for premenstrual stress. I hammered out the prose on the manual typewriter, paragraph by hard-won paragraph. I was desperate to please the editors.

I was on assignment on Capitol Hill Thursday, September 23, when the air traffic control piece came out. I arrived in the newsroom. It was bizarrely quiet. No typewriters were clacking. No one was talking. Every writer at every desk had the new magazine open to the same page. They were reading my story.

"I'm never going up in an airplane again," said Tom Arrandale, a writer.

"Hi there, Crash," said Marlyn.

The nickname suited me. Unfortunately, it was what I was about to do. I was putting more pressure on myself than I could handle. I was primed for a collapse.

I ditched my Georgetown roommates in October, when Mary van Briesen, my friend from the Fletcher School, arrived. She had taken a job as consular officer at the State Department and would study Afrikaans, the official language of South Africa, for six months before being deployed to Pretoria. She despised South Africa and its system of apartheid, the forced separation of blacks and whites at every level of society. It was an insult that she was being made a consular officer, an administrative position, rather than a Foreign Service officer who would delve into politics. But it was what the State Department expected of women, including women with Mary's brains, competence, and education.

Mary wasn't one to waste time complaining, however. She leapt into her studies and went after a social life. I'd been doing nothing but work, but she insisted we explore Washington and have people over to our apartment at the Arlington Arms, right next to the Iwo Jima statue in Arlington, Virginia. She reached out to friends from the Fletcher School whom I had forgotten. We had people over for dinners Mary cooked and which we served on paper plates.

"I'm supposed to do dessert," I complained to Char over the phone.

She suggested a jar of brandied peaches. Opening the jar and spooning the peaches out with a little juice was within my culinary prowess.

That autumn, my hands and feet felt numb and my heart took to skipping beats as I worked at my desk. Banging on the manual typewriter seemed harder than usual. I appealed for an electric typewriter, and the editors gave me an IBM Selectric, with a ball instead of type bars to strike the ink ribbon.

I was certain I was sick with something awful when I went home at Christmas. Char took me to a neurosurgeon friend, who decided I had multiple sclerosis.

Seelig Freund, our surgeon friend from New York, was skeptical. We biked a few miles around Bexley together on one of his and Charm's frequent visits to Columbus.

"There's nothing wrong with Vivian's legs," said Seelig.

I didn't want to believe him. Nor did Char. Instead of going back to the District of Columbia after the first of the year, I spent extra weeks at home recuperating from the spinal tap the neurosurgeon had ordered. It was negative, but he still believed I had MS.

It's hard to look back on an earlier self who was more or less consciously seeking a socially acceptable way to fail. If I hadn't kept a diary, I could have conveniently forgotten about the MS episode.

I can see now that Char aided and abetted me. She was sure the neurosurgeon was right and cried as she read my diary notations, which to her seemed rather brave. Fear of illness was real and constant for Char, and she was worried about me.

It was a bizarre ménage à trois at that time. Char confided in me that she was considering divorce, but I would still have a home in Columbus. That must have reinforced my sycophantic relationship with her. I did not discuss the situation with Dick but made it clear through my behavior that I was taking Char's side.

Perhaps Char had another motive. Keeping me close made it less likely that she would lose Dick and be lonelier, with her own parents old and ill. I didn't consider at the time that Dick would care if he himself had less time with me, but I'm betting now that he did. It was like a game of Diplomacy, where you have to have allies but somehow maintain your own coherent boundaries.

With all the emotional pushing and pulling, I suppose I could have become one of those spinster crones with unspecified maladies who mope in an attic. Instead, the thought of a debilitating disease turned out to be a miracle cure for whatever really ailed me. It concentrated my mind. The anxiety went away. Perhaps a doctor prescribed Valium or something similar. That alone could not explain my exuberance. I was suffused with happiness and eager to go back to Washington as soon as possible. It was a case of *reculer pour mieux sauter*: to jump higher, take a few steps back.

Dick bought me a small parrot to take back to the Arlington apartment. All my parakeets and parrots have been named after Supreme Court justices since Donnie got Clarence Darrow, a parakeet, soon after he read *Inherit the Wind* (not that Darrow was on the Supreme Court; the naming habit just grew out of that). Hugo Black was a conure, a small parrot, mostly green with a bright yellow and red forehead. He had no words, only a peremptory *awk*.

While I recuperated as 1970 began, the gubernatorial campaign started at home in Columbus, and I mean right at home, in Char and Dick's house. Jack Gilligan hired Mark Shields to manage the campaign. Char invited

Mark and Ann, who would be the office manager, to move into Melrose while they looked for an apartment in Columbus. They could use my brother Bobby's room.

We all ate dinner together as I prepared to go back to DC, surrounded by the temptation of a new campaign and the delights of living at home.

At dinnertime, Leroy took on the role of butler with the panache of Carson in *Downton Abbey*. Char, Dick, Mark, Ann, and I would be having a drink in the library and watching the end of the six thirty news when Leroy entered in his white jacket to pronounce in his deep bass voice, "The repast that has been prepared for your delectation is ready to be served." He'd vary the words, but the delivery was consistently suitable for the peerage.

Ethel James, Char and Dick's live-in cook, had taken to Julia Child's recipes like Dorothy Goins to *The Settlement Cookbook*. She was turning out sauces with homemade stock and could do a crème renversée that flipped perfectly, no sign of a crack.

Mark was bemused. "You realize what a seven-course meal is in Ireland?" he said. "A six-pack and a boiled potato."

Mark was familiar with six-packs at that time. It was only well after the Ohio campaign that he gave up drinking. As he tells it, on the day of his daughter's sixth birthday party, he had to officiate with a hangover.

"Try playing duck, duck, goose, goose with a headache," he said. It was an epiphany. He quit.

"Alcohol is the sickle cell anemia of the Irish," he liked to say.

I was surprised a couple of days after my return to Washington with Hugo when Chuck Riesz, one of *CQ*'s researcher-writers, asked me out. I hadn't paid much attention to Chuck the year before. For one thing, I thought he was married. He was interested in passenger trains, a topic within my purview as the transportation expert. I'd been forced to hand over a story to him in the fall when I had so much to write I had to give up something. At first I'd greedily tried to keep it, and he had been politely agreeable with my writing the piece.

"Malleable lad," were the first words I wrote about Chuck.

In trying to prove myself, especially to the editors, and avoid being fired, I'd accumulated responsibility for a mishmash of legislation in Medicare, Medicaid, hospital construction, welfare, aging, prescription drugs, and Social Security. The pile of copy I had turned out was higher than almost every other writer, though much of it was unimportant, routine, and easy. Hard as I tried, I could not cover everything I'd signed on to by that time. It would have been smarter to focus on one area and develop marketable expertise, but I didn't realize that.

I figured I was wrong about Chuck's marital status and accepted the invitation to see the movie *Z,* followed by beers at the Old Europe in Georgetown.

"I want you to know, Crash," he said over a mug of lager, "that I don't approve of girls who date married men."

It was a great line. The first of many.

Chuck was still raw from his recent divorce. On the plus side, it gave him an excuse to go into group therapy, and so far that was keeping him out of the draft. Military service was a threat, though when the air force called him in for a physical, he fainted from the blood test. Chuck was from Wilmington, North Carolina, but his parents were living in Richmond, Virginia. He'd studied piano as a boy and at one time had dreams of becoming a concert pianist. His father was a lifelong employee of the Atlantic Coast Line railroad (now CSX), hence the interest in trains.

That evening he waxed passionate about rail transportation. "It's ridiculous to have all that gasoline and traffic when people could take a nice, comfortable train," he complained in his gentle, southern accent. "Ridiculous."

I agreed as I took stock of my companion, a small, lean guy with thinning, cardboard-colored hair and a pair of glasses in front of bright-blue eyes that were full of passionate disgust with misguided public policy.

We established that he was friends with a college classmate of mine from Wilmington.

"I went to O-Woo myself," he said.

"Umm."

"Ohio Wesleyan," he explained. It was right up the road from Columbus, in Delaware. He had an Ohio connection.

"I had no money," he said. "My scholarship didn't leave much room for eating. I lived on peanut butter for the last couple of years. And had a hot plate. My fraternity brothers called my diet 'Viet Cong rations.'"

I commiserated.

"No. I felt wonderful. I was a journalism major. I'm a journalist."

I hadn't thought of myself as a journalist. That implied a career decision.

Like me, Chuck was ready to recover from a bad experience, although mine had been in my head. He was verbal, funny, and eager to break out of postdivorce anger and recrimination. We were meant for each other right then. Chuck and I bonded like a pair of comedians, except that neither of us played the straight man. He couldn't do Desi Arnaz to my Lucy or George Burns to my Gracie. Neither of us deterred the other from crazy, loopy, absurd, daffy tomfoolery, practical jokes, and endless punning. And we were not alone. Chuck and I were becoming two cogs in an engine that generated parties the way a helium pump spews out multicolored balloons.

❧

By February 1970, the *CQ* binge in hiring people straight out of college was spawning unintended consequences. The editors looked on in horror and admiration as their staid office erupted in a fit of twentysomething bliss. The newsroom was turning into no country for middle-age men, as all the editors were. Actually, probably some of them were only in their thirties, but that was enough older to be in a different category, with spouses and even children. One of the few women writers and I collaborated on a Valentine's Day collage for the editors we put on a large poster board. It was an exquisite mosaic that covered every editor's quirks and sayings with clips from newspapers and photos of our targets, which Chuck had taken and developed as eight-by-tens.

Tom Arrandale, the writer who said he was never going up in an airplane again after reading my air traffic controller story, was the unofficial social secretary. He'd wander by the desks and say something like, "Maybe we could all go to Baltimore for a basketball game," casually naming the precise day and time.

"But you don't have to come," he'd add.

"You don't have to come," Chuck mimicked, laughing. "Y'all come, but only if you really want to."

On the way to the basketball game, Carole Horn suggested we have a naked rooting section. We discussed it. I was a little nervous that she meant it. It was still the sixties, after all, and Carole was the closest thing to a hippie in the group.

The next week Tom said, "I'm thinking we could go ice-skating at Cabin John. You don't have to come."

Of course we came. A passel of *CQ* staff and Mary piled into a couple of cars to go to Cabin John in Maryland. I could skate a little from lessons at Rockefeller Center. Mary was the expert. She grew up in Milwaukee, where ice was as common as intrigue in Washington. She skated backward and in circles, while I tried to maintain forward momentum and negotiate the curves. Carole couldn't skate at all and hung onto the rail as she toddled forward. Chuck and I coasted until our leg muscles began to give out and were glad when all the skaters had to leave the rink for the Zamboni to grind slowly onto the chipped and abraded ice, grade it, then put down a new sheet of water that quickly froze. The Zamboni was exquisitely funny—a machine as ugly, ungainly, and powerful as the snow walkers in Star Wars. We cheered for the Zamboni as if it were the home hockey team. It was a thrill to go out on the silver-smooth ice when the Zamboni rumbled offstage to our applause. Our ankles ached a bit, but our blades cut satisfying new trails.

One Friday, as the editors conferred about the stories for the next week, one asked, "What was that that just went by?"

"I think it was a Frisbee," said another.

Of course it was a Frisbee. What better place for a whizzing game of Frisbee than an open newsroom, dodging among the desks, jumping for catches inches from bookcases stacked with *CQ Weekly Reports*, and spilling stacks of the US Congress's best hopes for solving the problems of the world and other purposes?

I was enjoying every minute of my strong-limbed life.

⚬

"How do you know you don't like grits?" Chuck asked. "Have you ever even had them? I'll show you southern cooking, Crash."

I was always happy to have someone else cook for me, especially something new. Chuck lived in an underground unit in a garden apartment building in Glover Park. I sat in the kitchen as he leaned over the deep skillet. It was filled to the brim with cooking oil. I should have known to be worried.

"You have to have plenty of oil," he said as the pan started to simmer, then bubble. He threw in a breast piece of a cut-up fryer, and a plume of hot oil shot up, making him leap back, tongs in hand, to avoid getting his button-down dress shirt spattered. He grabbed a couple of leg pieces and put an arm straight out to ease them in gently while he shied away from the stove. The chicken sizzled like a faucet opened after the water had been turned off too long, and the pan hissed and spat. Geysers of oil leapt up and splattered against the wall like the first moments of a thunderstorm.

"So this is southern cooking," I said.

"I could use a strainer," Chuck said, as he frantically searched the kitchen drawer for a cover of some kind, though he didn't turn down the heat. The sweet aroma of frying chicken spread through the kitchen, the apartment, and probably as far as Capitol Hill.

I tried not to laugh. But he was already laughing at himself.

If human beings who already had the Maslovian basics could be divided into those whose highest goal was power and those who loved truth, Chuck was above all a truth seeker. He despised lies, subterfuge, and unbridled self-interest. His humor sprang from Voltairian vision that pierced cant and façade. Chuck was meant to be a reporter, and *CQ* was an excellent place for him to start his career, as long as he could stay out of the military.

The chicken was delicious; the grits needed butter.

By May the ice rinks were closed, and I introduced Chuck to canoeing. At a quiet inlet off the Potomac River, we rented a boat, and I deferred to him to take the stern. Chuck was not a muscleman, but he was a good seven inches taller and much stronger than me. Unfortunately, experience is useful for canoeing, especially for the paddler in the stern, who is responsible for setting direction.

Somehow we drifted close to the wide Potomac. Then we were on it. From land, you ordinarily don't realize how fast a large river is moving. We were in full fathom five of deep trouble and about to head downstream, a tiny stick of a craft on a ruthless river. I like to paddle my own canoe, but not on the high seas.

"Pull to," I yelled back to Chuck above the roar. I pulled my paddle out to demonstrate, sticking it back in the water as fast as possible so we wouldn't lose another couple of feet.

I poured all my energy into a bow sweep, leaning dangerously forward over the river to try to get us turned enough to move at an angle back to the quiet water where we started. We maneuvered into a position we could maintain if I kept sweeping and if he paddled hard and straight on the downstream side. My shoulders ached as we crept a few inches at a time into the quiet, safe haven of the inlet and slid sideways quite neatly into the canoe rental dock.

It wasn't Chuck's fault that he hadn't been to summer camp and learned to paddle. But our deliverance reminds me of things that eventually did not work well between us. Chuck was better at mechanics than I was, but it wasn't too hard to be better than worthless. Despite a mutual interest in transportation, over the next couple of years, our vehicles persisted in breaking down. We had flat car tires, flat bike tires, and a flat tire with the car stuck in reverse. Paddling in the right direction was also a problem. We were unable to find each other at a bus station in Richmond when I went to visit his parents, unable to find a rugby game Donnie was playing in at Ohio State, and unable to find a party in German Village. When we got lost, we would give up and go home.

"When I go to Europe, I'm going with Babsie," Dick said at one point. "The two of you are a pair of incompetents."

The other issue was numbers. Chuck and I had better things to do than higher mathematics, like balancing a checkbook.

At lunch one day with our large *CQ* group, which was now going out several nights a week, not just Friday when the magazine was put to bed, Carole Horn decided we should make a movie. She looked at me.

"Crash, you'll be the leading lady."

We shot the black-and-white film on a Saturday in a park, a surrealistic background, considering the props were office furniture. Carole baked Alice B. Toklas chocolate chip cookies. (This was not the time I overdosed, however.) The managing editor brought beer. The way Carole had it planned, I was the thread who tied together half a dozen disjointed scenes. The camera lacked the equipment for sound. So there would be captions in the style of the original silent films. Chuck shot stills on his Miranda SLR. In the last scene, the managing editor played a sheriff wearing a badge. I entered the viewing field to talk to him about my job. We argued. He pulled out a cap gun, aimed it at my chest, and pulled the trigger. I contorted myself into a dramatic death scene. It was a little like something I had imagined in my first few months at *CQ*.

The *CQ* movie, made long before it was routine to shoot video and even longer before YouTube, was an example of neither craftsmanship nor humor, but it was a perfect reason for several parties. First, a party celebrated the cinematic achievement, with awards and speeches Oscar-style; then we had two screening parties, probably accompanied by more of Carole's mind-altering baking. Chuck's film hadn't caught when he tried to thread it in his camera, so there were no stills, and I comforted him. The movie itself turned out fine, and we all were mesmerized with every cell, from the moment at the beginning when, carrying a parasol, I sashayed past a group of *CQ* guys to the final caption: "You're fired."

Not only did I not get fired, *CQ* chose to give me a promotion. I was now a staff writer, not a mere researcher-writer.

When Mary moved out in April to head to Pretoria, Chuck moved in. He signed on to domestic duties, such as taking Hugo, the parrot, to the vet and trying to teach him to say hello. We bought plastic plates. No more paper ones. Tomorrow was years away, we thought.

✺

Tomorrow came on May 10 in the form of a purge. *CQ*'s budget was tighter than we knew, and the managers had decided that Chuck and Tom would be sent to Florida for a year to report for the *St. Petersburg Times*. It was a humane decision. They would have further training at a nationally respected daily paper. In retrospect, a year doesn't seem that long. *CQ* did end up keeping its promise to Tom; it became moot for Chuck.

One of Char's favorite sayings was, "You must hold those you love with an open hand," meaning people were going to do whatever they were going to do, and you had little control. It's a lesson all parents have to learn. If you think about it, though, holding with an open hand is still holding, and even a mother of adult children sometimes wishes she could clap the other hand down and embrace the loved one who is about to do something foolish and take care of the problem for them.

Another of Char's favorites was from *Hello Dolly:* "I've always been a woman who arranges things for the pleasure and the profit it derives. I've always been a woman who arranges things—like furniture and daffodils and lives." She knew perfectly well that the song applied to her.

"Maybe Chuck could get a job in Columbus working for the gubernatorial campaign," Char said over the phone as I vented my anger and frustration at losing him so fast. "I could look into it. You could volunteer. That way you could stay together."

I could move back to Columbus, have the excitement of a political campaign, and continue a relationship with a delightful guy.

I'd already brought Chuck to Columbus for a weekend in May, so he knew what it was like. I played Broadway shows for him on my record player and took him shopping at the store. Char took him to buy bagels at Block's on Broad Street. We went to Hoo-hoo and Pop-pop's house and played catch on their lawn, showing them how Frank Howard of the Washington Senators caught a ball in center field.

Chuck and I were both at vulnerable points. We wanted to find happiness, which we were under the illusion was normal. Chuck visited Columbus to interview for the campaign. He was familiar with central Ohio from his years at school in Delaware. He was delighted with both Dick, whom he saw as a Yankee gentleman, and Char, who was fun and voluble.

He also found she had interesting quirks—like her method for summoning the dog, a willful, intact male airedale named Buck.

Ethel, in her tinny little voice, would report Buck missing.

"Not again," Char would say, getting up from her lunch. Then she'd stop in the front hall, open a drawer, and pull out a gun. Chuck was dismayed the first time he observed this novel approach but realized that at least it was a starter pistol, not a live weapon. She would walk out the front door and stand on the stoop.

Crack went the pistol, loud enough to make them jump at Saint Alban's Church around the corner on Drexel Avenue. A moment passed, and Buck came running from whatever had attracted him this time.

Why Buck responded to Char's starter pistol, I don't know. I guess we all were in the habit of coming when she called.

Chuck first told *CQ* he would take the offer to relocate. But he decided to follow up on the Columbus possibility, with the idea that experience on a campaign could be good for him in the long run as a journalist. Char made the initial contact. Chuck went to Columbus for an interview, staying with Char and Dick. Jim Friedman, the deputy campaign manager, was impressed with Chuck's credentials and skills. The campaign offered him a job in the press department.

"*Awk!*" said the voice on the phone. Chuck had accepted the job and was calling to tell me.

As Ethel served lunch on the screen porch that Saturday, Chuck discussed the job and his plans with Char and Dick. The food was accompanied by a bottle of Lynch-Bages, a second-growth Bordeaux that Char and Dick enjoyed referring to as "lunch bags."

"Why bother with an apartment for only a few months?" Char said. "You can stay in Bobby's room." It had been vacant since Mark and Ann moved out. They took a look at the room, and Chuck remarked that the bathroom would not work as a darkroom. Char took him over to Hoo-hoo and Pop-pop's house, where they found a secluded nook deep in the basement.

My boyfriend would be living with my parents. Char was a woman who arranged things.

In the darkroom in Hoo-hoo and Pop-pop's basement, Chuck developed the photograph of Hugo. It was a mechanical, tedious process with many steps and quite a bit of angst to get it right, starting with making the room lighttight. We worked under a dim red bulb, an enlarger projecting the image onto photographic paper. It took several tries because the image of Hugo was dark and the light behind him flat white. Chuck dodged his fist between the enlarger and the paper to balance out the light. We put the exposed paper into a tray with developer and sloshed it around gently until the image miraculously appeared—a parrot looking remarkably large on an eleven-by-fourteen-inch sheet of paper, his mouth slightly open and a large black tongue sticking out sideways, his black eye ringed with white. We slipped the photograph into a bath to stop the chemical process and then into the hypo to fix the image permanently. Done right, prints like that don't yellow or fade for a very long time. The ones Chuck and I made in those long-ago days look the same today as they did then.

I had left my job before that enduring darkroom work. I knew it was for good, though the editors said they could make it a leave of absence and, even if I did not do that, would be glad to have me back. Chuck and I drove to Ohio on June 11, 1970, in the Red Baron. Soon after we crossed the Ohio border, we paused at a rest stop and Chuck made his first policy decision.

"Ohio has lousy rest areas," he said, emerging from the men's room. "North Carolina's are way, way better. First thing when we win is improve Ohio's restrooms."

In mid-August, Chuck and I went to Wilmington so he could introduce me to his maiden aunts. That's what he called the three of them, even though the oldest, Aunt Kate, had been married. Cahway (Caroline) was the middle aunt. Shishi (Virginia) was the youngest at seventy-three. All doted on Chuck and his younger brother, Saville, who was not there at the time but came to visit in Columbus later that summer. Shishi had been a revered teacher before she retired. She had a schoolmarmish authority.

Chuck took me crabbing in the low, brackish waters near Carolina Beach. It was not a high-tech endeavor. We cut a couple of lengths of kitchen string to which we attached fish heads. We had a long-handled net.

"You have to stay still," said Chuck as we stood in cool water with our jeans rolled up over our knees. The sand was smooth under my bare feet, and the hot sun beat down. Somewhere in the distance, a shrimp boat or pleasure craft puttered. A shadow scuttled sideways on the sandy bottom, headed toward Chuck's feet.

"Get the net, get the net, get the net," he whispered. A crab was nibbling the bait. My job was to slip the net stealthily into the water and under the crab without alarming his nearby friends. I scooped and scored a flat, dish-shaped lump with flailing claws.

"Dump it in the bucket."

I had to shake hard to get the thing to let go of the netting. One crab. Soon we had a dozen and took them to the maiden aunts to cook up.

When the maiden aunts were all presumably asleep, Chuck came into my bedroom as quietly as he could, worried that one might hear him. They expected him to be a southern gentleman, which he was. But the family standards were somewhat dated, even for the time. When Chuck had taken to wearing boxer shorts to bed instead of pajamas, for example, his mother told him he was becoming a savage.

Gilligan's campaign for the Senate in 1968 had been the labor of idealistic newbies. We had less money than hope. In 1970 the campaign for governor was bigger, slicker, and, while not quite cocky, had an undercurrent of self-confidence. The opponent, state auditor Roger Cloud, was implicated in what the *Columbus Dispatch* called "the Statehouse loan scandal." I don't recall what the foofaraw was about, only that it meant the big money was betting on a Democratic win.

Another advantage was that Cloud had a vaporous personality. "To know Roger Cloud is to forget Roger Cloud," his own press secretary was caught saying.

By 1970, opposition to the Vietnam War was widespread, even in Ohio. Gilligan now represented the majority on the issue. President Richard Nixon announced on April 30 that the United States was going to invade Cambodia. National Guard troops, responding to protests at Kent State University in northern Ohio, shot into a crowd and killed four students on May 4.[1] Gilligan gave a stirring speech. Even Americans who continued to tolerate fighting in Vietnam reacted with anger to expanding the war to Cambodia and horror at the mayhem on a college campus.

Once again the campaign was housed in the Lincoln-Leveque Tower. Instead of a newsroom-like layout, the offices had walls, which was a good thing because the campaign had at least twice as many staff members. We had a miraculous machine that could send printed copy to the Cincinnati or Cleveland campaign headquarters. An early version of a facsimile, or fax, machine, it weighed about fifty pounds. You fed in a press release, and a hard copy showed up in the other city. We had the money for color TV ads.

Jack Davis, the scheduler, worked next door to me and Chuck. Jack was a native of Columbus, our age, and newly graduated from Franklin University. His job was to make sure the candidate was constantly on the road, harvesting votes and money at high-octane events. Sheets of yellow legal paper covered one entire wall of his office, each sheet representing a day to be filled with appearances by the candidate. I didn't see much of—or *in*—this Jack Davis fellow, though he did stop in the press office every once in a while with some harebrained plan.

"I think two weeks from Tuesday," Jack would say, "I can get the candidate to a breakfast meeting in Akron, then down to Dayton for a rally, then to Toledo, over to Canton, to a dinner in Columbus, and to a meeting in Athens, where he can stay overnight."

The idea of hitting every corner of the state every day kept Gilligan irritated with Jack. Nor did it sit well with Gilligan's traveling companion, staff member John Daley, who complained that he had to watch out not to get his hand bitten off if he held out the orange juice for Gilligan too early in the morning. It was Jack's job, however, to scare up opportunities and offer them to the candidate.

I reported to the press secretary, Bob Tenenbaum, a smart, thoughtful man who was good at his job. Unfortunately, Chuck's boss horned in on Chuck's work and belittled it. Many campaigns have to deal with fervent amateurs who believe that without their early activism, the candidate would never be running for office. Chuck's boss was tough and hardworking, and she presumably did not think much of the staff brought in by moneyed backers. She had accumulated talking points during the primary, and Chuck's major job was to use them to write position papers.

At the end of the workday, as we hiked back to the Red Baron, parked about half a mile away in the Vets' Memorial lot, Chuck would turn his righteous anger, usually aimed at ruthless, money-grubbing, calculating lobbyists or incompetent, spineless, venal politicians, onto his low-level supervisor, who carried a grudge because she thought the whole gubernatorial campaign really belonged to her.

"Why can't you face her down?" I asked, irritated at having to hear the same thing over and over. But confrontation wasn't in him.

Chuck was also full of righteous indignation at the campaign itself. The innards of politics were, as he expected, full of egos and backbiting. It was indeed good experience, he was finding, but only strengthened his commitment to the high ground of journalism. I was more tolerant. Politics is often irrational and circuitous, I thought, but is the only avenue for positive policy change. Chuck's constant ranting was beginning to wear me down. I wasn't getting enough time by myself. We were both starting to think that our relationship might not be forever.

Something else came between us: an aquarium. My cousin John Sirak, at the age of eight, had a large collection of freshwater fish. He persuaded Chuck to try them as pets, and soon a noisy tank with neon tetras, swordtails, and angelfish appeared in Bobby's bedroom. The aquarium motor and filter puttered and burbled all night, and the room smelled a little rank. I started to sleep in my own bedroom. Chuck and I began a new riff of banter—this on which were smarter, fish or birds. Unlike before, a frisson of tension emerged in the back-and-forth. I started to turn silent instead of responding to teasing observations, such as how fish could blow bubbles and birds could not.

"Have we won yet?" a Gilligan staff member asked on November 2, the day before the election. It seemed over except for tallying up the votes. So we hoped.

In Cincinnati on election night, I headed up the adding machine, as in 1968. The numbers came in fast and positive. The election was over at seven forty-five. Cloud conceded. The governor-elect took the stage, and I wiggled my way up along with other staff. A rolling sea of happy people jammed the ballroom. Gilligan gave his acceptance speech. Mark, near me, looked tense. I soon understood why. As Gilligan finished, the crowd stormed the stage. We didn't have bodyguards or security of any kind. An advance man, sweat standing out on his brow, told me to get people back so they could make an aisle for the candidate to leave. It was a desperate situation if someone was asking me to help.

More vote tallying remained to be done. I worked until five in the morning, back and forth on the phone with a college student in Columbus, who was giving me voting counts to turn into percentages on the adding machines.

"Tell Chris to forget the goddamned bellwether counties and get me Summit and Cuyahoga," said Mark.

"Mark says to forget the bellwether counties and concentrate—"

"I said forget the *goddamned* bellwether counties."

➘

After the campaign, Chuck developed the pictures he took of the campaign staff. All of them were excellent. The snap of the two of us was disappointing. Whoever took it was less skilled than Chuck.

We visited New York, staying at the Freunds' apartment. We arrived at one o'clock in the morning to be greeted by Charm, wearing a black dress and carrying a glass of brandy. Chuck shot a load of pictures of Rockefeller Center and the Empire State Building. "Record shots," he said, to show where he'd been, as opposed to artistic effort. We rode bikes through Central Park, though we didn't have time for me to show him my rock.

We went to Washington and *CQ*, where the editors assured me once again that I could have my old job back if I wanted it. Chuck followed up a job lead at the *Dayton Daily News*, and when he arrived, four wonderful words greeted him: "When can you start?"

"After I go to Europe," he told them, and the two of us took off for three weeks to London, Madrid, Toledo, Barcelona, Rome, Florence, and Paris. I kept a photograph of Chuck from that trip in my wallet until 1990, when the wallet was stolen. It showed Chuck feeding a gaggle of pigeons in a square in Florence. The flight of pigeons flocked over and around him. A couple of them sat dimwittedly on his arms. He grinned happily.

I felt as though the trip were a coda, however—the conclusion of a lovely symphony.

"Just let it go. Let it die a natural death," Char said. "He's going to Dayton, and all it will take is time."

Against her good advice, on New Year's Eve, I dumped my anger on Chuck like a ball falling in Times Square, naming his faults one by one. He was uptight, timid, easily hurt, and too easily bossed around. He calmly rebutted my complaints, point by point, showing for one thing that he wasn't so easy to boss around. His calmness was a refutation of my emotional harangue. I couldn't help realizing that I could as easily as he be accused of being uptight, timid, and easily hurt. In addition, I was giving a good demonstration of self-indulgent intolerance.

"Carole Horn said it wouldn't work out because you're too particular," said Chuck, summing me up.

"She told me it wouldn't work out because southern men put their women on a pedestal," I said. "I don't want to be on a pedestal." I meant it—sort of. On the one hand, it was delightful to be worshipped like Guinevere in *Camelot* ("Shall a feud not begin for me? Shall kith not kill their kin for me?"). On the other hand, it was scary since I couldn't live up to it.

I had to stop arguing, there in the dark in Bobby's bedroom. Chuck leaned over to me and into my ear shouted "*Awk!*" as loud as he could. "*Awk!*" I yelled back, bumping my nose into his forehead hard enough that it hurt the next day, the day he was leaving to begin his life as a reporter. I cried because one and a half hours away wasn't far enough and because Chuck was kind and funny and I liked him near me.

The *Daily News* made Chuck a consumer affairs reporter. Every day he would be exposing the sleazy practices of some high-handed business trying to put one over on innocent consumers.

"I wish Vivian weren't so particular," Dick said to Char when I reported Carole's comment. "I like Chuck."

So did I. Just not all day, every day.

13

SIX STEAK KNIVES FROM THE CORNER GAS STATION

It was just me and Hugo. But Chuck had split up with *me*, not with Char and Dick. As 1971 began, he was a regular weekend guest at Melrose. He did the bageling at Block's for brunch on Sundays. We sat together at Gilligan's inauguration. I read books to him. I would like to believe we did not sleep together, having officially broken up. The diary suggests otherwise: "Ethel opened the door on us," I wrote in February.

I visited Chuck in Dayton, bringing the color TV set Char gave him for Christmas. He cooked French toast for breakfast, and I helped him arrange his furniture. He decided to get a Quaker parrot and told me he'd found one "real *cheep.*" Quakers are similar in size to conures like Hugo. The name comes from their gray plumage.

"You have to come with me," he said. "I don't understand why the one at the mall is four dollars less than the one I saw at the pet shop."

We went to inspect the one at the mall. I took a good look. The little guy was getting around quite well, considering.

"Chuck, that bird only has one leg," I said.

He bought the pricier one, and I helped him set up the cage.

I took a job at the Department of Public Welfare. It was an unclassified position, which meant it was a political appointment. My boss was the department director. He and Gilligan had big plans. We scrapped the department budget offered by the Republican administration of former Governor Jim Rhodes and crafted one of our own, adding a load of social services under Medicaid. We worked feverishly over a weekend with pencils, legal pads, scissors, Scotch tape, and a secretary to type so we could meet a legislative deadline.

I was shin deep in the small details that compose big policy change and as happy as if I were crabbing in the shallows of a Carolina inlet. It was meaningful. It felt like the sort of work I could do well. And it was in Columbus.

No greater authority than my gynecologist, a good friend of the family, told Char in August 1971, "I think Vivian's going to marry that little guy from Dayton."

That was two weeks after my first date with Jack Davis, the crazy campaign scheduler who was now working in the state personnel department. Jack and I saw *A Streetcar Named Desire* that night. We did not kiss when he dropped me at the front door. To my surprise, the nonkiss crackled with electricity.

Chuck and I had just spent the weekend together, much of it in highly domestic pursuits. We'd been to the bookstore, the movies, and

Lazarus, where we bought records and material to make a cover for Chuck's birdcage. We had decided to smoke some marijuana and tootled up to the OSU campus to buy head equipment. I felt as though I were getting outfitted for school, except that instead of pens and paper, we purchased a water pipe, incense, an incense burner, and cigarette papers. I already had the glass bong, of course. I almost picked up the only ungummed cigarette papers in the place, but the salesgirl put me wise. I had a hard enough time calling up the manual dexterity to roll the glue-stripped ones.

I got pleasantly stoned. Chuck didn't have the inhaling part down and intellectualized about what was happening to him rather than giving into it.

Chuck and I had dinner Saturday at the Japanese Steak House, where they cooked communal meals on the table and diners always went home with hair smelling of onions. We shared a table with three air force veterans. They said "negative" instead of "no," and one remarked that it would be fun to fly Governor Gilligan over Thule and drop him there. Chuck and I kept quiet.

The weekend was fun, but no bolt of electricity struck like that startling moment in the driveway with Jack.

Jack arrived at Melrose for the first time for dinner on August 23, a Monday. Chuck was at work at the *Daily News*. Char and Dick were out of town, and I had friends over. Jack glided into the long driveway in a Chrysler Imperial as long as a smallish yacht. Buck, the airedale, greeted the car by cheerfully slapping his muddy forepaws on the newly washed white paint. Jack wore a tie and jacket. His shirt, in muted blue and brown stripes, matched the tie. He helped with dinner by flawlessly opening the wine. Ted Celeste, who worked with me at the Welfare Department, did the dishes.[1]

Chuck had given me a three-foot-tall, inflated plastic penguin that emitted a wheezy squeak. That night Jack grabbed it and waved it at Buck, saying "back" and squeezing the penguin. The other guests gathered around to see the show.

"*Twee!*" went the penguin. Buck cringed. Jack laughed. It was the most uninhibited, happiest cackle I'd ever heard.

Jack sat the penguin on the floor. Buck crept up on his forepaws, rear end high in the air. Jack picked up the plastic toy and squeaked it again. Buck leapt backward. Jack laughed again. We all did.

When the other guests left, I suggested that Jack accompany me while I walked Buck. I pulled the leash out of a drawer in the front hall, where the dog was lying down recovering from the penguin incident. Buck bounded to his feet in anticipation. Dogs just don't know when to hold a grudge. The three of us headed down the dark driveway. The locusts were singing their late summer song, and the evening was cooling off.

"How's Chuck's bird doing?" he asked.

"All right."

He'd hoisted a crimson flag. Clearly he was interested in what was going on between Chuck and me. I didn't follow up. Jack and I walked up the long driveway back to the house. I unhooked the dog's leash. Jack said good night— no kiss.

Jack was grieving that summer. His mother had died of cancer a year before, during Gilligan's campaign for governor. He told me he was thinking a lot about death. I sympathized. My family was grieving too, because Hoo-hoo had died in July. We would be grieving again in another month when Michael Hoffman, Jean Lazarus Hoffman's youngest child, burned to death in a house fire in Woodstock, Vermont. His parents were in Bogota, where Junie was helping to found a new law school. Char and Dick drove to Vermont, identified the body, and signed the cremation papers while Jean and Junie made their way back from South America. The black-and-white photograph of Hoo-hoo and Pop-pop, their children, and their grandchildren, taken the year I was thirteen, now had two ghosts.

Jack had adored his mother, Mary, who I imagined was meek and kind—a quiet, accepting type like Jack's older sister, Donna. She was no boat rocker, but a traditional *Kinder, Küche, Kirche* type, the church in this case being Lutheran. Mary Davis's father, John Blackwood, had been a watch repairman in Columbus. The family was Orange Irish like my antecedents, the Butlers. Mary took joy in petit point and feeding the family, which included, in addition to Jack and Donna, Jack's older brother, Tom. The meals tended to be repetitious, Jack said. They sounded like my grandmother Belle's meals. Sweet potatoes arrived on the plate so often that in adulthood Jack would not touch one.

Labor Day weekend was approaching. Several weeks before, Chuck had invited me on a trip from Cincinnati to Chicago promoting the Turbotrain. Amtrak was rolling out the train with great fanfare, and news reporters were invited. I would pretend to be a *Daily News* reporter. It was definitely Chuck's kind of thing. I agreed and was looking forward to it.

Babsie answered the phone the Tuesday before. "Chuck is on the line," she said.

It was Jack, calling to ask me out for Wednesday night, before the Turbotrain expedition.

"They're Tweedledum and Tweedledee," said Donnie.

Jack and Chuck did not look much alike to me. After all, I could tell them apart. Of course, a mother of identical twins knows which is which too. They were similar in their glasses, height, complexion, and mesomorphic body types. They both had longish, blondish hair at the time.

There I was on Wednesday, September 1, having spent the previous weekend with Chuck and planning a long weekend with him in Chicago for the next one, trying to persuade Jack to come with our friends Alan and Karen Farkas to the state fair the next night. We sat in his car with the lights off in the Melrose driveway and talked for an hour.

I let him know my weekend plans with Chuck. In the dim light, I could see him blush.

"It's been set up for a while," I tried to explain.

"I have a meeting tomorrow night," he said. "And I'm sick of the fair." He had been advancing events for the governor, including long days at the fair.

Fairs were not one of Gilligan's favorite things. "I shear taxpayers, not sheep," became one of Gilligan's most quoted sayings, a foolish, extemporaneous remark delivered at the sheep exhibit one summer. His most lasting accomplishment would be the institution of an income tax in Ohio. It was badly needed to improve numerous government services, including mental health, prisons, and education. Unfortunately, the income tax was the major reason he would not be elected for a second term.

Jack was sick of advancing, period. A week earlier he'd had to go with the governor on a helicopter to the Lake County Democratic Picnic. The ride was long, bumpy, and loud.

"It lasted about three weeks," he said, referring to the helicopter trip, from which he returned with a strong need for aspirin and a fondness for helicopters that rivaled his love of sweet potatoes. Most of his work was by car. He only had to drive a route once to know it and be able to pass it on to the governor's assistants.

I told Jack it was over with Chuck. We were friends, and Char and Dick enjoyed his company. But there were no long-term plans and would not be. He listened quietly.

He suddenly reached across the front seat and pressed his lips to mine. There it was.

After a while, he pulled back.

"I've come to a revolutionary decision," he said.

"Which is?"

"I'll go to the fair with you and the Farkases."

Jack negotiated the route to the fair with liquid skill. He drove with the same assurance as my father. The fair's parking lots were chock-full, and it was cool to slide the Imperial into a spot reserved for the governor's staff. The four of us saw a horse show, chickens, swine, and cows. We checked in on the exhibit by the Department of Natural Resources. Alan was hoping for a top job at the Environmental Protection Agency the governor was setting up, which would pull responsibilities from the DNR and the Health Department. If that did not work out, he and Karen would probably leave Columbus. It did work out. Alan became associate director for policy development when the agency started up in 1972, and I went to work for him as a policy analyst, one of the best jobs of my life. Karen became personal assistant to Katie Gilligan, the governor's wife, managing her schedule and the operations of the governor's mansion.

"We have to go on the roller coaster," said Jack.

During the ride, I gritted my teeth to fight off panic. Karen screamed. Alan stayed silent. Jack laughed maniacally.

"Do you want to go again?" he asked, as I shakily tottered out of the coaster car.

Next, Jack persuaded us onto the "skydiver," a Ferris wheel with open cabins that spin every which way, and the only thing holding you in is a single restraining bar.

I went home queasy but impressed at Jack's fearlessness.

I daydreamed about Jack during the trip to Chicago with Chuck. When I came back, the courtship was on. Some of it, in fact, took place on a court. In the long, crisp evenings of September, we and the Farkases slapped away at mixed doubles on the Siraks' tennis court off Drexel Avenue, or sometimes on Chuck and Frannie Lazarus's court on North Columbia. Jack was a beginner, so I covered a good deal of the court for him. The two of us usually lost to Karen and Alan.

Karen and Alan had moved to Columbus so Alan could work on the Gilligan campaign as an advance man. He knew Jack from that intense, rewarding venture. Karen started work at the Welfare Department at the same time I did. They were East Coast, Ivy League people living in a small, lonely apartment off East Main Street. It helped them that Babs and Howard took them under their wings and often had the Farkases housesit. Karen and

Alan didn't at all mind taking up residence in a mansion filled with some of civilization's finest late-nineteenth-century and early-twentieth-century paintings. The Farkases were not particular friends of Chuck's, which was good. The four of us glommed onto each other for after-work frivolity.

Possibly as part of an effort to recover from his mother's death, Jack was trying new things all at once. He was learning tennis, practicing chess, studying French with a tutor in German Village, and reading deeply in Japanese history.

"The self-improvement award of 1971 goes to Jack Davis," said Karen.

Karen and Alan routinely invited us over to eat dinner and smoke dope, Alan with an enthusiastic joie de vivre. One night we had onion soup; underbaked, chewy French bread with honey; quite a bit of wine; and three reefers.

Alan took a huge pull on a cigarette and held the smoke deep in his lungs, his chest visibly, demonstratively expanded, then let go through nostrils and mouth.

'Wow!" said Alan. "This is great stuff." He passed the joint to the next person, adding a detailed analysis of how he felt, from the airy euphoria in his head to the numbness in his toes. "Sergeant Pepper's Lonely Hearts Club Band" spun from the record player. We were all in tune.

Like Chuck, Jack was not good at inhaling. I smoked a couple of tobacco cigarettes a day at that time, so I picked up on the new drug easily. People have always laughed at President Bill Clinton's claim that he smoked marijuana but did not inhale. But I think he may be telling the truth. Plenty of people went along for the ride but had throats and lungs that were less than flameproof.

Karen and Alan fell asleep on their couch, and Jack and I quietly departed.

"Boy, Alan was really stoned," I remarked sanctimoniously as Jack drove me home. "I wasn't. I wasn't really very high."

"Vivian," said Jack, "you spilled honey all over yourself and your plate, and you spilled wine on their tablecloth. Red wine."

The movie *A New Leaf* came out in 1971, but I don't think either Jack or I had seen it when he made that remark. When we did, Jack said it was about us. In the movie, Walter Matthau is a playboy who has run through his inheritance. He thinks of suicide but decides instead to marry money. Elaine May plays the heiress, a shy, klutzy academic—a botanist—whom Matthau first sees spilling her coffee into a saucer and juggling saucer, coffee, and cup in several minutes of hysterically funny ineptitude. Matthau marries May with the idea of a quick murder, but when his new wife falls into a river trying to reach a rare plant, he can't help but save her, and he commits himself to a life of trying to keep her tidy and safe.

Maybe I should have taken umbrage at the comparison. I never have minded. There was something to it.

We advanced from necking in the white car in the driveway to petting on a beat-up couch in a room in Melrose's basement where Donnie and Babsie had painted a wall in psychedelic colors and spiders roamed freely. I felt uncomfortable taking Jack into the house and certainly could not hang out in Bobby's room, which still seemed to belong to Chuck. I wasn't too worried about Char and Dick; it was mainly Ethel. She saw a threat to her "Chuckie" and would not approve of my behavior.

I introduced Jack to Hugo. They didn't hit it off.

"You know, it's hard kissing you with the bird on your shoulder," said Jack. "I don't think he likes me."

That's probably because Hugo was threatening to bite him.

"Chuck's on the phone," Leroy said one day.

It was Jack. He'd figured out a way for us to be together unimpeded: his father was gone on weekends. I started going the block and a half around the corner to Dawson Avenue to spend Saturday nights with Jack. It was as if I were having an affair.

Newton Davis, Jack's father, owned the Miller-Davis Electric Company on North Fourth Street in downtown Columbus. Miller was born "Mueller" but changed his last name to avoid sounding German in World War II. No Miller remained by the time I met Jack except for the office cat, named to keep up tradition. The war had been good for business. Columbus had a Defense Department construction center, and the company sold it electrical services. The Davis side of Jack's family had emigrated from Wales and settled in Oak Hill, Ohio, where they became farmers and strip miners of coal.

Newt was a drinking man. Jack thought he'd been a bootlegger during Prohibition, the country's great failure of an experiment in universal temperance. Newt and a friend bought a bar on the west side of Columbus as a sideline, with the idea that they could get free liquor. Railroad workers would come into the bar before work to get a shot and a beer. They'd come back after work for a shot and a beer. Or two.

Drinking unleashed Newt's temper. His wife, being handy, was often the target.

"I tried to get in between once when he was hitting her," said Jack. "I was a kid. I couldn't help."

My whole being resonated with his story. He'd had an experience that I understood too well. He seemed, despite that, exquisitely normal. He wasn't too special for me.

"You're the most affectionate person I've ever met," Jack told me.

He didn't say I was the shyest, the most self-centered, or the most particular. He said I was the most affectionate. I wasn't putting on a false face with him. I was already relatively open and easy with him, and it felt good. We seemed to be equals in important ways. I wanted to give him kindness and respect. Jack was making a monumental observation. I was ready to cross one bridge to maturity.

"You realize that Jack is never going to leave Columbus," said Alan. He thought that would be a negative.

My new boyfriend had graduated from Bexley High School in 1965, the same year as Bob Greene, a reporter and writer who documented the class in several books, including *Be True to Your School.*[2] Greene's parents, Bob and Phyllis, were frequent dinner guests at Melrose. Phyllis was Chuck Lazarus's stepsister. Char and Phyllis were close in age and had both gone to Columbus School for Girls and to Wellesley.

Jack knew Bexley as I knew Broadway lyrics. Not only could he give the names of current occupants, he also knew who had lived in the houses before them. It was and is a Bexley thing. The current residents are used to having their homes referred to as "the old Jeffrey house," or whoever had lived there. It is unclear how many centuries it takes before the house is thought of as yours.

Jack had enrolled at Ohio State but flunked out after one quarter and finished college with a major in accounting at Franklin University in Columbus. He did better than his parents or siblings, none of whom received college degrees.

He was miserable at spelling and mangled multisyllabic words, yet handled numbers and steering wheels brilliantly. He talked authoritatively about finance, politics, and history. I'd never met anyone like Jack before. The verbal stumbling was appealing, restful, in fact. It made me feel smart. Jack wanted a career in finance and was sure he would be rich. If Chuck's highest motivation was truth, Jack's was power, especially as represented by money.

My highest motive, as it turns out, is what is often called "speaking truth to power." I love treating public policy as a science, where you try to figure out what action is likely to be effective by using numbers, facts, and models. Usable knowledge for policy makers is my game. I'm not a leader but believe there is a place in the world for excellent followers. Not blind ones, of course, but people who can raise the level of policy argument. Unfortunately, politicians are not always receptive to policy that makes scientific connections between cause and effect.

"He's the youngest fifty-year-old I know," said older friends of Jack's. Jack was twenty-four, nine months younger than me. It seemed to mean I could rely on him. I would find out later that his maturity, like any I myself was trying to demonstrate, was in part a put-on built on shaky ground. Growing toward greater wisdom would be a mutual endeavor.

❧

Jack started coming to Melrose regularly for dinner, arriving in the white "boat" and wearing a tan cashmere coat. Having him there made me nervous. It made him nervous; you could tell because he would sit in the library before dinner and play with the buttons on the telephone.

One night, artichokes were the first course, and as Jack started bravely peeling off leaves, Dick said sharply, "Vivian, explain to Jack about artichokes." He guessed accurately that Jack had never eaten one before and was on course to pierce the soft lining of his throat with choke needles.

Another night, Jack sat next to Jean Hoffman, my aunt. She was in town to be with family as she dealt with Michael's death. Junie was still in Bogota.

"My great-uncle was president of Peru," Jack remarked.

Afterward, we went to the basement to play Ping-Pong. I held the paddle in my left hand and still beat him every game but politely did not let on that I was applying a handicap.

"Why did you say that to Jean about an uncle being president of Peru?" I asked.

"You're supposed to make small talk with your dinner partner."

"That wasn't small talk. That was weird." I had seen Jean suppressing laughter, and though that was good for her, I didn't want it at the expense of my new guy. "You're supposed to lead into it, like, 'I have an interesting story about Peru,' or something. Anyway, what did you mean?"

"I've waited for years to get that into a conversation."

"What?"

He explained that an aunt, his mother's sister, fell in love with a Peruvian guy at OSU whose last name was Leguia. They married. The man's father was the head of the secret service in Peru, and his uncle was president, Jack said.

Indeed, an Augusto Leguia served as president of Peru. It was one of those "illegitimate son of the illegitimate nephew of Napoleon"[3] relationships the Gershwins wrote about and that pepper so many family histories.

᳁

Gas stations were going through a period when they competed for customers by giving out gifts when you filled up. At Dorsey and Reynolds, at the corner of Parkview and Main Street, the bonus was steak knives with thin serrated blades and flimsy wooden handles. I got one, then two. They were on the light side, but one didn't expect the highest quality for free. I had absolutely no use for a set of knives, nor for any household item.

"Vivian's making a trousseau," said Dick.

"I'm snowed by Jack, but I feel closer to Chuck," I wrote. It's not surprising I felt closer to Chuck. I'd known him a good deal longer. I was framing the problem as a choice between Chuck and Jack. Today I know that's not what was happening. Chuck and I were best suited as a brother and sister type of pair. Chuck, in fact, did not especially want to get married, given his first experience with tying the knot. Looking back, I see how great the divide is between the easy come-and-go of dating and the formal vows of marriage.

Jack and I talked without using that heavily charged word. "Relationship" was the closest we could get. I wished he were going out of town for a bit so I could write him a letter. I would be able to express myself better on paper. Our intimacy had reached the prone, bedroom level, but we were scared of giving in completely, like two fish flailing against unrelenting hooks.

Leaves drifted onto the Sirak tennis court a few at a time, then in blowing spurts. Night was coming early. Tennis was over. Jack tried to teach me chess, but I was as good at chess as he was at Ping-Pong. We cheered at a couple of OSU football games and gamboled with the Farkases.

We probably could have used a year or two of living together. Unlike these days, that was not an option, at least not for couples wedded to tradition. Donnie Gilligan, the governor's older son, moved to German Village with a girlfriend he later married. His mother, Katie, was appalled and worried that the press would find out about the situation and headline it.

A night came when I couldn't fight Jack anymore.

We went to a movie, then to the International House of Pancakes. We ordered short stacks. I drizzled mine with melted butter and syrup, spilling on my blouse as we discussed the film, a depressing one.

"I really like musicals," I said. "They're never sad."

"I worked on a play," he said. "Junior year. The lighting. It was..." He twisted his head sideways as he tried to remember the name of the show. "... Annie Oakley."

"*Annie Get Your Gun*," I corrected him. Love, the kind where there is no going back, claimed me that evening.

I had to tell Chuck. Char had advised me not to, but that was when things were fluid, a whole two months earlier. It was time. Chuck and I went to Washington together to see our friends. I resolved to break the news on the plane home to Columbus. In the waiting area at National Airport, he told me he'd found out that a mutual *CQ* friend was having an affair with a *CQ* editor. She had visited Chuck in Dayton earlier in the summer and never said a word about it.

"Miss Sincerity," he said sarcastically. Sitting in a plastic bucket seat in the airport lounge, I started to feel airsick.

Aloft, Chuck read aloud from the day's *Washington Post.* An article dealt with the ridiculous fad of drawing insipid happy faces. It was funny, but I couldn't laugh. The feminist Gloria Steinem was visiting Richmond, where Chuck's parents lived. Was I a feminist or a conventional, soap-opera-watching cheater? Before he could get from the style section to the news, I took a deep breath and, feeling as if I were snapping on a parachute to jump out of the plane and wishing I could simply jump out of the plane with or without a parachute, said, "Remember how we agreed we could date other people?"

"Who?" he asked. When I revealed the name, he said, "That's incredible. I've known for a long time we aren't really compatible, but I thought for right now we were doing fine."

He told me that when he'd visited Wilmington over the summer, a former girlfriend was ardently affectionate as she told him about her new boyfriend.

"It isn't serial monogamy this country is headed to," he declaimed. "It's multiple monogamy."

He was drafting an editorial. The worst was over.

I came home from Jack's house on a Sunday morning the next weekend to find Char had invited Chuck to brunch, and Ethel was making eggs Benedict. Char said it was a special treat because she'd fed him meatloaf the last time he was at Melrose. We all knew it wasn't about the meatloaf.

✺

"What I want to know is, if you marry Jack, where are you going to eat?" asked Char.

I had an answer. Jack had worked in his father's drugstore, a sideline to the electric company, at one time doing short-order cooking. Julia Child was bringing French cooking to the United States via TV shows and fat cookbooks. Cooking was on Jack's self-improvement list. And mine. We would make gorgeous meals together in our own place, an apartment first, probably, and then later our own house. We would live neither too far nor too close to Char and Dick and Jack's father. We would start our own family, though I had far less of an understanding of parenthood than cooking. I had whole course loads to learn, and I wanted to. Jack and I were both raw recruits to adulthood. My parents probably saw our obvious naïveté as a drawback. But it was something we had in common. We were at similar starting points.

As it turned out, everyone made good decisions. Two years later Chuck met Joanne, a calm, organized person. They moved to Wilmington, where he took charge of the editorial page of the *Wilmington Morning Star.*

Joanne says, "If you and Chuck had married, your lives would have been frantic and silly." Chuck and I have similar temperaments.

Chuck says, "Crash, when two people get married, one of them should be able to balance a checkbook." Jack can balance a checkbook. Marriage isn't about "anything you can do, I can do better."

Chuck and Joanne have been together for thirty-five years as of 2014. Jack and I have been married forty-two years, almost as long as my brother Bobby and his wife Linda. Char and Dick stayed together and had celebrated their forty-fourth anniversary when they both died in 2003. The only divorce, if you can call it that, was eventually between Char and me when I started raising my family and had to assert my right to make mistakes. Eventually we rebuilt our deep connection.

By the end of 1971, I was on the road to having everything I'd wished for. For most of my career after Gilligan's four years in office, I worked at a public policy research institute at Ohio State. It gave me a career with ever-changing policy challenges. The job included travel throughout the country, with the benefit of always coming home to my man and my family in Columbus.

I'm not saying a magic wand was waved and life turned into Camelot. I wasn't cured of my failings. Over time I found ways to declare a truce with them. It was Jack who ended up getting MS, and it was not mild numbness but primary progressive MS that took away his balance and his ability to move his legs, then abruptly retreated, leaving him in a wheelchair by the time he was fifty-five. Bobby and Linda's daughter, Hattie, an only child born that crazy fall of 1971, also developed MS. It was strange, considering my diagnosis had been wrong.

All I'm saying is that some things worked out and some didn't. After three children, two shrinks, family illness, the death of many relatives and friends, and several episodes of misplaced hubris (Jack's fault as well as mine), I know what Leroy Hawkins meant when he said you do the best you can with the tools you got. That's exactly what I would want on my tombstone, grammar included. That's all a body can do.

As for Hugo, a serious misidentification was eventually revealed. Good birdwatchers we were not. When I was pregnant with Wit, Hugo laid eggs. Three of them appeared in his seed dish. Hugo was a she and apparently having a sympathetic pregnancy of the avian kind.

⊷

"I'm packed and ready for the honeymoon," I wrote in the diary in November 1971 as I prepared to go to New York with Jack. I had four steak knives, with more trips to the gas station and more steak knives expected.

Another item was still missing: the marriage proposal.

We checked into room 316 at the Plaza on Friday, November 19. On Saturday we had a lunch at La Côte Basque that began at two o'clock. We started with Dubonnet, then ordered artichokes for an appetizer, which Jack dealt with expertly. The main course was *aiguillette de boeuf.* We finished the meal with a dark-chocolate crumb cake. We slowly sipped *café filtre* amid the deep-blue, green, and white *trompe l'oeils* murals of scenes along the Mediterranean coast. When we staggered back to the hotel at close to four o'clock in the waning afternoon, we were certain in our hearts that our lives would be an unending continuum of oysters and profiteroles.

I'd always wondered what couples see in a literal roll in the hay. It would be prickly and probably damp and cold. Hay stalks would get in your mouth. Lumps of hay would give way at bad moments. It turns out that when you've lost yourself to someone, found yourself with him, or whichever, it doesn't matter whether you're on pressed sheets at the Plaza or in a field with cows standing around.

"I want you to be my wife," Jack blurted as he was getting dressed. Then he added, "Now I've done it." He looked up at the ceiling and waved his hands vaguely. "Nothing striking me down so far." He looked at me. His eyes were open as wide as they could go. "I meant to wait until after the new year."

Carole Horn was right when she told Chuck that I was particular. A spur-of-the-moment proposal in a hotel room didn't come up to snuff, even if the hotel was the Plaza. This was not going to be the story I would tell our children.

"I'm not going to answer you until you're stone-cold sober," I said. I needed sobering up myself.

He disappeared into the bathroom, where I could hear retching.

We went to the theater and dinner, though Jack ate little, said little, and looked defeated, or maybe just sick. We did not talk further. I don't know what Jack was thinking, but I was struggling to find reasons not to spend my life with him. It wasn't working.

I kept myself from saying anything the next morning in the Palm Court as I wolfed down my finnan haddie and Jack fiddled with his fork in the yolks on his eggs Benedict.

"I have someplace to take you," I said. We walked into Central Park and followed the path to the zoo. I took him directly to the sea lion pond. It was cold, the kind of damp cold that eats through a winter coat. My courage slipped down into my toes. I couldn't do it. We drifted away and visited the birdhouse, ape house, bear house, and everything-else house. That was it. We were about to exit the zoo.

I took a deep breath. "Can we look at the seals one more time?" I said.

A couple of the animals lay supine on bare rocks, doing their best to soak up the pittance of frail November sun. They did not bark. The water in the moat was still. It was quiet except for distant taxi horns on Fifth Avenue. I put my hand on the soft cashmere that cloaked Jack's arm.

"Will you marry me?" I asked.

14

MY FATHER'S ASHES

My father's ashes squat on a bookshelf in my loft office. An unopened tome, an unplumbed tomb. They have lain like a shadow on the second shelf from the bottom for eleven years. For several of those years, they sat next to the ashes of the family dog, processed by the same funeral home and packaged in the same type of cardboard, lead-lined box. I imagined a series, unpublished and uncatalogued, that my children would inherit.

"Is that one Mom's or Dad's?" they'd ask themselves. "Or that golden retriever who could hold three tennis balls in his mouth?"

Cremation, the quick way to death's dusty denouement, sounds simple. The body is oxidized and vaporized under extreme heat. All done. But what then? We finally buried the dog's ashes in the backyard, near the pond where he used to escape for a swim if he decided to risk the electric fence. Dick didn't say what I was supposed to do with his box. His remains can't go where Char's did. That alternative was closed off long ago.

I imagine places. I imagine other times. I think of less-sticky stuff he left behind besides a few pounds of thick, corporeal residue—stuff that is barely less ephemeral: the raised anchors on the brass buttons from the deep-blue navy uniform; the softly shaped Panama hat; the framed black-and-white photo of a little girl standing beside a 1950s sports car, shot by someone looking down into the square viewfinder of a Rolleiflex camera who advanced the film with a raspy whir and a click from the lever he turned on the camera's side.

☙

Char and Dick detested the American way of death, with unctuous funeral directors trying to sell bereaved families the fanciest caskets. Mortal waste invited economic foolishness. Though they were rich, they were always clear that money should be spent only on things that would be well used, and even then only at a bargain price. Large expenditures on weddings or funerals were anathema. Jack and I had our wedding on a bright May morning on the lawn at Melrose with about thirty people present. Chuck was the photographer. Dorothy, my grandparents' cook, made eggs Benedict. A rabbi officiated, and Pop-pop tipped him fifty dollars.

Char and Dick made clear to us that when they died they wanted the cheapest possible cremation. Judaism has traditionally disapproved of cremation, and the Holocaust with its mass furnaces fueled that sensitivity. But my parents' Jewish backgrounds didn't have anything to do with their choice. Char and Dick believed in neither God nor an afterlife.

Char refused to be confirmed in the Jewish faith as a child and stayed as far away from religious observances as possible. I believe it was partly because large assemblies made her uncomfortable. She even hated graduations. She could never see what was going on up front, and there were always people who recognized her and said hello though she could not tell who they were. It was also that religious observances infuriated her. She happened to be in Columbus when Rabbi Jerome Folkman arrived at Temple Israel in 1947. Hearing he was a terrific speaker, she went with other family members who were regulars for his first Yom Kippur, the most important Jewish holiday—not that she cared.

"What were all these people atoning for, they knew not for what? I loathed the service," she told an interviewer.[1] She found the nondenominational Christian atmosphere of the Columbus School for Girls or Wellesley easier to take. It was undemanding, and the hymns and responsive readings were fun to memorize.

The two of us were never good at Yom Kippur. We once tried to buy bagels at Block's, the Jewish deli on Broad Street, and were amazed to find it closed for the Day of Atonement. When Jack and I were engaged, he politely asked her what Yom Kippur was about, and she told him to look it up in the dictionary.

Even after leaving New York and moving back to Columbus, Char was able to ignore the call to be a full member of the Jewish community. She joined Temple Israel so Dick could play tennis and golf at Winding Hollow, a country club that at the time required temple membership. Jews weren't admitted to other country clubs. She never pretended to be interested in Judaism, except for the emphasis on family. That was of fundamental importance.

Dick wore Judaism like a scar under his white dress shirt. A third-generation American, he had no accent, either Jewish or New York-ish. Nor did his mother or her siblings. They blew right through the immigration experience, as far as I can tell; they must have come here from Lithuania with enough money to head uptown with never a look behind. Dick's father was a member of the New York Society for Ethical Culture, a humanist and civil rights group that does not find belief in a god necessary to live a moral life. But Dick never did anything with the Ethical Culture Society, either. Americans have been considered joiners of clubs, societies, and religious groups since Alexis de Tocqueville's nineteenth-century analysis of our culture, but Dick did not participate. In fact, Americans were pretty much beneath him. The English and the French, however, were admirable. He must have been taught in his generation exactly what I was taught in my cloistered private school, that the United States was a young nation, poor in history—read "inferior" for "young" and "uncivilized" for lacking history. If he had been faced with joining the revolutionaries in 1776, he would have become a Tory and moved to Canada.

Though they were divorced from religion, Char and Dick had a high opinion of Jews. By definition, Jews were smart. Watching College Bowl, a show that pitted teams of undergraduates against each other on general knowledge questions, Char summed up a game where Lehigh slaughtered Northern Michigan:

"Of course they lost. There were no Jews on the team."

George Steinbrenner once chewed out that rara avis, a Jewish baseball player. "What's wrong with you is you're dumb," he told the player. "Dumb, dumb, dumb."

"Of course he's dumb," said Dick. "If he were any brighter, he'd be a dentist."

If Dick had a religion, it wouldn't necessarily help me deal with his ashes. My friend Anand, who is Indian, was supposed to spread his mother's ashes over the Ganges, but it was a long way to go from Bexley, Ohio. He makes do by keeping the ashes in the kitchen and every once in a while sprinkling a few on the rosebushes outside the window.

The impulse has gotten ahead of ritual, and there is no set of givens on how to dispose of cremated remains. I like ritual. We had parties in Char and Dick's backyard soon after both of their deaths. My brother Bobby found some Two-Buck Chuck at Trader Joe's—two-dollar wine that was quite good—and bunches of friends and relatives stopped by for food and drink. Two days before Christmas in that dreadful year of 2003 we had a memorial dinner for Char and Dick at the New Albany Country Club for family only, including the Freunds. We talked about having it at Melrose, but the paintings were gone by that time, and the house too depressing.

⋘⋙

I could scatter Dick's ashes at sea. He kept a white-brimmed hat from his time as a US Navy officer in World War II and had an impressive collection of books about the war. The gold buttons from his uniform are in my vanity, the one that holds the bong. He almost never talked about the navy. Like many men of the "greatest generation," reticence was his style. No bragging. If his military service came up in conversation, Char would jump in with her own summary:

"Dick had a delightful war on the *Arkansas*," she liked to say to a group of dinner guests. "They cruised around the Atlantic and later the Pacific, enjoying the officers' mess. Fancy meals with the best silver. Menus. Uniformed stewards in white gloves to serve them. Nothing ever happened."

"The only thing that ever hit them was the *New York*," she finished up, and the guests would laugh.

Dick would smile wryly because it was a good line.

I don't think it could have been that simple. I suppose the *New York* and the *Arkansas* bumped each other in a docking effort. I don't know. And it is funny. Talking to Yogi Berra, the Yankees catcher and manager, Dick established that Yogi was in the navy on D-Day, June 6, 1944, carting soldiers to shore. Dick's ship was among those providing cover, a much safer position to be in. Somewhere along the line, I started to believe that Dick was a gunnery officer on the *Arkansas* when the invasion began that marked the beginning of the end of World War II. Char's point was, I thought, that it would have been much more dangerous to be infantry. As I remembered the report on the conversation with Yogi Berra, Dick was aboard and participating.

In his last year, I asked Dick what D-Day had been like. He told me how he was aboard the *Arkansas* when she moved out of Belfast, Ireland, on June 3, headed south as part of a fleet that would provide massive gunfire support and bombardment. Three days later, long before dawn, his ship was in position off the coast of Normandy. They fired on the Germans. The Germans in their embattled pillboxes shot back.

It was a great story. Hero stuff even. "Present at D-Day," we said in his obituary in the *Columbus Dispatch* and *New York Times*.

Ten years after Dick died, in the summer of 2013, I read up on the Normandy invasion. My son, Josh, adored his grandfather, modeling his strong, silent personality. Josh read omnivorously about World War II. The *Arkansas* bombed Cherbourg in the days immediately after June 6, Josh told me. The family of Josh's wife, Lorraine van Dommelen, lived in Normandy, not ten kilometers from Omaha Beach. Lorraine's grandmother and great-aunt both were war brides. They married GIs and came to the United States. Josh and Lorraine were expecting a baby, a son, my first grandson. It would be a wonderful story to put together as an heirloom for him.

From Steven Ambrose's book on D-Day, I found out that the *Arkansas* was scheduled for disposal before World War II broke out and was among three battleships considered "expendable."[2] I wondered if Dick knew his ship was expendable. I imagined the high winds and rough seas as he passed Land's End and the Isle of Wight. He would feel excited, even relieved, to have the tension of training for the invasion over and the sharp, defined anxiety of impending action take its place. I thought how in the predawn hours of June 6, he would not be able to see the thousands of ships and landing craft that had snuck up on the French coast. All was quiet. He was eighteen kilometers off Omaha Beach. Like other sailors, Dick would have heard the rattle of the anchor chain running through the hawsepipe so violently loud that he was scared the Germans heard it. D-Day has been called "the longest day," but the hour before combat must have been the longest hour for the men aboard ship. I thought about Dick standing ramrod still, waiting. He was always good at looking composed, his nerves in some other mental compartment.

At 5:50 a.m. the battleships fired their opening salvo, a brutal weight of noise. It's no wonder Dick grew deaf as he aged, I thought. Eardrums aren't meant to be pounded by the coordinated thunder of a modern armada. The force of the guns shoved the *Arkansas* sideways. Dick would have had to move his feet quickly to keep his balance. He had been a goalie on the University of Virginia lacrosse team and was always quick on his feet.

The *Arkansas* may not have taken a hit on D-Day or any other day. It was, however, fired on by cannon from a German shore battery at Longues-sur-Mer shortly after dawn and retaliated with the support of two French cruisers. Perhaps time stood still, and my father held his breath as the swift, dark explosives emerged vengefully in the lightening sky and spent their strength in the gray Atlantic.

In my research on my grandfather, William Butler, fiction had gotten in the way of truth over the years. I didn't expect that to happen with Dick, who was habitually honest about facts and motives, though he skipped out on emotions.

Besides the box of ashes, several other boxes came my way after Dick died. The box of ashes is rubbish of the simplest kind—organic matter crushed and mixed. The boxes of photos, records, and oddments were rubble, like what an archaeologist uses to reconstruct something. I set about rebuilding my father's life, thinking how strange it is how quickly complexity is lost when the central organizing fact of a living human being is gone.

Richard Jules Witkind was only twenty-three years old when his life was interrupted by all-engulfing war. He was barely out of the University of Virginia and signed up with the navy to make it less likely that he would be dead before he reached thirty. Dick was sent to training at the University of Notre Dame, where the squads were organized by last name. Training took three months, and newly minted officers such as Dick were called "ninety-day wonders." Amid the rubble, I found his yearbook, the *Capstan*, for the US Naval Reserve Midshipmen's School, class of January 1943. It includes Dick's photograph, along with those of a whole lot of guys whose last name was Williams. I found a Christmas 1943 menu from the *Arkansas* that bolstered Char's recounting of Dick's war. It began with cream of tomato soup and concluded with cigarettes, cigars, and coffee. The young Maryland turkey and baked spiced Hawaiian ham were accompanied by oyster dressing and giblet stock gravy.

Then the story fell apart. A highly official-looking "officer qualification record jacket" listed Dick's naval duties, typed in a form. It said he was a junior watch and division officer assigned to the number 4 turret on the USS *Arkansas* from January 1943 to March 1944. Beginning in May 1944, he was at a naval base in New Guinea, and he finished out the war on an APC boat based in Puerto Rico. I didn't want to believe it. I found another form filled out in Dick's own hand after the war. "Papua and Australia," he wrote for his whereabouts in 1944 and 1945. As if that wasn't enough, I found a card certifying that my father crossed the equator on board the

SS *Alfred C. True* on April 16, 1944. While the *Arkansas* was getting ready for D-Day, Dick was headed in the opposite direction.

Why did he begin to lie about his war service? It must be like the moth in James Thurber's fable who repeats the story of flying into a flame so often that he begins to believe he did it. Why did Char go along with the story? She was a stickler for truth, although when she turned seventy, she decided that was too old and began to count backward—on her seventy-first birthday, she said she was sixty-nine; On her seventy-second, sixty-eight. After that, she stopped counting down and simply said, "Sixty-eight and holding."

Why did Dick keep documents that showed up his story? Theory one: he forgot about them in his old age. Theory two: he never thought anybody would actually go through his old stuff. Theory three: he wished he had been at D-Day.

Theory four: Dick kept his stuff as a memory of exciting times. Char told an interviewer Dick did not leave service until the summer of 1946. She said, "If it had not been for the fact that by that time Vivian had arrived and he felt that he needed to be more available, I think he might have stayed in."[3]

I caused my father's dream to drown. He accepted that his greater duty was to me. I always resented what seemed like his unnecessary absence, but thinking it over, Dick gave me all the presence he was capable of. I am profoundly grateful.

The sea would be a good place for Dick's ashes even if he didn't attend the biggest shows. He did love the navy. He had the cremated remains of his brother, Lloyd, disposed of at sea for fifty dollars; the bill from the funeral parlor was in the rubble.

I could throw Dick's ashes into the Atlantic Ocean, maybe at Jones Beach, where he took me on summer outings. The trouble is that the wind comes in from the ocean. The ashes could blow back at me the way they do in *The Big Lebowski*. The tears in my eyes would be grit.

❦

If not the sea, how about the air? A newsletter from the 1940 "Who's Who" of Zeta Beta Tau, a Jewish fraternity, introduced Dick Witkind this way:

> This half-baked addled egg is trying his best to become an eagle. Spends his time at the airport spinning and turning which makes it hard to tell if he's plastered or just air-sick. Wonder what will happen when he takes his date for an airplane ride, parks, and tries to get in the back seat? He's the official photographer for house party bedroom scenes. Note: Girls please sit in the dark room and await development.

It's hard to think of my father as a partying college student, though he told me the University of Virginia at the time was not known for studiousness. He disliked it for that reason and always wished he'd gone to a more serious and prestigious school. For most of my life, I thought he didn't go to an Ivy League school for lack of money after his father died. In his last summer, however, he said he was not accepted at Princeton.

"I'm sure if I had been, my mother would have scraped up the money for me to go," he said. He was fessing up about one thing while lying about D-Day.

Dick got a private pilot's license while in college and took a course in flying seaplanes after the war. In Columbus, he took a few lessons on a

Cessna but gave it up. In the rubble, wallet-size copies of his pilot's license arc incxplicably attached by a rusting paperclip to my wallet-size high school graduation photo.

If Scotty, the engineer from *Star Trek,* can be shot into space, why can't I have Dick's remains spread over Ohio Stadium from a Cessna? It's flashy, it's a party, and it's a good way to give death a slap in the face. Char and Dick sat in the Lazarus box in B-deck for many decades before it was remodeled and luxury boxes took over. The men were ranged in the back row in suits and ties and the women in front—"orthodox-style," said Char. Dick would sing "The Star Spangled Banner" in his off-key voice. Phyllis Greene wrote in *It Must Have Been Moonglow* that everyone looked forward to his rendition.[4] It was as much part of the tradition as the drum major with the baton bending backward until the tip of his hat's pompon touches the ground.

Perhaps I could book the Ohio State marching band to play "Anchors Aweigh" while the plane dropped the ashes just before the game started. The last flecks of ash would flutter to the fifty-yard line as the referee tossed the coin. Looking up, the ref would see them, black against the afternoon sun.

Dick would be mortified at such a show. It would be like the guy Chuck told me about who worked in pyrotechnics in Disneyland and took charge of arrangements for a reclusive, shy, ancient aunt. He arranged for his aunt to be shot from a cannon on the Fourth of July. Not what she would have wanted.

Maybe I need to think more about earthly resting places and maybe beyond the United States. Dick loved France, and I have memories of accompanying him and Char on road trips through the provinces, the kid in the family selected as the most able to appreciate it, or perhaps the one with the weakest social life. Other families travel for sightseeing or culture, but with Char and Dick, a trip was planned around food. We would stay, for example, for a few days at the Auberges de Noves, which at the time had three Michelin stars, looking out over the rolling vineyards of the Châteauneuf-du-Papes while nibbling on anchovy-stuffed olives at cocktails, waiting for our palates to be further entertained in the dining room. Driving routes were built around where we could get a one-star lunch, often not as overwhelming but just as satisfying as a three-star dinner.

Char loved to repeat the story about the time Dick "ate the menu" in Le Mans. She meant he ordered *le menu* (several courses for a fixed price) rather than a la carte, but she liked saying he ate it—the whole menu from escargots a la Bourgogne to the Napoleon. A Napoleon in French is *milles-feuilles* (a thousand leaves), but he pronounced it *milles filles*. We would grow quietly hysterical into our napkins when he ordered "a thousand girls."

Dick did all the driving in a rented Peugeot because Char could not see well enough. She handled the maps, bringing them up to her nose to puzzle through, and my major job in the back seat was to keep the chocolate out of the sun.

"Is the chocolate out of the sun?" Dick would ask, my cue to break off a piece of the pistachio or raspberry Lindt bar to hand forward. Dick adored all kinds of chocolate, even Hershey's, which he complained was plebeian but happily consumed nonetheless. At home Char hid the chocolate from him deep in the kitchen flour bin so he would not overindulge and they would not constantly be running out.

If I scatter Dick's ashes in a Châteauneuf-du-Papes vineyard, they might add something to the *terroir*. Some taster years later would ask herself, "How can I describe this wine? It's earthy, but a special kind of earth."

To be safe, I would have to keep the box in my carry-on luggage. I'm not sure how that would go over with the TSA. I'd take out my electronic gear and the little containers of mouthwash and such and put them in a basket with my shoes, leaving the ashes in the roll-on suitcase. I'd watch from past the checkpoint as the security dude ran my bag through, backed it up, and looked into its contents with a gimlet eye. There'd be the French dictionary, eyeshades, a cardigan, and my father's ashes. He would turn the whole bag over to another TSA official while I quaked in my socks.

I don't think I'll risk it.

Here's another idea. Dick liked chocolate so much I could have his ashes wrapped up like bonbons and placed in a tin box. I have a handsome, old-time box left over from last Christmas. "Chocolate butter crunch," it proclaims in mid-twentieth-century lettering—Dick's era. I could take a bonbon out every once in a while and sprinkle the contents on the purple coneflowers in the backyard.

If the idea of a box of chocolates sounds weird, take a look around to see the crazy ideas people are hawking. Ash containers are being made into wind chimes, pendants, "diamonds" compressed from the carbon ash, birdfeeders, and pencils. One person makes about 250 pencils.[5]

I could take the pencils to meetings with me.

"I need something to write with," someone would say, as they often do.

"Have a pencil."

"Interesting. It says RJW 1920–2003."

"Yeah. It's my dad."

Would she use it then? Would she sharpen it later?

Two hundred and fifty pencils out there scratching out shopping lists on the backs of envelopes, or more probably stuck in drawers because nobody knows what to do with them.

Then there are the urns. They come as starfish, dolphins, and a "huggable bear" with a zippered pouch in the back. Urn-a-Matic, made from a vacuum cleaner, has a built-in screen that shows home movies and plays the 1970s pop song "Season in the Sun."

Isn't part of the point of cremation to skip the foolery? I know that's what Dick felt. If you don't want a tombstone, why would you want "a useful pot to put things in," like Piglet and his deflated balloon?

᧞

"When one of us dies, I'm moving to California," Char or Dick would say in their later years, trading the barb with glee.

The line was a joke, but they did rent a house in La Quinta, near Palm Springs, every winter, following a family tradition that began with Char's parents. Dick loved it out there.

Char fell ill to pneumonia in La Quinta the winter of 2002. She had chronic, progressive lung disease from too many years of smoking Parliaments. By then, tubes carrying oxygen into her nostrils went with her always. Pneumonia is extremely serious for someone with pulmonary limitations.

I drove to the Eisenhower hospital from the Palm Springs airport on a Sunday evening. It gets dark early in California in the winter, and the sky was filled with stars as I pulled into the parking lot. Char was in the Bob Hope suite, the biggest room with the best view. As sick as she was, she might as well have been anywhere. When I walked in, giving as casually normal a hello as I could, she looked like a small length of dough in a wide bed. She had no energy, no resistance to gravity. Yet she did respond with a weak hello.

I sat on her bed, simply being there. As always, she had things to say. She segued into song—"Nowadays," from *Chicago*.

"It's good, isn't it? Grand, isn't it? Great, isn't it? Fun, isn't it? Nowadays," she sang, the hum of the machines that were keeping her alive providing the accompaniment. "In fifty years or so, it's gonna change, you know. But, oh, it's heaven nowadays."

Her voice was low but steady. No quavering. No reaching for breath. I should have known right then that she wasn't ready to check out of the hospital and into that blockbuster musical in the sky.

If I scattered Dick's ashes on the Mountain Course at La Quinta, maybe it would make up for his conviction that I was never a help to him and not as bright as he wanted or as outgoing or as successful. The house that Jack and I rent each winter overlooks the eighteenth hole in a wide gully. I could walk down through the wild sage and up to the green fairway, then up some more to where the bare, crag-toothed mountains rise, just beyond the men's tee, and sprinkle the ashes where no one but coyotes roam. I'd do it at dawn, before the cool air of night gave way to the desert's hot sun.

Char died at home on May 18, 2003. After forty-four years, I had my father to myself again. The only trouble was that he was dying too. Neither Char nor Dick were fans of hellacious, no-holds-barred treatment of disease, whether chronic obstructive pulmonary disease or metastatic cancer. So they kept it a secret that his cancer, once confined to the prostate gland, had spread.

By 2003 Char had full-time nursing care at Melrose. Six or eight registered nurses spelled each other around the clock, seven days a week. They included two Michelles, a Patty with a *y*, and a Patti with an *i*. The nurses took care of her and were good company. Char loved having people to talk to twenty-four hours a day. She did not like being nursed, however. That wasn't the idea. She caught her caretakers keeping a record of her vital signs and tore up the book.

"I'm not being treated like that," she said, meaning like a patient. It was tough on the nurses, who were doing their jobs. Information from one shift was supposed to be passed over to the next one.

After Char died, we asked the nurses to stay on to take care of Dick.

"We didn't know he was sick," one of the Michelles said to me. Her arms were folded across her chest, and she looked distressed. "He's such a gentleman. He never asks for anything."

Dick invited Seelig Freund, our surgeon friend, to come visit from New York. Charm was gone by then, so Seelig would be alone. After he arrived and had a visit with Dick, he walked with me out the front door of Melrose to talk.

"I thought I was coming to visit an old friend," he said. "Nobody told me he was terminal."

In *Once Upon a Mattress*, the king is under a spell that prevents him from talking. At the end of the show, when Winifred, the princess, has passed the queen's pea-under-the-twenty-mattresses test, the queen suddenly can no longer speak.

"The queen can't talk!" a courtier shouts.

"But, I…I…I can," says the king. "And I have a lot to say."

In the last months of his life, Dick had a lot to say. The stories popped out unexpectedly. Relatives and friends exchanged laughs at the new, chatty Dick.

It was during those last months that he told me, though briefly, about D-Day, how they started from Belfast and provided cover for the landing troops near Cherbourg.

He told me he had cousins who instigated an invasion of Mexico. The cousins, brothers with the last name of Shapiro, had a store in Columbus, New Mexico. According to Dick, they sold Pancho Villa, the famed bandit warrior, a bunch of unsatisfactory guns. Not having a Better Business Bureau or consumer advocate to appeal to, Villa came back to Columbus in the dead of night on March 9, 1916, to take revenge by burning the town.

"One of the brothers was in Albuquerque on a buying trip," Dick said. "The other rolled himself in a rug to hide from Villa and his soldiers when they blasted into the store. He wasn't hurt."

The attack on Columbus infuriated President Woodrow Wilson, who sent the US Army into Mexico in an unsuccessful attempt to capture Villa.

The online encyclopedia Wikipedia says the reasons for Villa's raid on Columbus have never been fully established. I added Dick's story to my trove of possibly-somewhat-true family tales. The connection is insufficient for getting rid of his ashes, anyway. I'd probably be caught by border patrol if I got too close to Mexico.

"What have you got there?" an armed guard would ask.

"It's just my father's ashes."

"Looks like heroin. I'll take that."

"No, wait. He wasn't even Mexican."

❧

The Columbus in Ohio makes much more sense. In those last months, from May to October 2003, Dick was confined to the whitewashed brick house on South Columbia Avenue, and my siblings and I would rotate visits, particularly lunch and dinner duty. I stopped at Melrose first thing in the morning on my way to work, bringing Danishes from Panera's that he would nibble at. I went by again late in the afternoon after work if it wasn't my turn for lunch or dinner.

At lunch we used the screen porch, with Char and Dick's rose garden and perennial garden in sight. Tea roses bloomed in profusion all summer, and we missed seeing Char out there bending down to cut a few and bringing them to the flower room for her or a servant to arrange. We feasted on corn picked that morning and tomatoes as ripe and perfect as they can only be in Ohio in deep summer and thought of how much Char would enjoy them and how fast time was speeding. We remembered how once, when Hoo-hoo was alive, Char reached for a seventh ear of corn and Hoo-hoo said, "This time, Char, you've gone too far," which became a family saying.

Afterward, Dick would sit on the lawn in a camp chair near where a spreading beech tree had been torn up by a tornado and a Japanese maple planted in its place. He wore his tan Panama hat with its thin, black ribbon and the soft peak pressed to a point. Jack would inherit the Panama hat and wear it to the parade the next Independence Day, looking quite the geezer.

As Dick grew less able to get downstairs, even with a ride on the chairlift—a machine with a passenger seat that attached to the stairs on a rail and made a dull roar that sounded like a train pulling very slowly into a station—Jack and I ate in the master bedroom at a card table with a white tablecloth and polished silverware while Dick mostly observed from a chair. We poured from a bottle Jack had pulled from the wine cellar. Dick saw no point in waiting for the wine to age, and though he could drink little himself, he liked seeing us take care of a bottle of Château Cantemerle or Lynch-Bages, or, of course, Châteauneuf-du-Papes. When even sitting in a chair was too much and he was confined to bed, Jack and I did all the eating, keeping up a front.

The house has new owners. They've converted the rose garden into a beach volleyball court. My father's ashes would mix well with the sand, wouldn't they?

The owners are nice people, but I can't imagine suggesting that I toss the ashes where their bare toes would feel them, or at least where the players would be distracted by the sense of leaping on someone's grave. And I don't think I like the idea of my father pounded down by sweaty feet.

Maybe I could just go by the house in the dead of night in my red car, slowly, with only the running lights on, and toss the contents of the box out the window. Drive-by ashes. I'd have to be in the left lane to get close enough from the driver's seat.

I remember Dick driving in England one summer directly from Heathrow airport into the Cotswolds. He was always an extremely relaxed, capable driver. But not that day, with the steering wheel on the right and the right-hand turns, though of course he kept his lips closed tight about it. The hotel was a quaint English cottage, and our rooms were on the top floor, with a ceiling too low for Dick to stand up. I remember him collapsing on the bed, exhausted, drained, and no doubt wishing we had never come, while Char, who was delighted at how well everything was working out, planned what time we would go down for dinner.

So there I'd be throwing handfuls of ashes out the window in Bexley, Ohio. Along would come someone I know returning from a movie at the Drexel Theater or dinner at Giuseppe's on Main Street.

"You OK?" the friend would say, leaning out the window.

"Umm."

"I mean you're driving on the wrong side of Dale."

"Oh, right," I'd say, trying to adopt a John Cleese/Monty Python style. "So sorry. Just leaving. See you at book club."

How about the Lazarus mausoleum at Greenlawn Cemetery? Maybe there's room.

Or the Golf Club, where Dick spent so many days?

He complained that golf was a ridiculous game. "All you have to do is hit a little ball into a hole," he said with one of his joking grins. "The ball sits there and waits."

But he loved the game and loved belonging to the Golf Club, which didn't allow women on the course or even in the front door. Char, who bought him the membership, fumed about that. "You'd think I could at least come and ride in the cart," she said.

Dick liked feeling exclusive and didn't mind getting away from home for an afternoon every once in a while. He was the first of his heritage to be accepted as a member of the Golf Club, which in 1976 was under pressure to find a suitable Jew so they would look more ecumenical. Dick did nicely. He was hardly Jewish at all if he could help it. As soon as he was assured of the Golf Club membership, Dick and Char resigned from Temple Israel because he no longer needed the membership at Winding Hollow, the Jewish country club that required a religious affiliation. Chuck Lazarus, for one, was thoroughly miffed to have them leave the temple.

Early in the last months of his life, when he could still come downstairs, Dick sat me down at the card table in the living room with a big cardboard box of ancient black-and-white photographs in a jumble of sizes, many curled at the edges, warped into a curve, stained yellow, or stuck together. It was one of the boxes I would inherit. I am not allergy prone, but the smell of mold seeped into my nose, and my eyes threatened to water.

Without introduction, he began to go through them and identify the subjects. Almost all the photos were close-ups of serious-looking people. Dick at various ages was frequently in the pictures. So was Belle, my grandmother, and someone I recognized as Dick's father, Charles, who died when Dick was a boy. I also recognized Lloyd and my cousin Bob Wacht, called Caithness. One by one, Dick identified aunts, uncles, and cousins. He was handing his personal history off to me.

I felt overwhelmed. It was too much. There were too many people and no talk of what we were really doing. We made it about halfway through the box. I was relieved when he put it away again.

A month or two later, I asked him, "Don't we need to finish going through your box of family photos?"

It was too late. He did not have the energy, and his mind was clouded with OxyContin.

After Dick died, in a belated effort to be a good daughter, I contacted Belle's family, whom I had not been in touch with since her funeral in 1962. It turned out there was a family cemetery plot.

"Maybe that could be arranged," suggested one of my cousins. Another possibility.

Central Park would be more meaningful, if I went the New York waste-management route. There's my rock, of course, and the seal pond.

Probably better to think about the Rambles, which are more secluded.

On the other hand, I should keep in mind what happened to my friend Nancy. Before her father died, he said he wanted his ashes to be scattered high in the Rocky Mountains, in the national park near Estes Park, Colorado, as he had done with her mother's. Nancy kept the ashes on a bookshelf for several years—it's a modern tradition. Finally, she was able to fit in the trip to Denver, where, despite winds that were ripping up airline schedules, she met a cousin.

"You know it's illegal to dump ashes in national parks," her cousin remarked as they entered the woods.

"Now you think of that," Nancy said, and to herself thought, *Gee, Dad, that would have been a useful piece of information*. It was a blustery day, and hikers, nature watchers, and whole families clogged the paths and popped up around the bends. It was going to be as easy to find a spot to pee as one to scatter the detritus of a life. They imagined themselves as the family in Faulkner's *As I Lay Dying*, dragging a casket across the Mississippi counties.

Increasingly desperate, they came to the edge of a cliff with a pleasant prospect and for a moment were alone. This would have to do. Nancy pulled her package out of the backpack. But the hard wind was coming directly at them; the ashes would fly back in their faces—*The Big Lebowski* effect I mentioned earlier. In a last-ditch effort, they spied a rock with a gap in the dirt below and, looking around furtively, shoved Nancy's father safely under.

Sitting on the runway at the Denver airport, where a hot, dry wind made the atmosphere too thin for planes to take off on time, Nancy contemplated the experience not as a final act of filial devotion but as an endurance contest.

Dumping ashes in the thickest greenery of Central Park, Olmstead's urban masterpiece, is probably illegal. But I might get away with it if I planned well.

I wish he had told me. Whether it's cardboard boxes, exotic locations, or urns in the shape of candlesticks to be brought out at dinner parties, what kind of burden are you foisting off on your heirs and their bookshelves, mantelpieces, basements, and travel plans when you choose cremation?

Where is the ritual, the statement honoring the dead, the way to ring the bell on the first round of grief? Thomas Lynch, the undertaker and poet, is passionate about the importance of a burial celebration. Of Irish extraction, his expectations of death are embedded in a history of outsize wakes. He sees cremation and truncated ceremony as evidence of declining values:

"If death is regarded as an embarrassment or an inconvenience, if the dead are regarded as a nuisance from whom we seek a hurried riddance, then life and the living are in for like treatment."[6]

Let's note, however, that Lynch is selling a service. He has faith in its value, and well he should. We all must believe in what we call on others to support, especially those caring for our most intimate needs. Otherwise, how can we ask the customer to pay?

How is it that a box of ashes can weigh as much as Grant's tomb?

"It's time to have death at the dinner table," said an article in the *New York Times*, advising that parents tell their children ahead of time what they want done with human dust.[7]

"Say, this pot roast is delicious, Dick," I should have said as we sat at the card table in his bedroom eating while he was too ill to pretend to touch any food. "It's too bad it got a bit charred around the edges. Have you thought about what exactly you want me to do with your ashes after you're out of here?"

The problem applies to Jack and me as well.

"Say, Josh, you did a great job grilling the burgers," I could say casually to our son. "Have your dad and I told you we want our ashes scattered in the Moremi Game Reserve in Botswana? I'm sure you guys will manage."

Jack and I do have our denouement figured out. He wants his ashes tossed over Windrush Pond in our backyard, just like those of the golden retriever Hobbes. The full name was Hobbes Descartes Beau Soleil of Blacklick, given my penchant for fancy names for ordinary dogs. Hobbes loved the pond. Even in his decline, it was hard to keep him out of it. A few months before the vet came to our house to stick the euthanizing needle into Hobbes's forepaw, I took him on a retractable lead too close to the shallow, muddy, unhealthy pond, where carp grow three feet long, and he casually slipped in, smiling.

Goldens do smile, you know. Hobbes had a heavy head with a racing stripe down the middle of his nose, a cowlick of fur as if his muzzle was stitched like a stuffed toy. He wasn't thinking about how he would climb out—though I was, considering his bad hips. I let him happily wade for a while, the water deep enough to come midway up his torso. As it turned out, I did not have to roll up my jeans and lift his hind half to get him back to the grass. He hauled himself up when I tugged on the leash, but only after he twisted his head to the side for a moment to grab a juicy, water-soaked stick. Hobbes reminded me of my father. He was quiet and gave the humans around him plenty of rope. But he knew how strong he was and what he could get away with.

As for me, Gahanna Woods Park will do. It's where I walk Bertrand Russell now. A public place, it's less likely to be torn up than our development, though who knows. At my back I always hear time and change, like a brass band that refuses to yield, tubas braying.

None of the choices for my father's ashes seems to nail the coffin shut, or hoover up the dirt. Not city, suburbs, countryside, in the sea, or over the sea. Ashes to ashes. Then what?

I've lost my father, the person who was in my life the longest of anyone, from babyhood until I was almost sixty years old. When I was young, I assumed he was a hero. In my teens I was painfully aware of his flaws—an inability to see the Vietnam War as a disastrous misuse of power and, on a personal level, his resistance or inability to assume the behavior of a regular family guy.

I guess I could hold on to all the boxes, whether ashes or memorabilia. But I want an honest conclusion, or at least a marker, in the physical act of placing the ashes somewhere that shows respect, honor, and love. I need to bury my regrets. Dick was full of inconsistencies—that is, he was like everyone else on the planet. Yet he was not everyone else. He was my dad. He was always there for me in his own way. And I didn't make it easy. The opposite, in fact.

I honed avoidance of emotion to black-belt level, living with and being separated from Gladys. It's a useful discipline, though not so much if it means you fail someone you love. I treated Dick's last illness as a job to be done. I did it efficiently and made sure not to fully take in what was happening. It was a matter of working with my siblings to ensure that the nurses were scheduled, meals coordinated, and my visits adjusted to my day job at the university. I made his dying into a routine.

One afternoon when he was terminal, Dick said, "I feel like we should be talking about the affairs of the world."

I knew what he meant. We should be talking about him and us.

"Not much in the newspapers," I replied, deflecting him. Then I thought better of it and apologized for having to go to him and Char for money and support when Jack's electric company failed.

He didn't answer. That was the end of the conversation.

I have an excuse: the nurses' monitors were on in the bedroom, and they could hear us. That's not why I ducked, however, and I don't think it's why he did. It was our usual mutual inability to talk about important things straight on. We both would rather make jokes. He'd be good at making jokes about cremation.

But it's not funny that he's gone, and I miss him. I suppose that while he was dying and for a long time afterward, if I had let grief in, it would have been like a mile-high wave at Jones Beach with no hand to hold on to.

⁖

The box problem was beginning to remind me of the time I made a list of my faults and wrote down fifteen of them before thinking to add "overanalyzing" and "self-critical." Then I had two breakthroughs. I read *Saving Fish from Drowning*, in which Amy Tan's dead narrator wishes she had thought to give boxes of her ashes to her friends in "different and delicate proportions." The nine friends would each take an exotic trip and scatter the ashes in a lovely place. "The boxes, being museum quality, would have increased in worth over the years, and made people remember me 'with growing appreciation.'"[8]

When a problem is not getting solved, one thing to do is relax the constraints. Tan's multiple boxes were an inspiration, though I knew I didn't want more boxes. The solution was her idea that one can divide and distribute.

The other eureka moment came when I started to wonder why Dick's ashes were my problem. What about my siblings? What about Pop-pop's message that a family must keep the lines of communication open? Somehow I had wanted to keep Dick to myself. But I have two brothers and a sister who have been with me and Dick since 1958.

I will enlist Bobby's help. We can scatter some of Dick's earthly remains on the soccer field in the park where the old Yankee Stadium stood, as close to a goal as we can get. Babette lives in Bexley, and we will scatter another batch of ashes near Melrose. The Golf Club doesn't allow ashes on their pristine premises, but Donnie is a member, and we can find the plaque they have already put up for Dick and take pictures.

I will scrape the last few spoonfuls out of the cardboard box and pitch them into Windrush Pond. And I will remember the sea, the air, the vineyards, the white-painted brick house, the chocolate bars, the eighteenth tee, the airedales, the golden retriever, and "The Star Spangled Banner."

I end with a grandson, born to Josh and Lorraine on August 22, 2013. He has a *V* at the beginning of his name like I do, though Vincent is not a name that has been used before in any of our families. Like him, it is brand new. George comes from Lorraine's beloved stepfather, killed in a truck accident the day after Christmas in 2012. In Vincent George Witkind Davis is contained a past and a future, an upright *V* for now and an inverted one that will spread out to new generations with new stories.

The next generation arrived earlier than expected, eight weeks before his due date and six weeks before the tenth anniversary of Dick's death October 1, 2003. Vincent's first home was at the Ohio State University Medical Center, in an isolette with tubes and monitors attached.

I stood by the incubator two days after his birth. Machines hummed and beeped. My grandson was awake, and his eyes, which I knew could not yet focus, were aimed straight at me. They looked exactly like his father's, once my own sweet baby boy. The portholes to the incubator were open to the air, but I did not want to reach inside to touch the four-pound living person whose tiny ribcage expanded and contracted as he drew each breath. I was afraid of disturbing the wires attached to him. Vincent was listening as I talked to him—I swear he was—and I listed members of his large, caring family and told him how glad they all were that he was here on this blue earth. *I'll never let you down*, I thought.

Aloud, I sang to him, with the hum of the machines that were keeping him alive as accompaniment:

"It's good, isn't it? Grand, isn't it? Great, isn't it? Fun isn't it? Nowadays. In fifty years or so, it's gonna change, you know. But, oh, it's heaven nowadays."

ACKNOWLEDGMENTS

The first set of thank-yous belongs to the Thurber writing group—Marty Ross-Dolen, Margaret Feike, Patricia Liddle, Shirley Nyhan, Shelley Hoben, Linda Hutchison, and Holly Bardoe. Their pointed questions and comments on style, sequence, and motive were invaluable as I submitted chapter after chapter of roughly cobbled stories for their sharp eyes and hard-nibbed pens. Best of all was the support they gave in the hard work of writing.

My sister, Babette T. Gorman, the family historian, read the book for accuracy in its final stages and applied her skills to preparation of the photographs. (The photographs are from my collection unless specified otherwise.) She made many excellent substantive suggestions. Along with her numerous other accomplishments, Babette is a superb proofreader and editor.

Chuck Reisz, who beat me to it in completing a book after his retirement (*Tar Heels in Wooden Shoes*—a must-read), gave advice and encouragement all along the way. My friend Nancy Krasa, also an author (*Number Sense and Number Nonsense*—another must-read) repeatedly nudged me to "keep writing," probably the most valuable recommendation a writer can receive.

I bothered several relatives with repeated e-mails and phone calls to clarify events and check facts. Mary Lazarus, John Lazarus, Chuck Cooper, and Karen Zichterman deserve special thanks. I pestered friends too.

Thanks to Ann Hill, Cathy Miller Berkley, Frosso Iossifoglu Vasiliades, Georgia Kingson, and Lynn Mooney Hickey.

Thank you to D. G. Fulford, who subjected the first complete draft of the book to a high-level reading. Her enthusiasm was a big boost.

CreateSpace does not identify their editors by last name, but I am supremely grateful to the mysterious Joan and the enigmatic CN, who put the book into Chicago style, giving me an apparently badly needed lesson in the use of commas. They made excellent suggestions on issues of content as well as craft throughout the text and found errors of fact that had somehow escaped me. All remaining errors are, of course, the responsibility of the author.

I thank my teachers for starting me on the path to becoming a writer of creative nonfiction: Rebecca McClanahan at the Kenyon Review Writers' Workshop, Lee Martin at The Ohio State University, and Katherine Matthews, whose course at Columbus's treasured Thurber House led to our informally named writing group.

Finally, I owe my best friend and husband, Jack Davis, unlimited gratitude for enduring years of patiently respecting "the book" as an excuse for being unreachable and uncommunicative; then, at the end, patiently and thoughtfully listening to me read the whole thing aloud from the first syllable to the last.

NOTES

Introduction

[1] Ann Morrow Lindbergh, *Bring Me a Unicorn* (New York: Harcourt, Brace Jovanovich, 1972), 145. Lindbergh's quotation is in French and says, "Il n'y a pas de vie heureuse. Il y a seulement des jours heureux!"

[2] Bill McKibben, *The End of Nature* (New York: Random House, 2006), 4. Using thirty years as the length of a generation, McKibben estimates there have been 330 to 400 human generations since rudimentary settlements were first made in northern Mesopotamia 10,000–12,000 years ago. He points out that this is a large number, but "not inscrutably large."

Chapter 1

[1] Margaret Mead, *Blackberry Winter* (New York: William Morrow, 1972), 3.

[2] George and Ira Gershwin, "The Illegitimate Daughter," *Of Thee I Sing*, 1931. Available as George S. Kaufman, *Of Thee I Sing: A Musical Play in Two Acts* (New York: French's Musical Library, 1963).

[3] US Census, 1930.

[4] Thomas Cahill, *How the Irish Saved Civilization* (New York: Doubleday, 1995), 213.

[5] McKibben, *The End of Nature*. Using McKibben's thirty years for a generation makes the reign of King John about twenty-five generations ago.

[6] Eleanor and Herbert Farjeon, *Kings and Queens* (London: British Library, 2011), 17.

[7] Allan M. Brandt, *The Cigarette Century: The Rise, Fall, and Deadly Persistence of the Product That Defined America* (New York: Perseus Books, 2007), 26.

[8] Malcolm R. Burns, "Outside Intervention in Monopolistic Price Warfare: The Case of the 'Plug War' and the Union Tobacco Company," *Business History Review* 56, no. 1 (Spring 1982): 45.

[9] Bernard M. Baruch, *My Own Story* (New York: Henry Holt, 1957), 113.

[10] Ibid.

[11] Alex Lichine, *Alex Lichine's Encyclopedia of Wines and Spirits* (New York: Alfred A. Knopf, 1971). See the discussion of American whiskey types, pp. 352–4. Irish whiskey is made mostly from barley.

[12] Baruch, *My Own Story*, 114.

[13] Burns, 49.

[14] Edwin G. Burrows and Mike Wallace, *Gotham* (New York: Oxford University Press, 1999), 1071–3.

¹⁵ In 1883 Caroline Astor and Ward McCallister were the decision makers who made the list of "The Four Hundred." Mrs. William Kissam Vanderbilt, born in Mobile, shattered the social glass ceiling by scheduling a party for 1,200 people that at first did not include Mrs. Astor. Negotiations ensued, and Mrs. Astor caved. Burrows and Wallace, *Gotham*.

¹⁶ Nicholas Wade, "Cheney and Obama: It's Not Genetic," *New York Times*, October 21, 2007.

¹⁷ "New York Dogs Take Laurels at Newport," *New-York Tribune*, August 10, 1913, 9.

¹⁸ "Yachts Reported," *New York Times*, May 31, 1895.

Chapter 2

¹ "Mrs. W. H. Butler's Funeral Today," *New York Times*, October 21, 1927. She died in Paris on October 4.

² I have not been able to find the date of William Butler's death.

Chapter 3

¹ Lithuania today is a small Baltic state. At one time it included modern-day Ukraine, Belarus, and parts of Poland and Russia.

² Jackie Buster, e-mail message to author, August 29, 2007. Julius Shapiro was her grandfather, and Archie Speyer her father.

³ Masha Greenbaum, *The Jews of Lithuania: A History of a Remarkable Community, 1316–1945* (Jerusalem: Goffen Books, 1995). Their settlement was called "the Pale" in English, like the Irish "pale" or

boundary. When you live "beyond the pale," you are outside of a bounded area.

[4] Ibid., 134. Most immigrated to the United States, but also to England, South Africa, Argentina, and Palestine.

[5] Dorothy Sehring, long-serving and beloved fourth-grade teacher at the Columbus School for Girls, is another example.

Chapter 4

[1] St. Patrick's Hospital was founded by the satirist Jonathan Swift in 1757 to house "idiots" and "lunaticks." It is the oldest psychiatric hospital in Ireland and one of the oldest in the world. Swift was not a "lunatic" himself but probably suffered from side effects of Ménière's disease that made him seem so. No cures were available at the time, but St. Patrick's from the beginning treated the mentally ill more humanely than the alternatives, such as the notorious Bethlehem Hospital (Bedlam) in London. See Elizabeth Malcolm, *Swift's Hospital: A History of St. Patrick's Hospital, Dublin, 1746–1889*, viii–xii and 1–31.

Chapter 5

[1] The bronzing undoubtedly was completed by BronzShoe, a local company headed by Bob Greene, whose wife, Phyllis, was a Lazarus cousin. Their son, Bob Greene, is a well-known author, as referenced in chapter 11. Their daughter, D. G. Fulford, is an editor of this book. I asked my sister Babette to explain the Greenes' relationship to the Lazaruses. She replied as follows: "Phyllis's mother, Amy Weiler Lazarus Harmon (most likely not related to the Columbus Weilers), was the second wife of Pop-pop's brother Simon Lazarus Sr. after he and Amy were widowed. So Phyllis and Chuck were step-brother and -sister. That would make Phyllis to me a first (step-) cousin once removed, because Char and Phyllis were

first step-cousins, just as she and Chuck were first cousins. And to you, first (step-step??) cousin once removed? The hell with it, too many steps, I'm falling! First cousin once removed. Just say she was your aunt."

Chapter 6

¹ David and Beverley Meyers and Elise Meyers Walker, *Look to Lazarus: The Big Store* (Charleston, SC: The History Press, 2011), 14.

² The recipes for both are in Meyers and Walker, *Look to Lazarus*, 165–8.

³ Ibid., 69.

⁴ Tom Mahoney and Leonard Stone, *The Great Merchants* (New York: Harper & Row, 1966). See chapter 7, "F&R Lazarus Company: Ohio's Famous Department Store Dynasty," 100–115.

⁵ Meyers and Walker, *Look to Lazarus*, 21.

⁶ Ibid., 56. The references to the alligator, blimp, and serving tea are also from Meyers and Walker.

⁷ James Thurber, "The Day the Dam Broke," in *The Thurber Carnival* (New York: Harper, 1945), 190–5.

⁸ Meyers and Walker, *Look to Lazarus*, 50–52.

⁹ Ibid., 109–10.

¹⁰ Bob Lazarus, in discussion with the author, November 17, 2013.

¹¹ Meyers and Walker, *Look to Lazarus*, 101.

¹² Ibid., 121.

¹³ In fact, it turned out that Lloyd did father a child, Martin Whitkind, which is another story for another day. And descendants of Dick's uncle Maurice are out west. Max and Annie Witkind divide their time between Arizona and Colorado.

¹⁴ Joe McGinniss, *Never Enough* (New York: Simon and Schuster, 2007). The woman is Nancy Kissell, daughter of Jean Stark, a grandchild of Fred Lazarus Jr. McGinniss says Lazarus women were not encouraged to graduate from college or develop marketable skills (p. 18). The first statement is not true: Lazarus women did splendidly in college. As for the second, until the early 1970s, women were not expected to work outside the house.

¹⁵ The descendants are the following: Bobby and Linda Gorman, their daughter, Hattie Sima, and grandchild, Michael Sima; Donnie and Lisal Gorman and her children, Cody and Morgan Hondros, from her first marriage; Donnie's daughter, Jenny Speas, from Donnie's first marriage, her husband, Dave, and their children, Donald, Taylor, and Shelby; Babette T. Gorman, her boyfriend, Jack Buckingham, and her daughter, Amelia Thomson; and me and my Jack and our kids, Josh and his wife, Lorraine, Babette (called Wit), and Charlotte. Geez, what a crowd. The *T* in Babette Gorman's name stands for "the." She does not have a middle name so decided to stick that in.

Chapter 7

¹ Alvin Toffler, *Future Shock* (New York: Random House, 1970), 68.

² Ibid.

³ Andrew Kerensky's time in the spotlight of history was brief but pivotal. In 1917, toward the end of three years of World War I—the Great War, the war

to end all war—Russia underwent two revolutions, one in February and the other in October. We remember the October revolution that brought Lenin and the Communists into power. Between spring and fall, a more centrist form of socialism was in the ascendant under the leadership of Kerensky. He appointed himself commander in chief and peremptorily declared Russia a republic. He tried to rally the troops, but the country was exhausted. Lenin and the Bolsheviks promised peace and bread. They took over Petrograd without a single shot. Kerensky headed for cover but still received little military support and had to flee to Paris, where he lived until 1940.

[4] Radcliffe students carried this type of book bag in the prebackpack era—hence "Cliffie."

[5] Thomas J. Hamilton, "Peace Race Urged," *New York Times*, September 26, 1961.

Chapter 8

[1] Tom Brokaw, *Boom: Voices of the Sixties* (New York: Random House, 2007), 27.

[2] Hillary Rodham Clinton, "1969 Student Commencement Speech" (Wellesley College, Wellesley, MA, May 31, 1969), available online at http://www.sojust.net/speeches/hillaryclinton_commencement.html.

[3] Carl Oglesby, *Ravens in the Storm: A Personal History of the 1960s Antiwar Movement* (New York: Scribner, 2008). Oglesby describes himself as a Kerensky-like figure who was drummed out of SDS for not being radical enough. He was, however, on the speakers' platform at the protests at the Democratic convention in 1968 where police charged the crowd. Tom Brokaw in *Boom*, cited above, documents the personal history of all kinds of people from the period—politicians, musicians, soldiers, writers, and more. Brokaw includes his own sixties story, titled "What Was That All

About?"—exactly the question I wrestle with when I try to understand what I lived through.

⁴ She went on to a career as an assistant district attorney specializing in child abuse cases for Monterey County, California. Ann is a scissors-hands in white gloves. The male defense lawyer who thought he was going to have it easy with a sweet, blond, soft-spoken lady with a gentle laugh was in for a surprise. I imagine innumerable attorneys twisting in the honeyed blades of Ann's reasoning and realizing, in a moment of truth, that their clients were in for lengthy periods of secluded existence.

⁵ According to Cathy, the guy who made the crack about the cookie went on to become a dentist. She suggested that the cookie may have changed his life, convincing him never to eat more than one cookie to avoid dental harm, or "maybe it evolved into a family tradition—one cookie on a big plate left for Santa." Cathy Miller Berkley, e-mail message to author, April 28, 2014.

Chapter 9

¹ Tom Wells, *The War Within: America's Battle Over Vietnam* (Berkeley: University of California Press, 1994), 136–7.

² Ibid., 137–8.

³ John Lazarus, e-mail message to author, April 27, 2014.

⁴ *Missouri v. Holland*, 252 U.S. 416 (1920), cited in Herbert W. Briggs, *The Law of Nations* (New York: Appleton-Century Crofts, 1966), 874. The US Supreme Court ruled that a state could not prevent a US game warden from enforcing the Migratory Bird Treaty concluded with Canada. Professor Gross assigned it as a seminal Tenth Amendment decision.

[5] Brokaw, *Boom*, 95. New Hampshire was easy to reach for several politically active campuses in New England, including "Harvard, Brown, Yale, Amherst, and Wellesley," noted Brokaw. The students had to cut their hair to be "Clean for Gene." They had a good time. Sam Brown, one organizer, said, "Hey, I'm 22, the testosterone is running pretty high, and a lot of pretty, liberal women are going to be on the bus."

[6] The student was Jeremy Rifkin, who afterward made a name for himself as a radical thinker on a variety of global issues.

Chapter 10

[1] Memorial Service for Governor John J. Gilligan, Ohio Statehouse, Columbus, Ohio, September 5, 2013, available online at http://www.ohiochannel.org/medialibrary/Media.aspx?fileId=140235.

[2] For an excellent biography, see Mark Bernstein, *John J. Gilligan: The Politics of Principle* (Kent, Ohio: Kent State University Press, 2013).

[3] See *Monet to Matisse: The Howard D. and Babette L. Sirak Collection of the Columbus Museum of Art* (Columbus: Columbus Museum of Art, 2005) for the story of the collection and reproductions.

Chapter 11

[1] Columbus Jewish Historical Society, "Interview with Charlotte Witkind," November 2, 1999, http://www.columbusjewishhistory.org/oral_histories/Interviews/HTML/witkind_charlotte.htm.

[2] Ibid.

[3] Richard Sandomir, "Praise for Steinbrenner from Limited Partners," *New York Times*, July 15, 2010.

[4] Unpublished letter from Charlotte Witkind to George Steinbrenner, November 18, 1987. "Dan" could have been limited partner Dan McCarthy.

Chapter 12

[1] Governor Jim Rhodes sent in the troops after a student or provocateur set fire to a campus building that housed the Reserve Officers' Training Corps (ROTC) on May 2. Rhodes told the guardsmen the students were "scum." The guardsmen fired into a crowd of two hundred students who were two hundred feet away from them and withdrawing. Some of the students who were shot or killed had been protesters. Others had not actively opposed the Cambodian intervention or ROTC training. The guardsmen claimed they fired in self-defense. Subsequent reviews of the events conclude that it was simply a massacre. See Carl Oglesby, *Ravens in the Storm* (New York: Scribner, 208), 298–9.

Chapter 13

[1] Ted's brother Dick Celeste would become the next Democratic governor after Gilligan. Ted himself was elected to the state legislature and is a staunch supporter of good causes, meaning the ones I believe in.

[2] Bob Greene, *Be True to Your School* (New York: Atheneum, 1987). As noted above, Bob Greene and his sister D. G. Fulford, one of the editors of this book, are *mekhutonim*, the Yiddish word Char used to label relatives whose relationship to us was complicated.

[3] Gershwin, "The Illegitimate Daughter."

Chapter 14

¹ Charlotte Witkind, interview, transcript, Jewish Historical Society.

² Stephen Ambrose, *D-Day June 6, 1944: The Climactic Battle of World War II* (New York: Simon and Schuster, 1994), 257.

³ Witkind, interview.

⁴ Phyllis Greene, *It Must Have Been Moonglow: Reflections on the First Years of Widowhood* (New York: Villard, 2001), 117.

⁵ Patricia Leigh Brown, "In Death as in Life, a Personalized Space," *New York Times*, January 18, 2007.

⁶ Thomas Lynch, *The Undertaking* (New York: Penguin, 1977), 25.

⁷ "No Longer Avoiding That Talk about the Inevitable," *New York Times*, September 16, 2006, http://www.nytimes.com/2006/09/16/business/16shortcuts.html?pagewanted=print&_r=0.

⁸ Amy Tan, *Saving Fish from Drowning* (New York: G. P. Putnam's Sons, 2005), 10–11.

Made in the USA
Lexington, KY
27 December 2014